THE MAKERS OF
ENGLISH POETRY

THE MAKERS OF ENGLISH POETRY

BY

W. J. DAWSON, *William James,* 1854-1928.

NEW AND REVISED EDITION

KENNIKAT PRESS, INC./PORT WASHINGTON, N. Y.

MAKERS OF ENGLISH POETRY

Copyright 1906 by Fleming H. Revell Company
Reissued in 1968 by Kennikat Press
Library of Congress Catalog Card No: 68-16291
Manufactured in the United States of America

ESSAY AND GENERAL LITERATURE INDEX REPRINT SERIES

Progress is
The law of life, man is not man as yet
Nor shall I deem his object served, his end
Attained, his genuine strength put fairly forth,
While only here and there a star dispels
The darkness, here and there a towering mind
O'erlooks its prostrate fellows : when the host
Is out at once to the despair of night,
When all mankind alike is perfected,
Equal in full-blown powers—then, not till then,
I say, begins man's general infancy.

BROWNING, *Paracelsus*

PREFACE

THE publication of this, and the companion volumes, *The Makers of English Prose*, and *The Makers of English Fiction*, completes a task commenced fifteen years ago.

At that time I published a volume entitled *The Makers of Modern English*, which attempted to give a coherent and critical account of the makers of modern English poetry. But even then I had in mind a much larger design, viz., a critical history of modern literature which should include not only the poets, but the great masters of prose and fiction. For fifteen years I have steadfastly kept that design in view, working on it as the circumstances of a busy and laborious public life permitted. The design now stands complete. The three volumes stand coördinated as one whole, and the original title, *The Makers of Modern English*, now has a justification which the single volume on the poets did not possess.

The earlier volumes now take their place with *The Makers of English Fiction*, which was published but a few months ago. They have been carefully revised, a task rendered the more necessary by that process of time which in fifteen years has removed from the arena of literature some of the greatest of those men of genius who have given glory to our time.

It is with a sense of sadness rather than of relief that I now relinquish a task which has become so much a part of myself. But I am consoled by the knowledge that my work now appears in the form which I first designed

7

for it, and I trust that it may serve its purpose in stimulating among the increasing multitude of those who feel
the attraction of books that love of literature which has
been my own lifelong solace and delight.

W. J. DAWSON.

New York, May, 1906.

CONTENTS

10 CONTENTS

I

INTRODUCTORY

THESE studies have a certain aim, and it is hoped will have a certain coherence, which may make them acceptable to the class of readers for whom they are intended. It may be well to state in a few words what the aim of the writer is.

In the first place, it is somewhat difficult to define where what is called modern English literature commences. In the truest sense English literature is a unity. It has grown up out of small and semi-articulate beginnings into a great organic whole. It may be compared with a tree which has passed through various stages of growth, and has at certain seasons put forth foliage and blossom, passing through adolescence to maturity, at last becoming rooted in a stately strength, and bearing a perpetual harvest. Or it may be compared with a river which has broadened and deepened in its course, until at last what was a feeble and insignificant stream is a mighty tideway, on which the leviathan may float, or the craft of many and diverse masters sail at ease.

Whichever illustration we may select as most appropriate, the point to be remembered is, that English literature is an organic whole. There are no deep dividing fissures, and the divisions which we have invented to help us in our survey of it are purely arbitrary. Not the less, however, it has its periods. A just criticism and discerning eye perceive how, at certain eras of national life, a seemingly new force has flowed through the old chan-

11

nels, or has made a new channel for itself, and has produced distinct and definite results. The great literary
battle of Victor Hugo's life between classicism and
romanticism has had its counterpart again and again in
English literature. In the days of Pope and Dryden we
had a certain theory of poetry which was thought to be
perfect and all-sufficient. Poetry was treated almost as an
exact science, and the laws for its manufacture were reduced to a precise code, and stated with axiomatic clearness. There were even certain phrases for natural facts,
which were universally adopted as current coin, and the
west wind was always spoken of as " the gentle zephyr,"
and the north wind as " the blast of Boreas." The aim
of poetry was not to startle, but to instruct. It was to
put into lucid and authentic phrase certain facts and
teachings which the individual poet thought it well that
his generation should learn. Poetry was not the vehicle
of passion, not the expression of imagination, not the
voice of the emotions, so much as the vehicle of philosophic thought and reflection. To say that the poetry
produced under such circumstances was not poetry is
false ; but it is poetry in fetters. Every one knows that
Byron loved and defended Pope, and looked upon Pope
as an impeccable master ; and Pope deserved the recognition of Byron. For lucidity, for sharpness and brilliance of phrase, for delicate force and effect, it is hard to
surpass the finest work of Pope.

But gradually men came to see that Pope's *Essay
on Man* was not the last possibility of English poetry.
The new social and political forces at work in the world
spread a revolutionary ferment through the realm of letters also. Men were tired of the artificial glitter of didactic poetry ; they began to yearn for the freshness and

wholesomeness of a more natural style. As if in answer
to this new yearning, in 1726, Thomson published his
Seasons, which sounded the note of recall to nature.
Then, in 1765, Bishop Percy published his *Reliques of
English Ballad-Poetry*, in which the note of recall became an imperative and irresistible voice. There was yet
to be a long pause before the tree burgeoned with its new
spring, or the river burst its old banks into a wider channel; but at last the ear of the world caught the voice of
a Scotch plowman singing, at the plow's tail, " A man's
a man for a' that," and at the brookside to his " Mary
in Heaven"; and then, in the fullness of the time, came
Wordsworth, speaking from the dewy calmness of the
English mountains, and Shelly from the passionate air of
Italy. But all this was not revolution : it was development. The change was not arbitrary : it was inevitable
from the nature of things, and was part of that vast process of evolution which in the world of letters is as distinct a law as in the world of nature.

Where, then, modern literature may be said to begin it
is difficult to determine, and is a point one can scarcely
determine without adopting some arbitrary law of criticism, such as the general order of history forbids.
Speaking generally, however, it may be said that the old
movement' exhausted itself in Pope, and from that point
a new era did begin. The poetry of Goldsmith and Cowper is entirely different from the poetry of Pope and Gay.
Recurring again to our illustration, we may say that
while the stream flows on, one and indivisible, swelled by
many rivulets and springs, yet it is quite possible to follow its banks, and to mark certain alterations in its character as it passes onward to its fuller life. We notice differences of colour, of speed, and of temperature. As

the volume of English literature has increased its variety has also increased. It has become more flexible, more various in power, more complex in its manifold results. It reflects the lights of thought and passion more clearly, and it is readier to catch the shifting side-lights of the times. In a thousand ways the literature of to-day differs from, and in a hundred ways transcends, the literature of the eighteenth century. Into this vast subject it is not my province to enter; it is enough for me to point out, even in this general way, what I mean by modern English.

The second point to which I would ask attention is the nature of the studies contained in this series. The age in which we live is an age of many books and few readers. Does this appear a paradox? It is explained by what we mean by " a reader." The true reader is a man who applies patience and industry to books, and is contented with nothing less than their actual mastery. He is in earnest in his work, and " reads, marks, learns, and inwardly digests " his books. How many do this? There is reading in plenty, but digestion is rare. The very plethora of books has produced literary dyspepsia. But there is another reason for the growth of books and the haste with which they are devoured—not digested. The pace of life has vastly increased since the nineteenth century dawned. Leisure has almost disappeared. The railway has altered everything. It is true that he who runs may read, but much of our reading has to be taken running. The vast mass of readers have no time to devote to intricate literary problems and the ever-multiplying details of literary history. They are interested in books, they feel the fascination of literature, but they are destitute of that leisure for contemplation in which a just criticism grows up, and a sound personal opinion on the problems of literature can be formed. They have " no shelter to grow ripe, no leisure to grow wise "—to quote the pregnant line of Matthew Arnold. It follows, therefore, that for this vast mass of readers a sort of middleman is needed, who will do for them what they cannot do for themselves, and the critic may shelter himself under Mr. Leslie Stephen's tolerant assurance, that he who tells us sincerely what he thinks always tells us something worth knowing. It may not be a very dignified description of the critic to call him a " middleman "; but that is what he really is,—the middleman of literature. But if it is not a very dignified appellation, certainly the function performed is a very useful one, and one that in this age of many books and little leisure is becoming an increasingly important office.

For instance, take in illustration of this statement such a history as Shelley's. The Shelley literature has now become almost a library in itself. It ranges through every variety of detraction and adulation. To one biographer Shelley is a monster of pollution, to another a saviour of society, who, " under favourable circumstances, might have become the saviour of the world." Mr. Cordy Jeaffreson has written a huge book on the subject, and Mr. Edward Dowden has written a still larger. Mr. Jeaffreson's book was the unauthorized version of Shelley's life, in which men complained that everything against Shelley was stated with a sort of malicious veracity, and often with a lack of insight and sympathy which led to actual perversion of the truth. On the other hand, Mr. Dowden's critics complained that he glossed over the really difficult points in Shelley's strange history, and was misled by his sympathy into

an equal perversion of the truth.   Then, besides these
two great representatives of the two essentially divergent
views of Shelley, there is a host of writers, essayists,
poets, and critics of the first water, who have written
with more or less acuteness, and more or less diffuseness, on the same subject.   Shelley has been pronounced
viler and more dangerous than Byron, and has been
pictured as a pure and holy being, whose boots Byron
was not worthy to black.   Every shade of vituperation
and praise lies between these extremes.   Nor is the
battle of the books over.   It is very well for Mr.
Dowden to write *Last Words* on Shelley, but the last
word is not said yet.   At this very moment probably
there are half-a-dozen writers who believe that they
have a fresh view of Shelley to present, and are determined to produce an epoch-making book thereon.

Now, what is the plain practical man, the intelligent but unleisured reader, to do amid this babble of
tongues ?   Obviously he cannot for himself sort all the
evidence, and study all the books on Shelley, and yet,
perhaps, he feels a deep curiosity to know more of that
strange and visionary spirit whose winged words have
fascinated him.   He wants to know what relation his
poetry has to the other poetry of his time, and what is
the true secret of his wayward life.   To such a reader
the literary middleman is an ambassador of peace.   He
may not know everything, for " we are none of us
infallible, not even the youngest of us " ; but he knows
more than the reader who can only take his literary
diet by snatches.   It is for him to give as fairly as he
can the result of his own reading, the impression which
a famous poet's poetry has had upon him, the general
estimate which he has been led to form both of the

man and his works. Of course, it may be objected that all the busy man gets from the critic, then, is after all the critic's mere personal view of the matter. But after all that is what the most accomplished critic gives us, and he gives us no more. The worth of his verdict, and the laws by which it is attained, depend on the qualities of his own mind. According to his discernment will be the worth of his judgment; but his own personal judgment is, when all is done, the one gift the critic has to give.

This then is, in brief, the object of this book. It is to put before the reader in a compact form what can be said of the character and worth of writers who have made English literature glorious. The estimate may be imperfect, the verdict may be wrong: but it will be honestly given, as far as the knowledge and conviction of the writer are concerned; to which it is only necessary to add, that every wise reader will reconsider the verdict for himself, and will, as far as his opportunities allow, avail himself of those legitimate sources of information on which any estimate of any writer must be based. The astonishing cheapness of books puts such sources of information within the reach of almost all to-day, and the process of education will in another generation leave no excuse for those who have not read the great masterpieces of that long line of English writers who have made the nineteenth century famous.

II

THE INTERVAL BEFORE THE DAWN

WE have seen that in Alexander Pope one great period of English literature found its consummation and its close. He was the last master of a style of poetry distinguished by a species of hard and artificial brilliance, intellectual rather than emotional, dealing with philosophic niceties rather than the great passions and common thoughts of men, excelling in epigrammatic force and satirical incisiveness, but destitute, or nearly destitute, of tenderness and pathos, and, above all, marked by a total indifference to nature. It is a clipped and gravelled garden in which the poets of Pope's school walk, never in the fresh fields and true presence of nature. Their treatment of love is as artificial as their treatment of nature : it is mere conventional rhodomontade of " Dying swains to sighing Delias." They hear no lark singing at heaven's gate as did Shakespeare, and travel through no morning meadows fresh with dew as did Chaucer.

The childlike simplicity of Chaucer, garrulous, unaffected, bewitching by the magic of an art that scarcely seems to be art at all, was entirely forgotten by the men of the earlier decades of the eighteenth century. The magnificent force of the Elizabethan poets was even abhorrent to them. In Marlowe they saw nothing but the violent and untrained imagination of a barbarian, and Shakespeare himself was disallowed the full diploma of their approval. Spenser was left in complete obscurity,

18

and the passionate and fanciful lyrics of Elizabethan literature, excelling as they do in the most delicate and tender workmanship of which poetry is capable, were wholly forgotten. Then came the faint signs of a new era, but they were slow and intermittent. There was an interval before the dawn, an interval between the dying of the old and the birth of the new. The voices that heralded the return to nature were solitary voices, like the unaccompanied song of the lark in the gray morning skies, when the light is thickening and before the day has broken. It will be well before passing to the world of modern English to enumerate those who stood upon its threshold, and were its heralds and its architects.

There is, first of all, a group of writers, in which the spirit of Pope's poetry survived, and in whose work the ideals of the didactic school made their last stand. Dr. Johnson's *Vanity of Human Wishes* is a sample of this school. It is a stately and pompous poem, full of careful phrases, polished into epigrammatic force, and not without a certain pathos in its descriptions, which, however, springs largely from what we know of the early struggles of Johnson himself. Young's *Night Thoughts* and Churchill's *Satires* belong to the same school, but still further mark the process of disintegration. The poems of Gray and Collins contain a different element, and in one sense may be said to stand unclassed and isolated. They are among the finest examples we possess of studious, scholarly, exquisite workmanship in poetry. Every word is weighed in the finest balances of judicious criticism, and every phrase is turned with the utmost nicety. They breathe the spirit of classic and artistic culture. They are not wholly free from the affectation of their age, but their work is so excellent that we are rarely conscious of this defect. Goldsmith reckoned that ten lines of poetry was a good day's work, but Gray calculated that years were well filled in the perfecting of so short a poem as the *Elegy*.

Gray is also remarkable for another element which was to be a very striking feature of the new school of poets, viz., a sense of the romantic past. The old wild stories of chivalry and daring fascinated him, as they fatally fascinated Chatterton a little later. In Chatterton indeed we have the first and fullest expression of the romantic element of modern poetry. The old grandeur of phrase which distinguished the Elizabethan writers leaps up again in him, and the stern simplicity and tragic force of the older ballad-writers is again exemplified. And yet another writer who in no small degree helped on the change was James MacPherson, who published his *Ossian* in 1762. To many modern readers *Ossian* seems a wild farrago of formless bombast; but to the men of the latter part of the eighteenth century it was a revelation. It is known that it powerfully affected Scott, and was to him a valuable stimulus to poetic creation. Wild and chaotic as it was in form, it occasionally reached a grandeur of imagination and largeness of phrase wholly astonishing and new to those who looked upon didactic poetry as the final consummation of all poetic form and utterance. It was steeped in nature, it painted the impressiveness of savage scenery, the lonely vastness of moor and ocean, the broken magnificence of wild seacoasts, as no one had done before, and with the freshness and frankness of an evident delight.

To poets who never ventured beyond a park or garden, and thought that Fleet Street provided every interest that human imagination could desire, the wild work of Mac·

Pherson was a revelation. He had managed to utter a
need which had long been silenced in the hearts of men,
the need of communion with nature. Not the distorted
nature of trim gardens and well-ordered parks, but nature
in her solitude, her sternness, her terror ; the majesty of
her scarred and tempest-riven rocks, the pomp and splendour of her skies and seas, the " mountain glory " and
the " mountain gloom," the nature that Turner was to
paint, the skies that Shelley was to picture, the sea whose
boundless and eternal freedom Byron was to sing, the
mountains whose ever-shifting pageant, ranging from the
vision of magic colouring and airy distance to the sublimity of tempest and trailing storm-cloud, Ruskin was to
describe with unapproachable fidelity and eloquence.
Strange as it may seem to those who disinter from their
obscure grave the tiresome tirades of James MacPherson
to-day, and read them with impatience and disdain, yet
the first note of all the wealth of work represented in
such names as Turner, Shelley, Byron, and Ruskin is
struck in his forgotten *Ossian*.

There was yet another writer in whom the new spirit
was to find a still higher expression ; that writer was
William Cowper. The pathetic story of Cowper's life
is well known. What a strange contradiction the man
seems ! The writer of *John Gilpin* and the *Olney Hymns*,
the despairing suicide and the brilliant humourist ; can
the force of contrast go farther ? How incomprehensible
it seems that the man who wrote " God moves in a mysterious way " should also write about himself thus :—

> Hatred and vengeance—my eternal portion,
> Scarce can endure delay of execution —
> Wait with impatient readiness to seize my
>   Soul in a moment.

Man disavows and Deity disowns me ;
Hell might afford my miseries a shelter,
Therefore Hell keeps her ever-hungry mouths
All bolted against me.

How tragic is the reflection that the sweet singer who has done so much to inspire cheerfulness and trust in others should write of himself, " I feel a wish that I had never been, a wonder that I am, and an ardent but hopeless desire not to be ! " The secret of this immense despair was in the fact that Cowper's delicate spirit was crushed beneath the weight of intolerable theological problems—the riddle of " this unintelligible world." It was Cowper who introduced the theological element into English poetry, and it has worked unsuspected results both for poetry and theology.

But Cowper also introduced another element—the utmost simplicity and unaffected naturalness of style, and a true and beautiful love of nature. Far away from the vexed and crowded life of cities he lived in the heart of nature, and his own heart was ever open to her inspiration. When he described the flowers, the clouds, the weather, he did so with an inimitable fidelity. He put down just what he saw with the utmost simplicity, one might say almost with a scientific simplicity. In this Cowper was intensely modern. Nothing is better worth study, or would prove more interesting, than to trace how the scientific spirit of description has grown in English poetry. The earlier eighteenth century poets describe what they never saw, and what they had never taken the trouble to identify. Hence, because they have never really studied nature for themselves, they perforce fall back upon the stock phrases of artificial description. In this they stand aloof both from the earliest English

poets and the latest. Chaucer tells us just what he sees—
he makes us feel that he has seen it, and we see it too.
Tennyson, in like manner, has brought the most vigilant
observation to bear on all natural phenomena which he
has described. The botanist cannot improve on his description of a flower, nor the naturalist on his picture of
the way in which a bird flies or a wave breaks. We have
now become used to this species of scientific accuracy in
poetic description, and we resent the loose and inaccurate
generalities of which many poets are still guilty. But
the true author of this change was Cowper. He was the
forerunner of Wordsworth. He wrote of nature, not
because it was part of the stock business of a poet to do
so, but because he loved her. He, too, had felt the
"impulse of a vernal wood," and he knew that nature,
when reverently studied, has secrets to teach which
neither sage nor scholar can unfold. Few read Cowper
to-day. His *Task* has verified its title, and men weary
of it midway. Cowper is known rather by his hymns
and a few brief lyrics than by his more serious and ambitious poems. But it was nevertheless William Cowper
who was the herald of the modern school of poets, and
who sang the glories of the day when the dawn had
scarcely broken.

Not less marked was the change effected in poetry in
relation to its human interests. Cowper loved man as
well as nature. In this he was the precursor of a great
line of great poets. In place of violent satire on the
follies of the great, Cowper gave us sympathetic descriptions of the labour and sorrows of the poor. In this he
was followed by George Crabbe, whose descriptions are
equally sympathetic, but more realistic. Crabbe has
even fewer readers than Cowper to-day, and is only

known to many readers as the " John Richard William Alexander Dyer " of Horace Smith's *Rejected Addresses ;* yet he was a true poet, and deserves a better fate.   John Murray said truly that Crabbe said uncommon things in a common way, and perhaps it is the homeliness of his verse which has done much to obscure its great qualities.   Byron called him " Nature's sternest painter and the best "; Wordsworth predicted for him immortality; Scott read him with renewed and fresh delight in old age; Tennyson says, " Crabbe has a world of his own "; while Newman, in one of his " Addresses to the Catholics of Dublin," tells us that he had read one of his poems " on its first publication with extreme delight," and again, twenty years after, with even more emotion, and yet again, twenty years after *that*, with undiminished interest, and adds that " whether for conception or execution " it is one of the most touching poems in the language.[1]

It seems strange that a poet whose claims are so unanimously endorsed by the most competent judges should have fallen into such complete oblivion, and perhaps the real reason lies in the deficiencies of metrical art which appear in Crabbe's poetry, and the carelessness of his diction as compared with the metrical refinement of later verse.   Crabbe is a poet who wears worsted; but, homely as he is, his writings have some of the qualities of the greatest poetry.   It is in realism that his force lies.   He has little humour; he is in deadly earnest.   He goes to the jail, the workhouse, the hospital, the half-ruined cottage, for his themes.   He pictures the shameful squalor, the hard life, the unpitied ignorance, and the humble heroisms of the poor.   He tells his tale of shame and ruin with a grave simplicity and directness of state-

[1] Vide *Literary Remains of Edward Fitzgerald*, Vol. iii, p. 490.

ment which is wholly tragic. He is the spokesman of
the ignorant and neglected. He utters their appeal
against the social system of their time, and in this Crabbe
was the literary herald of the great Revolution.

With the French Revolution an entirely new spirit
was breathed into European literature. The social
problems of the times were forced upon the minds of all
men of letters, and especially of the poets. This is again
one of the most distinctive features of modern English
literature. The social problem is to-day the great problem
of Europe. It engages the perpetual thought of states-
men, and it presses heavily upon the hearts of all
imaginative writers. A large section of the poetry of
our day is full of bitter invective on the tragedies endured
by the poor, and an increasing section of our fiction is
animated by the same spirit. The beginning of this
movement is in Crabbe and Cowper. With the dawn of
the Revolution, there rose up poets who uttered the same
cry with infinitely greater bitterness, and expressed the
same spirit with an agonized intensity, a passionate daring
and poignancy, wholly transcending the works of Crabbe
and Cowper. But, as we have seen, these poets lived
in the interval

> Between two worlds—one dead,
> The other powerless to be born.

They, however, were its prophets. They struck the first
note of the new music. They perceived the drift of
thought, and watched the first trailing vapours of the approaching storm. By the time their work was done new
spirits were at work, and Burns, Wordsworth, Byron, and
Shelley were inaugurating the new age which is our
heritage to-day.

III

ROBERT BURNS

Born at Halloway, Ayr, 1759. Poems chiefly in the Scottish dialect, published 1786. Reprinted with additions, 1787. The Prayer of Holy Willie, 1789. Tam O'Shanter, 1790. Address to The Deil, 1794. Died at Dumfries, July 21, 1796.

WE have named Robert Burns as truly the first singer of the new era, and since Burns represents so much, he demands more than the concise brevity of a paragraph. He accepted the ideals of Crabbe and Cowper, and carried on the revolution they had commenced, but it was with large and important differences. It must not be forgotten that these great poets were contemporaries. While Crabbe in 1783 was beginning his series of life-pictures of the poor, and Cowper in 1785 was feeling his way towards a more simple and unaffected style of poetry, Burns in 1786 was rousing genuine enthusiasm in Scotland by the publication of the first poems of genius in Scottish dialect which had enriched the literature of Scotland for many years. Like Cowper, he described nature with admirable simplicity, but with a terseness and exquisiteness of expression which Cowper never gained. Like Crabbe, he described " the short and simple annals of the poor," but it was with a more moving sympathy, a deeper pathos, and a concentration and brilliance of phrase which Crabbe never acquired.

So far the work of Burns resembles the work of Crabbe

and Cowper, but no further.   Burns brought to his task
a broad humour and incisive wit which neither of his
English rivals could emulate.   He was himself a poor
man, a man of the soil, a son of labour, and he described
what such a life was, not from the calm heights of observation, but from actual experience.   Above all, he did
what neither Crabbe nor Cowper could accomplish—he
sang of love.   He sang of it with a full, passionate utterance, a grace and a fire unknown in English poetry for
upwards of a century.   There was the magic of enchantment in his song.   His lyrics have a sweetness and a
poignancy all their own.   They sing themselves into the
universal heart.   As a love-poet he is unsurpassed and
unapproachable.   Such lines as

> Had we never lov'd sae kindly,
> Had we never lov'd sae blindly,
> Never met—or never parted,
> We had ne'er been broken-hearted,

are immortal.   Scott said they had the essence of a
thousand love stories in them.   They utter in the simplest
but most pathetic fashion the experience of multitudes.
And in all his lyrics, whether of love or nature, there is
an abandonment and freshness which are captivating.
It is beautiful to remember, when we read these exquisite
love-verses, that the women who inspired them were
farm-girls, domestic servants—Scotch maidens met at a
dance or in the harvest-field, all of them used to toil, and
born to toil, and living a life far more akin to drudgery
than romance.   Yet no heroine of ancient or mediæval
song ever had more beautiful things said of her than this
child of the plow addressed to the comrades of his labour.   In nothing does the manliness and originality of

Burns's genius show to better advantage. He was so truly a child of the people that he found among the people with whom he lived all the elements needful for the nurture of his genius, all the materials requisite for his immortal songs.

There is not much that is new that can be said about the life of Burns. The story has become an epic, and the epic is known to all the world. It is something of a misconception which describes Burns as a plowman : he was rather a small yeoman, born of a race of small farmers, hard-headed, industrious, fond of reading, sober, religious ; precisely that class which is the strength and pride of Scotland to-day. His father was a man considerably superior to the class in which he moved ; and a strong taste, almost amounting to a thirst, for knowledge, was one of the leading characteristics of the home in which Burns was born. But whatever was the precise social position of Burns, there can be no doubt about one thing—viz., his passionate love of the people. In his poetry it is the human element that is supreme. For the mere picturesque side of nature, as such, he had no great love ; nature is everywhere in his poetry the background for man. Not that he did not love nature ; he loved her as few poets have loved her. His poems are full of those short, crisp phrases, those felicitous touches of description, which bring before us in an instant, with magical clearness and beauty, the aspects of nature in all her seasons, and all her moods. But when Burns looked at a landscape it was not to brood over its beauty, and to invent exquisite phrases with a laborious skill to interpret it. That is Tennyson's method, and living and beautiful as his touches of natural description always are, yet they are seldom quite spontaneous. We are pretty sure they have been corrected, sublimated, refined to the very last degree before they were submitted to the test of publicity. When Burns describes nature, it is always with a rapid and easy touch, as one who thinks less of nature than of the human toil and passion for which nature is the background. Nothing remains to-day of Burns's brilliant conversation among the notables of Edinburgh, during his first visit to that city in the early days of his fame, but one little story which Dugald Stewart recalls. He and Burns had climbed the Braid Hills in the early morning, and were looking down upon the fair plains, full of the dewy freshness of the morning glory. Stewart expressed his admiration of the beauty of the scene, and beautiful indeed it was. But Burns had his eyes fixed upon the little cluster of cottages at his feet, with the rising clouds of blue smoke trailing in the morning air, eloquent of the labourer's early meal, and said the worthiest object in all that fair scene was this little cluster of labourers' cottages, knowing as he did the wealth of true character, the piety, and happiness, and contentment, which they enshrined. It was a speech that was characteristic of the man. His mission was not to describe nature, but to sing the epic of man. He has himself given excellent expression to this idea in his well-known lines :—

> To mak a happy fireside clime
> To weans and wife,
> That's the true pathos and sublime
> Of human life.

There are certain passages in Burns's letters which do not exactly tally with this simplicity of nature, but the letters Burns wrote are the only bad things he ever did write. They are artificial and stilted, and were unworthy

of him.   For among the many weaknesses of Burns was
the temporary desire to be a polite letter-writer, and consequently he has left a mass of letters conceived in false
sentiment, and written in false taste.   It is true these letters occasionally give us vivid insight into the heart of
the man, but upon the whole they distort the true image
of Burns.   They give us an unpleasant feeling that under
the fascination of society the sturdiness of Burns's character suffered some deterioration.   It would not have
been wonderful if it had.   But any such lapse was entirely temporary, and limited in its results.   A worship-
per of wealth and power Burns never was, nor could be.
He was, indeed, at times fiercely Republican, and got into
frequent trouble for his outspoken political views.   His
heart was with poor folk, and he was happiest amongst
them.   How fully he understood their ways, their noble
struggles, their social difficulties, let this passage from
The Twa Dogs declare :—

> But then to see how ye're negleckit,
> How huff'd an' cuff'd, an' disrespeckit!
> Lord, man, our gentry care as little
> For delvers, ditchers, an' sic cattle,
> They gang as saucy by puir folk
> As I wad by a stinkin' brock.
>
> I've noticed, on our Laird's court-day,
> An' mony a time my heart's been wae,
> Puir tenant bodies, scant o' cash,
> How they maun thole a factor's snash ;
> He'll stamp an' threaten, curse an' swear,
> He'll apprehend them, poind their gear,
> While they maun stan', wi' aspect humble,
> An' hear it a', an' fear an' tremble !   .   .   .
> There's mony a creditable stock
> O' decent, honest, fawsont folk,

Are riven out baith root and branch,
Some rascal's pridefu' greed to quench,
Wha thinks to knit himsel' the faster
In favour wi' some gentle master,
Wha, aiblins, thrang a parliamentin',
For Britain's guid his saul indentin'.

Any student of Burns could cite at will a score of passages setting forth with equal or superior force of diction the condition of the labouring poor, and full of honest admiration for their virtues, and sympathetic understanding of their lot. What wonder is it that Burns is the poet of the poor ? What wonder that he is the singer best known in the field, the factory, the mine, the wild settlements of distant lands, among crowds of horny-handed men who have known nothing but hard toil all their lives, and have found but one poet who loves them and understands them perfectly, who has written songs that they can comprehend, which bring a new light of sweetness and contentment into their difficult lot ? Burns is the poet of the common people, almost the only one, and the common people receive him gladly.

Another element in Burns which had a wide influence on literature was the mixture of jovial fun, pervasive humour, and excellent wit and satire in which he abounded. He commanded laughter as well as tears. He had an irresistible power of ridicule, and knew how to use it with consummate effect. All that he did he seemed to do easily, without the least sense of effort, drawing upon the resources of a rich and wholesome nature, which never showed the remotest sign of exhaustion. With him a song was the joyous work of a morning, or even of an hour, and that most matchless example of jovial and rollicking humour, *Tam o' Shanter*,

was written in a single day.   As for the satire of Burns,
that also at its best is unsurpassable.   He knew how to
strike with swift and deadly effect.   He had a wholesome
hatred of cant, and a fearlessness of conventional opinion,
which were the sources of his satirical vigour.   *Holy
Willie's Prayer* is the most tremendous blow ever dealt
at the Calvinistic dogma of Predestination.   Burns rushed
into the theological combat of his times with no knowledge of theology beyond that of the ordinary yeoman,
but with a splendid endowment of common sense and
brilliant satirical force, which enabled him to do more
for the demolition of the rigid Calvinism of Scotland than
any other writer who has assailed it.

The two forces by which poets link the hearts of mankind to themselves are love and admiration.   We may
admire, and almost worship, but not love: we may love,
and yet be unable to worship.   We do not love Shakespeare, Goethe, or Milton.   They tower above us in an
inaccessible majesty.   They are the mountain heights of
humanity, and are sacro-sanct with a sublime isolation.
We approach them with awe and reverence, and it is with
reverence we habitually remember them.   But there is
another class of poets whom we love.   Their very frail-
ties interpret them to us and endear them.   They are
" not too bright and good for human nature's daily food."
We cannot revere them, for they were full of faults and
blemishes.   They have no claim to majesty, but they
have the tenderer claim to sympathy.   Milton was
scarcely the sort of man we should have cared to live
with.   His own daughters found it particularly difficult
to live with him, and his first wife found it so difficult
that she ran away from him.   His friends always approached him with a solemn etiquette such as a monarch

might demand. But we should all have felt it a privilege
to live in the company of Burns. The geniality of his
presence would have filled any place with sunlight. Our
love would easily have made us " to his faults a little
blind." We should have forgiven him his excesses, and
have run eagerly upon the errands of ministration when he
was sick. His words of tenderness, his pathetic glances,
his wholesome wit, his abundant laughter, his brave
struggles with poverty and temptation,—even his weaknesses, would have endeared him to us. As a matter of
fact, they did endear him to his countrymen, and they
have endeared him to posterity. He has now the love of
countless thousands of human beings who never saw his
face, and know him only by his history. He was so intensely human that no human heart can find it easy to
deal harshly with him. He exerts a persuasive fascination
on mankind, quite independent of his genius, his song,
his exquisite creations in poetry. It is the fascination of
a true, loving-hearted man, a man who sinned much and
suffered much, who had a hard life, and fought it out
bravely as best he could, and in the very prime of mid-
manhood lay down to die in poverty and broken-hearted-
ness. The secret of the fascination of Burns, as it was
with Byron, is in the man himself as much as in his poetry,
and it is the individual note in his poetry, the strong
personality which speaks through it, which gives it so
wide a mastery over the hearts of all kinds and conditions of men.

On the other hand, genius is no apology for breaches
of the moral law. The sort of explanation which the
apologist of Burns sets up for his lapses from sobriety
and virtue to-day is an explanation which Burns himself
would have indignantly repudiated. He was under no

delusion as to himself. He mourned his follies, and he
expiated them in bitter suffering. There is no sadder
tragedy than the closing days of Burns. Undoubtedly
it is a reproach to his time that the greatest of Scotch
poets should have worn his heart out in ineffectual
struggles with financial embarrassment. But there were
other causes also which deepened the gloom of those
dark days at Dumfries. Partly by his own errors of conduct, partly by his injudicious violence of political opinion,
he had estranged his best friends. He was sick, poor,
and in debt. The last letter he ever wrote was a pathetic
appeal to his cousin to lend him ten pounds, and save
him from the terrors of a debtor's dungeon. It would
not have been much to expect from that brilliant society
of wealth and culture in Edinburgh that some help might
have been forthcoming to soothe the dying hours of the
man it had once received with adulation. But no help
came. There he lay, wasted by fever, his dark hair
threaded with untimely gray; poor, penniless, overwhelmed with difficulties, but to the last writing songs,
which won him no remuneration then, but which are
now recognized as the choicest wealth of the nation
which let him die uncomforted. Then at last the end
came. Those dark eyes, which Sir Walter Scott said
" glowed " with such an intense fire, flamed once more,
but it was with anger. His last word was an execration
on the impatient creditor who had striven to drag him
from a dying bed to prison ; and then the troubled spirit
passed. It is the old story : we slay the prophets, and
then build their sepulchres ; to the living in their need
we measure out neglect, and reserve our praises for the
dead who are beyond our charity.

IV

LORD BYRON

Born at Holles Street, London, January 22, 1788. His first poems printed at Newark, 1807, followed in the same year by Hours of Idleness. First Two Cantos of Child Harold, published 1812. The Waltz, The Giaour and the Bride of Abydos, 1813. The Corsair, Lara and The Ode to Napoleon, 1814. Hebrew Melodies, 1815. The Siege of Corinth and Parisina, 1816. Beppo, Mareppa and Don Juan, 1818. Marino Faliero and The Prophecy of Dante, 1820. Wernez, The Deformed Transformed, Heaven and Earth, and the Vision of Judgment, 1822. Died at Misso-longhi, Western Greece, April 19, 1824.

THE later science tells us that we do not come into this world with a nature like a sheet of white paper, waiting for any inscriptions we may choose to write thereon, but we carry our ancestors with us in our brains and blood. We inherit tendencies, and are apt to reproduce them. The laws of heredity and environment condition all human life. If this be so, it must be confessed, nothing could be more disastrous than the environment of Byron's life. His father was a ruined profligate, and his mother a woman of coarse instincts and violent temper. It was his mother's habit to mock his deformity, and then to smother him with caresses. She had a tongue full of bitterness and a hand swift to smite, and her habitual treatment of one of the proudest and most sensitive natures ever fashioned was a process of alternate violence and affection. There was something to be said for the poor woman : her profligate

35

husband had squandered the fortune for which alone he had married her, and then had left her to the emptiness of an embittered and lonely life. There was absolutely no good influence ever shed upon the boyhood of Byron. His only reply to his mother's outbreaks of temper was a fit of silent rage, which occasionally frightened her into a tenderness as odious to him as her brutality. Then this lad, full of strong passion and strong pride, is launched upon University life as it was in those bad days, and it is little wonder that he should instantly become the leader of the fastest set the University could boast. Full of humour and equally given to melancholy, sensitive to a degree beyond the comprehension of ordinary men, fond of all athletic sports, but debarred from them by his deformity, with an imagination brilliant, powerful, intense ; easily swayed by either good or evil influences, yet also full of pride altogether morbid in its excess, and, when once his mind was made up, absolutely stubborn, and of indomitable will—what future could the most charitable augur for such a youth as this ?   The future was precisely the future such an endowment indicated.   The only difference between the boy of sixteen and the man of thirty was that the good qualities had diminished while the evil qualities had ripened.   The pride, the stubborness, the morbid sensitiveness increased with years ; the susceptibility to the influence of better natures decreased as his own nature developed its own forces of will and individuality, and that developed individuality became a power to subdue others by its own imperious fascination.

On the verge of manhood Byron awoke and found himself famous.   What were the sources of his fame ? First of all there was, of course, the genius which deserved it.   He brought into poetry an intensity and pas-

sion altogether his own. All the strength of his own
nature, and all its weakness too, were interpreted in his
poetry. No poet was ever more fearless in putting himself into his work. He wrote with perfect self-knowl-
edge, and he made the public the confidant of his most
secret thoughts. He had no reticence, no self-respect in
one sense ; he flung himself on the public sympathy, and
poured all his bitterness into the public ear. He did so
in language of unequalled force and beauty. He said
what he had to say with an energy which compelled attention. He cared little for mere felicities of construction in his verse, his heart was surcharged with emotion,
and he poured it out in an intense and overwhelming volume. The poetry he gave the public was intensely individual poetry. Every character he sketched was himself
in various disguises, and the disguise deceived no one. A
more undramatic dramatist never lived. He set up a
puppet and tried hard to make it work, but it was useless :
before the first scene had ended, the puppet was always
kicked aside, and it was Byron himself who was pouring
out the story of his pride, his wrongs, his passionate
hopes, and infinite despair. And not only did he interpret himself, but in a certain degree his times also. The
old order was perishing, and the air was full of revolution. Without in the least sympathizing with the
people—for a prouder aristocrat never lived—he caught
up the inarticulate cry of the people and uttered it. He
wrote with just that scorn, that fierce anger, that reckless
revolt against the conventional order of things, which
was seething in thousands of hearts in the last days of
George III, and the infamous period of the Regency.
Just as Swift served the Irish people, but despised them
and their plaudits, so Byron served the democracy, but

scorned them; and just as the Irish people made an idol of Swift, so the English people made an idol of Byron. His books sold by thousands on the first day of issue. They were the solace of the student, the inspiration of the democrat, the secret delight of the schoolgirl; they were read by noble lords and needy apprentices, society beauties and sympathetic dressmakers, atheists and Methodists, all kinds and conditions of men. The English people love a fight, and Byron was fighting the Reviews, the solemn critics whose word had hitherto been as the law of the Medes and Persians, the social proprieties, the edicts of conventional opinion, the King and the Court —and the people cheered him on. He became, in a word, the idol of the people, and every excess, every audacity of opinion or of conduct, was eagerly condoned to one so young, so brave, so famous, and so splendidly endowed.

Then, also, we must take into account the personal beauty of Byron himself. With that one terrible exception of the club-foot, which was his torturing thorn in the flesh, he had the face and figure of an Adonis. Both face and figure were cast in the very finest mould of manly grace. Some one spoke of his face as being like a mask of perfect alabaster, lit up by a great light which glowed within. The shapely head, with its close clustering curls, was like the head of a Greek god. Nor was his grace merely physical: there was an exquisite charm of manner which distinguished him. He was a perfect actor, and the sadness of broken hope which he had set himself to write about he constantly strove to personify. Of course, society was at his feet. He was the observed of all observers. There was an aroma of delightful wickedness about him dear to many female hearts which would shudder to confess the feeling. Byron had to deplore errors enough in conduct which were real and circumstantial, but he always loved to exaggerate his own wickedness. He called on earth and heaven to witness that it was not his fault that he was wicked. He had never met the heart that really loved him, or if he had, like the young gazelle " it pined and died." All things were against him, the fates pursued him with relentless fury. Such an attitude in the ordinary man would simply expose him to ridicule; but we must remember that Byron was not an ordinary man. When this theatrical wickedness, this melodramatic despair, this passionate sadness, is interpreted by a man of marvellous physical beauty, in language of matchless force and energy, it is not difficult to understand the success that would attend the representation, or the applause that would greet the consummate actor.

It is because Byron has projected so deep a shadow of himself over all his literary work, that we are bound to take the fullest cognizance of the conditions and character of his life. What is the effect produced upon the mind by his works? It is an intense but unwholesome brilliance. They leave an evil taste upon the palate. The taint of a morbid despair is on all he has written, and on much that he has written there is the worse taint of moral depravity. No satirist has surpassed him in the keenness of his irony, no controversialist in the violence of his invective, no humorist in the grotesqueness of his imagination, no writer of any age in the masculine good sense which he can manifest when it so pleases him; and yet in all, and through all, there runs an element of depraved egotism, a contempt for virtue curiously allied with a remorseful loathing of vice, a perpetual bitterness and cynicism which leave upon the mind the unhappiest and most perilous deposits. In truth, Byron's was a great but morbid genius. His character was destitute of moral cohesion. He was the child of impulse, never unconscious of higher ideals, but habitually swayed and governed by the lower, or the lowest. His poetry was the exact reflex of his life. He was perpetually sinning, and blaming other people for his sin. He lived in a hard-drinking, fast-living age, and he drank harder and lived faster than anybody. He never seems to have known a good woman. His views of womanhood are simply brutal in their callous carnality. The purity and chivalry of woman's nature had no existence for him. It is the pure in heart who see not only God but the Godlike, and it is the genius that is pure-hearted which scales the loftiest heights of achievement; but to Byron such heights were impossible. The distractions of vice disturbed and poisoned his genius. The only form of womanly purity he ever met was unsympathetic purity. It is needless to enter here into the vexed controversy of Byron's relations to his wife, but it is pretty clear that Miss Millbank was the last woman Byron ought to have married. She was precise, formal, and cold; he was passionate and impulsive. A man with a record like Byron's, if he is to be reclaimed, can only be reclaimed by the most patient sympathy, the most prudent and delicate tact. But of this faculty Lady Byron unhappily had little. Fletcher, Byron's valet, said that any woman could manage his master except her ladyship. That she irritated Byron by her coldness is beyond dispute; and that he behaved badly to her is equally clear. But beyond that there is no evidence. The foul and odious myth evolved from the lively imagination of Mrs. Beecher

Stowe has been repeatedly disproved, and may be consigned to the shameful oblivion which is its due. Byron was a bad man in his relations to women, beyond all question, but he was not so bad a man as Mrs. Stowe imagined him. The chief thing for us to note, in our attempt to estimate the significance of Byron in poetry, is that his life coloured his poetry absolutely, and that that life was one long series of misadventures, follies, and errors, for the most part conditioned by the lower instincts of his nature, and embittered by the usual results of unbridled passions and undisciplined desires. Byron sowed the wind; in his poetry the world has reaped the whirlwind.

So much in relation to the moral aspects of Byron's worth every just critic is bound to admit. The plea that genius is a chartered libertine was one which Byron perpetually paraded, but it is a plea which the common sanity of the race instinctively rejects. We must repeat of Byron, as of Burns, that genius has no more inherent right than dullness to break the moral law. It is, indeed, the more bound to respect it, because, as genius is the highest effluence of the intellect, so its example should be the highest manifestation of the soul. Every man of genius ought to say with Milton, " I am not one who has disgraced beauty of sentiment by deformity of conduct, or the maxims of the free man by the actions of the slave; but by the grace of God I have kept my life unsullied." But, leaving the question of Byron's life, what are the distinctive features of his poetry? They are superb force and imaginative daring, a masculine strength of style, an intensity of conception and vigour of execution which few English poets have ever rivalled. He has little play of fancy; it is in imagination he excels. His verse has a large and noble movement, and inspires the mind with an exhilarating sense of freedom. He was not a thinker, but he insensibly perceived and absorbed the new thought of his day, and gave it courageous expression. He did much to accelerate the decay of old institutions and the birth of new. He swept like a storm across the mind of Europe, and uttered in the language of the storm the new thoughts which were then trying to liberate and express themselves. To say that Byron is a great poet is not enough; he is among the greatest. It is the fashion now to depreciate his claims, and Matthew Arnold and Swinburne have both demonstrated the looseness of his rhymes, and his ignorance of metrical construction. To do this is easy. Byron aimed at force rather than art, and art was less fastidious in his days than ours. He wrote carelessly because he cared little for the criticism of his age, and was at war with it. But for a man ignorant of metrical construction he has done exceedingly well. He won the praise of Goethe, and the foremost place of influence in his time. He alone of the writers of his time shared with Scott a European reputation, and his reputation entirely eclipsed Scott's. Hitherto English poetry had been insulated; he lifted it into a cosmopolitan currency. In the large and startling effects of imagination few can surpass him. What picture of a Swiss glacier, in the early morn when the mists are rolling off, can excel in truth of description and daring of imagination such lines as these? —

> The mists boil up around the glaciers ; clouds
> Rise curling fast beneath me, white and sulphury,
> Like foam from the roused ocean of deep hell,
> Whose every wave breaks on a living shore,
> Heaped with the damned, like pebbles !

It is in passages like these that the strength of Byron is seen: it is in virtue of poetic power like this that Byron has taken his place among the great poets of all time.

The last chapters of Byron's life are familiar to everybody. His life in Italy was one profound disgrace. Shelley said the best thing to hope for Byron at that time was that he might meet with a violent and sudden death. But it was at this period of moral decadence that some of his most extraordinary work was done. It was in Italy he wrote *Don Juan*, one of the cleverest books the world has ever seen; one of the saddest and most wonderful, but also one of the most immoral. Then came the sudden kindling of patriotic fervour for the cause of Greek independence. It seemed as if Byron, after all, would triumph over his lower self, and at mid-manhood begin a new and noble career of public service. But it was not to be. On the 14th of April, 1824, the fatal fever struck him at Missolonghi. On the 19th, with his last thoughts on his wife, his sister, and his child, he died. Like a sudden shock of sorrow the news ran round the world, " Byron is dead! " Tennyson, speaking many years afterwards, said, " Byron was dead. I thought the whole world was at an end. I thought everything was over and finished for every one—that nothing else mattered." " I was told it," writes Mrs. Carlyle, " in a room full of people. Had I heard that the sun and moon had fallen out of their spheres, it could not have conveyed to me the feeling of a more awful blank than did the simple words, ' Byron is dead.' " Mrs. Shelley, who had known him on his worst side, and had little cause to love him, wrote in that hour of loss and consternation, " Beauty sat on his countenance, and power beamed from his eye. I knew him in the bright days of

youth. Can I forget our excursions on the lake, when
he sang the Tyrolese hymn, and his voice harmonized
with winds and waves? Can I forget his attentions and
consolations to me during my deepest misery? Never!"
Even Lady Byron sent for Fletcher, and was overcome
with passionate grief; but, as he observed, was "perfectly implacable." That indeed was the general attitude
of public opinion towards him: remorseful, but implacable. Greece would have buried his remains in the temple of Theseus; England refused them Westminster
Abbey. The Grecian cities contended for his body, but
the country of his birth turned from him with cold dis-
favour. It was therefore in the quiet churchyard at
Hucknall, on the 16th of July, 1824, that his unquiet
dust at last found rest.

In Mrs. Browning's *Vision of Poets*, in which the poets
of ancient or modern fame are described with a brief precision and beauty of phrase altogether admirable, there is
no verse more appropriate than that which describes
Byron:

> And poor proud Byron! sad as grave,
> And salt as life; forlornly brave,
> And quivering with the dart he drave.

The pity which the poet-heart of Mrs. Browning felt
for Byron will always be the predominant feeling of the
world towards him. Much there was in him altogether
contemptible—his vanity, his insincere vapourings, his
coarseness, his selfishness, his devotion to what he describes
as that most old-fashioned and gentlemanly vice—avarice;
but when all is said and done, Byron attracts in no common degree the sympathy of the world. Before we
measure out hard judgment upon him, let us consider
the environment of his life, and remember that with what
measure we mete it shall be measured to us again.

V

SHELLEY

*Born at Field Place, Sussex, August 4, 1792. Poems first pub-
lished 1810. The Necessity for Atheism, published 1811. Queen
Mab, published 1813. Alastor, published 1816. Meets Lord Byron
at Geneva, 1816. The Revolt of Islam, published 1817. Rosalind
and Helen, and the Cenci, 1819. Prometheus Unbound, 1820.
Epipsychidion and Adonais 1821. The Triumph of Life 1822.
Drowned in the Bay of Spezzia, July 8, 1822.*

THE name of Shelley is irresistibly suggested by
the name of Byron, and the connection is a
vital one. They were contemporaries, and their
lives interlaced in many ways, and profoundly affected
each other. The influence of Byron upon Shelley was
comparatively slight; the influence of Shelley upon Byron
was high and stimulating. In life, in habits, in modes of
thought, no two men could be more diverse, and yet both
shared a common obloquy and exile. Both were at war
with society, and each has left an imperishable inheritance
in English literature.

The main point that unites spirits so different as
Shelley's and Byron's is that they were both poets of
the Revolution. Southey, Coleridge, and Wordsworth
were equally fascinated by that immense awakening of
Europe, and in the early days of its Titantic movement
could feel that at such an hour " it was bliss to be
alive." But as the lurid light of the days of the Terror
fell upon the scene, each receded in astonishment and
horror. Coleridge watched the transformation in silent

dismay; Southey took refuge in violent Toryism;
Wordsworth retreated to the cloistered calm of Nature.
Byron and Shelley alone remained, and still cham-
pioned the cause of human liberty. But Byron's was
the cry of despair; Shelley's the trumpet-voice of perpetual hope. The one gazed like a dark spirit on the
general overthrow, and uttered mocking, bitter, angry
words, and felt the wild storm of the nations akin to
the storm within his own heart, and the ruin of his
own life ; the other rose above the red scenes of revolution, and built up in the realms of fantasy a new
and golden age. It is this idea that colours Shelly's
poetry throughout. He really believed in an age of unrestrained personal liberty and consequent happiness.
He believed that he was helping it on. The fine thrill
of a rapt enthusiasm is felt in all he said and wrote.
He denounces the old with the fervour of a prophet, and
heralds the new with the passionate joy of a poet.
Queen Mab marks the rise of this conception of a golden
age in the mind of Shelley ; the *Revolt of Islam* expresses the sacrificial side of the revolution he desires ;
the *Prometheus Unbound* paints the apotheosis of his
thought, and is his completed picture of a regenerated
universe, the magnificent song which ushers in a liberated
world. Shelley sets the French Revolution to music ;
but he does his work with such an ethereal magic, that
its earthly and faulty aspects are forgotten, and it is lifted
into a realm of pure enchantment, where all its errors
are obliterated, and all its boundless hopes are crowned
with a more than human fulfillment.

It is necessary always to recollect how controlling
was the force of these ideas upon the life of Shelley,
if we are to gain a clue to the strange vicissitudes of

his career. The circumstances of his life and the
peculiarities of his thought have been so variously
represented by his biographers, that it is quite possible
to rise from the perusal of one life of Shelley with the
impression that he was a gifted madman of impure mind,
and to close another biography with the feeling that of
all poets he was the most spiritual, the most unselfish,
the most ideally pure-minded. In point of fact, there
is evidence to sustain both conclusions, that is, to the
critic who has a cause to plead, and enters on the study
of Shelley in the spirit of a special advocate. There
were certain ideas which Shelley held which almost
savoured of a disturbed sanity. The very recurrence
and insistence of such ideas leads the leader to suspect
a mental flaw. To the staid and respectable people of
his day, who only knew him by his advocacy of these
ideas, it is not surprising that he was—to quote his own
phrase—" a monster of pollution whose very presence
might infect." When a serious and fatal error in his own
conduct added impetus to the resentment which his sentiments had produced, it is easy to understand the position Shelley occupied in the opinion of his contemporaries. Yet, on the other hand, there was about Shelley
an atmosphere of unworldliness and purity, which struck
all who knew him with surprise and admiration. It
was a sort of unearthly charm which invested him
with the purity and irresponsibility of a fairy or a
spirit. There was a boyish impulsiveness, a childlike
simplicity and unselfishness about him which he never
lost. He was in truth an eternal child. He was unfitted
for the rough shocks of life, and never grew familiar
with, or tolerant of, the compromises on which society
is built. When he believed in an idea he was always

ready to carry it to its utmost logical sequence, and to
suffer martyrdom rather than forswear it.

Of the generosity of Shelley's impulses there can be
no question. When Harriet Westbrook, the daughter
of a London coffee-house keeper, threw herself on
him for protection from the persecutions of home, he
instantly married her. When he discovered the recklessness and injustice of British government in Ireland,
he at once proceeded to Dublin to proclaim a revolution,
which should be accomplished by the moral regeneration of the people. When he found a Sussex school-
mistress who sympathized with his vast schemes for
the regeneration of Ireland and the world, he instantly
persuaded her to sell all she had, and live with him
forever in platonic friendship. He was incapable of
prudence; the tide of impulse always mastered him.
He never paused for the mitigating caution of the
second thought. If he did an act of charity—and he
did many—he performed it with complete self-forget-
fulness. He could pinch himself to be munificent to
others, and when most in want of money always found
ways of relieving the embarrassments of his friends.
His wants were few and of the simplest. He was
perfectly content with a couple of rooms, cold water, and
a diet of bread and vegetables. Delicate and frail as he
appeared, he could endure the strain of prolonged intellectual toil, and was absolutely happy if Homer or
Euripides shared his shabby solitude.

It was in such a lodging in Oxford Street that Leigh
Hunt discovered him, and said that, with his slight figure,
his bright colour, his flying hair, he only wanted a
green sod beneath his feet to become a sort of human
lark, pouring out in the sunlight a song of unearthly

sweetness. Every one who knew Shelley realized something of this feeling which Hunt expressed in his graceful fancy. They felt that Shelley was an ethereal creature, whose life was so purely one of the imagination that he seemed outside the world of common human action, with its customs built upon the traditions of the centuries, and its prudence taught by the sorrows of experience.

This, then, was the sort of nature which was given to the world on August 4th, 1792, when the first thunders of the great Revolution were already in the air. We can easily picture Shelley, the frail and visionary child, of quick imagination, eager, resolute, and yet brooding, moved by the strangest impulses, and acting on them with an utter scorn of consequence. His imagination was his life, and it took very little to set those delicately-strung nerves of his vibrating and tingling with ecstasy or terror. As was the child so was the man. The first movement of his mind was towards the supernatural, and his first published writing a worthless romance, in which the supernatural and the terrible were the chief elements. The first man who really influenced his mind was a Dr. Lind, of Eton, who shared the revolutionary ferment of the times, and dropped its fiery leaven into the inflammable nature of Shelley. Even at Eton the wild and dreamy lad was known as " mad Shelley." Then followed the brief residence at Oxford, from which he was expelled at seventeen for having published a pamphlet on the *Necessity of Atheism*. There can be little doubt that in his expulsion from the University unnecessary harshness was displayed. The pamphlet was a declaration of ideas—not of convictions, and was really a series of logical propositions, in which Shelley challenged the first minds of the University to dispute after the fashion of the mediæval schoolmen. It was one of those impracticable notions with which the mind of Shelley was always teeming. The learned dons of an ancient University did nothing, of course, to convert the sinner from the error of his ways : their method of conversion was expulsion. Such a course might have been readily anticipated. But such a result had never occurred to the unsophisticated calculations of Shelley. The issue of his expulsion was that Shelley's mind, already alienated from Christianity, was now embittered against it, and that at seventeen he was master of his own career.

Byron spoke of being " lord of himself, that heritage of woe "; certainly no man was ever less fitted by natural endowment, or acquired experience, to administer the difficult heritage of himself than Shelley. He was flung upon the world with a heart hot with anger, a mind fermenting with revolution, and a character destitute of the discipline of self-control, and regulated by no knowledge of life or affairs. The wonder is not that he erred, but that he did not err more widely. As it was, from that hour he became the poet of revolution. He practiced what he preached. He had none of the cold selfishness which was the underlying stratum of Byron's character. His view of the brotherhood of man literally led him to share all he had with the poorest, and to meet the most remote from him in the social scale upon a level of frank equality. All the fervour of an exceptionally ardent nature was given to the work of spreading his ideas, and as these ideas passed through the alembic of an extraordinary imagination, they were transformed into the noblest poetry.

There is nothing more remarkable in English literature

than the rapid advancement of Shelley's intellect to the highest victories of poetry. His first poem, *Queen Mab*, like his first romance, was poor stuff, flimsy and incoherent, and it was against his expressed wish that it was ever included in his works. *Alastor*, his second long poem, is equally incoherent, but the beginnings are in it of his marvellous mastery of language, and the first bright glory of his extraordinary imagination. Every year that Shelley wrote he wrote better, and his style increased in purity and condensation. It reaches its highest point of splendour in such poems as the *Prometheus Unbound*, the *Adonais*, an elegy on John Keats; the grave and terrible drama of *The Cenci*, which is unmatched by anything since the Elizabethan dramatists; and lastly the *Epipsychidion*, which has been well described by his most relentless censor as the greatest love-poem in the universe. The *Prometheus Unbound* is, without question, the mightiest and most majestic production of modern English poetry. It stands alone in the magnificent scale of its conception, the splendour of its diction, the harmony and perfection of its workmanship. It is in itself a world of beauty, and the highest power of word-painting and the finest gifts of word-music which Shelley possessed found in it a worthy theme for their fullest exercise. It was written in Italy, as were all the great poems of Shelley, and is steeped in the light and beauty of that brightest and most beautiful of lands. To Shelley nature was the spirit of beauty, and he worshipped her with adoring fidelity. He was not destitute by any means of that minute accuracy of observation which distinguished Wordsworth, but his power lay rather in those large and startling effects of magnificence in nature, which none but he could adequately paint. He has been called the " Turner of Poetry," and the phrase is as just as it is beautiful. Shelley's power, like Turner's, was in depicting the pomp and splendour of evening skies, the weird and changeful glory of atmospheric effects, the terror of tempest, those rare and more awful manifestations of nature, when she puts on a supernatural grandeur, and seems indeed to be alive, a spirit of strength and beauty, whose rainbows blind us, whose ethereal loveliness awes and masters us, whose half-dreadful charms at once inspire and subdue us. Majesty is the key-note of Shelley's highest poetry.

Just as Wordsworth treated nature as something alive and breathing, so did Shelley, but his conception of nature differed from Wordsworth's. The difference is exquisitely touched by Mr. Stopford Brooke when he says : " While Wordsworth made the active principle which filled and made nature to be Thought, Shelley made it Love." There is a passion and sensuous warmth of imagination in Shelley's view of nature which is wanting in Wordsworth's, and there is a certain indefinable exultation which no other poet possesses. He speaks of nature in the tone of a victorious lover. He does more than this ; there is not only exultation but exaltation in the poetry of Shelley. He seems transformed by the stress and intensity of his passion into a spiritual form, a being of fire and air, an Ariel " of imagination all compact," a weird and unearthly creature who dwells among " the viewless winds," and lives in the hidden heart and secret place of nature. This passionate adoration of nature is nowhere so apparent as in his lyrics. They have the true lyrical fire and sweetness. They are the perfection of music. And through them all runs another element, the element of a most pathetic sadness. He pours out in his lyrics the cry of his heart, with all its intense yearning, its disappointment, its insufficiency. Of these feelings the famous *Ode to a Skylark* is the best example, and is in itself the most perfect lyrical production of modern poetry. It is sweet, strong, and tender; perfect in senti-ment, perfect in expression, perfect in workmanship. It is known wherever the English language is known, and if every other writing of Shelley's were lost, would be suffi-cient to give him a place among the greatest lyric poets who have used the English language with mastery and music.

Matthew Arnold has hazarded the strange verdict that Shelley will live by his prose rather than his poetry, but the saying does more to illustrate the eccentricity of the critic than to define the position of the poet. In poetry Shelley is described as " an ineffectual angel, beating in the void his luminous wings in vain," but in prose Mr. Arnold describes him as a master. The fact remains, however, that his prose has rare qualities of force and eloquence. It reflects in a singular degree the precision and purity of the great classic writers of antiquity. The real value of the assimilation of the great classics is the mastery of language which they confer. A ripe classical knowledge ensures purity and justness of lan-guage; it teaches its students to value and discern the delicate shades of meaning in which language abounds; it confers that accent of distinction upon the style of a writer, which, in its highest manifestations, is, as Matthew Arnold has told us, the great secret of im-mortality in literature. Preëminently is this result to be observed in Shelley. The English of his early romances is fustian—commonplace, incoherent, turbid; the results of his lifelong study of the ancient classics are seen in that splendour and purity of diction which distinguish his poetry, and have made his writings part of the English classics.   Shelley was one of the finest of classical scholars, in the sense not merely that he found the daily bread of his intellect in Plato, Homer, and Lucretius, but that he has in some respects more perfectly assimilated and reproduced the Greek spirit than any other English poet. The great poets of antiquity, especially Lucretius, whose breadth of view and majesty of style fascinated Shelley as an undergraduate, were his daily companions, and in his coat pocket, when dead, was found a well-worn copy of Sophocles.

The remoteness of theme which characterizes Shelley's poetry is both a gain and a disadvantage.   Often the thread of human interest is attenuated to the last degree. Mrs. Shelley, than whom no poet ever had a nobler intellectual helpmeet, felt this, and when he wrote the *Witch of Atlas* expressed her disappointment that he had not chosen a theme of more general human interest.   But, on the other hand, it is this remoteness of theme which does much to invest Shelley's poetry with so unique a charm. One of his biographers [1] has well said that in naming Shelley most readers feel they name a part of everything beautiful, ethereal, and spiritual—that his words are so inextricably interwoven with certain phases of love and beauty as to be indistinguishable from the thing itself. We may say so much to-day, but the practical effect of Shelley's insubstantiality of theme in his own day was that he had few readers, and to write without a public for many years is always a serious disadvantage to a poet. It represses ambition, it discourages effort.   Much of Shelley's depression of spirits arose from this sense that he wrote in vain.   " Mine is a life of failures," he said.

---

[1] *Vide* Mrs. Marshall's *Life and Letters of Mrs. Shelley.*

" Peacock says my poetry is composed of day-dreams and nightmares, and Leigh Hunt does not think it fit for the *Examiner*. I wrote, and the critics denounced me as a mischievous visionary, and my friends said that I had mistaken my vocation." At the time of his death there was practically no sale for his works, and his father only acted in accordance with the general sentiment about them when he made the suppression of his posthumous poems the condition of a niggardly allowance to his widow. The very expenses of the publication of his posthumous poems had to be guaranteed by the generosity of private friends. Is it wonderful that Shelley cared little to please a public who at the best studiously ignored him, or reviewers who received everything he wrote with virulent scorn, and were capable of writing after his death, " He will now find out whether there is a hell or not " ?

That the poetry of Shelley should reflect the sadness of his life is natural, but it is noticeable that, as he grew older, his mind became more serene and hopeful, just as the violence of his early opinions died away with years, and left him writing an admiring essay on the Christ he had hated as a youth. But it is almost absurd to speak of Shelley as growing old, for he died at thirty. In one sense he had lived long, for he had lived much, and intensity of life adds age to life not less than length of days. He himself felt this, for only the day before his death, when he left the house of Leigh Hunt at Pisa, he said that, if he died to-morrow, he would be older than his father—he would be ninety. What he might have done had long life been his it is possible only to conjecture. It is certain that, every year he wrote, he displayed more mastery over his own powers, and produced results more marvellous in themselves, and more worthy of fame, than the work that went before them. But long life was not granted him; he died with the song on his lips, at the very moment of its utmost power and sweetness.   On July 8th, 1822, he left Leghorn for Lerici, on a sailing-boat which he had bought from Byron, in company with Captain Williams. No sooner had they gained the open sea than a tremendous squall struck the boat, and a thick darkness shut her off from the anxious watchers on the shore.   When the darkness lifted the boat was gone forever. A few days later the body of Shelley was found, and in his hand was still grasped the volume of Keats which he had been reading when death came upon him. His body was burned, in the presence of Byron, Leigh Hunt, and Trelawney, on the shore near Pisa. From the flame the heart was taken uninjured, and was afterwards given to Mrs. Shelley. The ashes were buried beside the body of John Keats, at Rome, in the English cemetery, near the pyramid of Caius Cestius—a spot so beautiful that he himself said it may well make one fall in love with Death.   Thus, by the tragedy of fate, within eighteen months the writer of *Adonais* was laid side by side with the great poet whom he had thus commemorated in the most splendid elegy which the English language possesses. *Adonais* is less the elegy of Keats than the monument of Shelley, and it is of Shelley rather than of Keats that we think when we read the prophetic lines :

> He has outsoared the shadow of our night ;
> Envy and calumny, and hate and pain,
> And that unrest which men miscall delight,
> Can touch him not and torture not again ;
> From the contagion of the world's slow stain
> He is secure, and now can never mourn
> A heart grown cold, a head grown gray in vain.

VI

JOHN KEATS

Born in Moorfields, London, October 29, 1795. His poems first published 1817. Died in Rome, February 23, 1812.

ONE of the saddest themes for consideration in the literature of this century is the ill-starred life and early death of four of its greatest poets. Byron died by misadventure, one might almost say, at the very moment when he had begun to throw off the poisonous morbidity of earlier years, and certainly at a time when there was no token of failing powers. Shelley was drowned at a time when his genius had begun to show a magnificent promise of ripening power, and when his early errors had not only been amply atoned for, but were repented and forsworn. Burns, after a long series of misfortunes, died at an age when the latter poets of the Victorian epoch had scarcely put forth their powers. John Keats completes the list of poets of great genius and commanding influence, overwhelmed by misfortune, and cut off in the very prime of hope and achievement; and in many respects Keats' is the saddest history of them all. Byron, Burns, and Shelley, at least, had some recognition of their powers accorded them, and the two first had both ample and generous awards of fame in their own time. But Keats passed out of the world before the world had in the least perceived the rare spirit which had been in it. Even those who were his most intimate friends, Hunt and Haydon, had no commensurate understanding of the height and scope of his genius; both of them lectured him pretty severely, and Hunt even aimed to instruct him in style. The rare lovableness of the man, his sweetness of temper and simplicity of nature, his straightforward honesty and contagious enthusiasm, they both admired and acknowledged in no stinted terms of praise, but neither the painter nor the poet really perceived the originality and freshness of the genius they admired. As for the outside world, it was both contemptuous and indifferent. The reviews of that day were full of a wicked partisanship, and the criticism was venomous and brutal in the extreme. It was quite enough for the *Quarterly* to know that Keats was the friend of so prominent a Radical as Leigh Hunt; such knowledge afforded ample provocation for attacking him with every fair and unfair weapon it could lay its hands to. Indeed, it was not so much a matter of weapons as of missiles. Keats was not attacked in fair fight, but was virtually mobbed off the stage. To taunt a young poet with his lowly birth was an offense against every canon of gentlemanly feeling, not to speak of the good traditions of honourable criticism; to tell him to go back to his gallipots and stick to his pill-boxes was an access of brutality of which even critics in that bad age were seldom guilty. Byron said he would not have written that article in the *Quarterly* for all the world was worth; yet even Byron at an earlier period had written to Murray that if he did not get some one to kill and skin Johnny Keats he would be forced to do it himself.

The brief life of Keats is soon sketched. He was the son of a livery-stable man, and was born on the 29th of October, 1795, at the sign of The Swan and Hoop, Finsbury Pavement, facing the then open space of Lower

Moorfields. His father had married his employer's daughter, and appears to have been a man of integrity, and with some charm of character. He was killed when Keats was a child, and after a twelvemonth his widow married again. Keats received his education at a private academy at Enfield. For the first part of his time there he gave no promise of anything beyond athletic power; then suddenly his mind seems to have blossomed into life, and he became an ardent reader and student. Spenser was the first poet who fascinated him, and Spenser, who has been called " the poet's poet," was a potent influence to the last. On leaving school Keats was apprenticed to a doctor, and began to study medicine. But he never really took to it. In one of his later letters he says he could never have been a surgeon. He was far too abstracted for the skillful exercise of surgery, and he never could have taken fees. The fact was, his mind was not in his profession, and he soon left it, and began to write poetry. There was a considerable sum of money due to him on his mother's death, and on the interest of this, and latterly on the principal, he contrived to live in a frugal way sufficient for his tastes.

He soon found friends, and the love his friends bore him is very marked and touching. He was by all accounts a youth of singular beauty. Mrs. Proctor said, not more finely than truthfully, that his face was like the face of one who had looked upon a glorious sight. It was a delicate and refined face, with large and sensitive mouth, the eyes a brilliant hazel, the forehead low and broad, the hair auburn, and curling softly; a face which once seen was seldom forgotten. In frame he was slightly but compactly built, and the general testimony of his friends is that he always struck them as one destined to long life. He was full of vitality and energy, of enthusiasm and hope, and had sufficient physical powers on one occasion to administer a severe thrashing to a big butcherlad who was molesting a small boy. Indeed, the common idea of Keats, so far as the first period of his life goes, is about as far from the truth as it can well be. He was no puling, sickly youth, but energetic, buoyant of spirit, creating in all his friends the idea of strong vitality, which was likely to ripen into vigorous old age. Coleridge's description of him, as a slack, loosely-dressed youth, with a thin nervous hand, of which the older poet said when first he grasped it, " There is death in that hand," was written long afterwards, when disease had made serious inroads on Keats' strength. The true picture of the Keats who wrote *Endymion* is of a bright and brilliant youth, impressing all beholders with an idea of great powers, a youth who was bound to succeed in making his mark broad and deep upon his times.

It is, however, not the Keats who wrote *Endymion* we know most about, but the Keats who was the lover of Fanny Brawne and the butt for the ridicule of the *Quarterly*. It seems to us that there are two totally distinct John Keats'—the John Keats before decay began, and the John Keats tortured by the sense of great powers unappreciated and soon to be eclipsed forever. The impression which John Keats in the days of health and hope produced upon his friends we have already described. The impression one derives from the study of the doomed and dying Keats is very different. It is in his love-letters to Fanny Brawne, which never ought to have been published, that the John Keats of tragedy is revealed. The letters are full of violence, despair, jealousy : the ravings of a tortured youth, pouring out with-

out regard for himself all the weakness and intemperate
passion of his nature. There is something pitiable in the
display, something that makes a sane and self-sufficient
nature shrink back in severe distaste. They are, in fact,
the revelation of a disordered nature, a nature of diminished moral fibre, and in this view the words of his contemporaries confirm us. Haydon, who knew him perhaps
better than any man, says emphatically, " His ruin was
owing to his want of decision of character and power
of will, without which genius is a curse." Nor does
Haydon speak in the spirit of a censorious critic. He
loved Keats. He says in another place, Keats had " an
eye that had an inward look, perfectly divine, like a
Delphian priestess who saw visions. Poor dear Keats!
had nature given you firmness as well as fineness of
nerve, you would have been glorious in your maturity as
great in your promise!" It is difficult to sum up the
impressions such words as these create, but unquestionably they describe a nature in which the artistic and intellectual forces were not balanced by the moral forces.
There is not the firmness of nerve Haydon speaks of.
There is something, on the contrary, that strikes one as
sensuous and unwholesome. Keats says of himself, he
has an " exquisite sense of the luxurious," and writes,
" Oh for a life of sensations rather than thoughts!"
There is a story of his once having covered his tongue
with cayenne pepper, that he might appreciate more exquisitely the sense of the coolness of the claret he was
about to drink. The story is slight, but it appears authentic, and it coincides with the impression of character
which Haydon's criticisms and Keats' own words convey.
How far the pressure of disease may account for these
morbid excesses it is impossible to say: but it is certain

that this touch of the morbid ran through all Keats' later period, and occasionally gave his poetry a sort of false and hectic splendour. It is a dying poet who writes; and there is something of the preternatural brilliance of disease in his poetry.

Turning from the poet to his poetry, there are considerations of great interest which readily suggest themselves. Keats is the youngest and last of the great band of poets who laid the foundations of the poetry of the century: but he is not of them. The Revolution woke no echoes in his nature. He professed, indeed, the most advanced democratic opinions, and reverenced Voltaire; but there is no trace either of political or religious bias in his poetry. He is destitute alike of love to God and enthusiasm for humanity, so far as his poetry is concerned. Byron was never free from the haunting presence of religious problems; Byron and Shelley were both filled with the fervour of the revolutionary spirit; but in Keats there is no trace of either. He had no interest in man. In the passion and tragic struggle of ordinary human life he discovered no food for poetry. To him poetry was a world of the imagination only, a sealed and sworded paradise, a realm of enchantment where only those might dwell who saw visions and dreamed dreams—a land of voluptuous languor, where magic music filled the air and life passed like a dream, measured only by the exquisiteness of its sensations and the intensity of its delights. In order to create such a world, he went back to the legends of ancient Greece and the stories of mediæval life. To him the vision of modern life was tame and vulgar; he needed a realm more remote, and consequently obscured by the haze of distance, in which his imagination could work unhindered. The world he thus lived in was a completely ideal world, jealously closed as far as he could close it against the intrusion of ordinary human affairs. So saturated did his mind become with the imaginations of the past, that Leigh Hunt said of him, " He never beheld the oak-tree without seeing the Dryad." The only thought he has ever elaborated in all his writings is that beauty is worthy of worship, and loveliness should be worshipped for its own sake. The worship of loveliness he thus substituted for the worship of truth, and this seems to have satisfied all the religious instincts of his nature.

Essentially this is the artist's view of life. The cant of art now is that art exists for its own sake, and has nothing whatever to do with morals. Of this view John Keats was the true, though perhaps unconscious, originator. He created the school of ornate and artistic poetry —poetry which has no human robustness or passion about it, but which excells in the exquisiteness of its workmanship, and the delicacy and remoteness of its imagination. He himself said that a perfect phrase delighted him with a sense of intoxication. His view of poetry was that it should aim at the production of perfect phrases, beautiful enough to be welcomed for their own sake, apart from any thought or lesson they might convey. Here is his own poetic creed : " 1st. I think poetry should surprise by a fine excess, and not by singularity ; it should strike the reader as a wording of his own highest thoughts, and appear almost a remembrance. 2d. Its touches of beauty should be never half-way, thereby making the reader breathless instead of content. The rise, the progress, the setting of imagery should, like the sun, come natural to him, shine over him, and set soberly, although in magnificence, leaving him in the luxury of twilight. But it is easier to think what poetry should be than to write it. And this leads me to another axiom —That if poetry comes not as naturally as the leaves to a tree, it had better not come at all." This is, in brief, Keats' creed, and his work exemplifies it. He does little to quicken the sympathies, nothing to liberate the moral impulses, or to instruct the intellect. He surprises us by the "fine excess" of his imagery; he weaves a fabric of phrase wonderful for its colour and beauty, and he does no more. With that he is content; to dazzle us with loveliness is, according to his view of poetry, a sufficient end and aim. We have spoken of him as helping to lay the foundations of nineteenth-century poetry: it would be juster to say that he waited till the foundations were laid, and then covered the superstructure with an intricate arabesque of strange and gorgeous beauty.

Endymion, the first work of Keats, reveals the artistic nature in its primal struggle to realize these ideals. It has nothing to teach, no thought, or scheme of thought, to unfold, no real story to tell, nothing but its own wealth of phrase and imagery to recommend it. Of course it pretends to have a story, but as the poem proceeds the story is reduced to extreme tenuity. It aims, moreover, at being a love-story: but there is no human vigour in its love. To read it consecutively is almost impossible. The nuggets of gold lie far apart, and between them are dreary intervals, where the work of reading is indescribably toilsome, and the toil yields but the scantiest result.

The cardinal fault of *Endymion* is that it is confused and unequal, and is overlaid by excessive imagery. No one felt its defects, however, more keenly than its author, and no criticism could be more just than the criticism of his own preface to it. He says, the reader " must soon perceive great inexperience, immaturity, and every error denoting a feverish attempt rather than a deed accomplished. This may be speaking presumptuously, and may deserve a punishment; but no feeling man will be forward to inflict it; he will leave me alone with the conviction that there is not a fiercer hell than the failure of a great object. The imagination of a boy is healthy; and the mature imagination of a man is healthy; but there is a space of life between in which the soul is in a ferment, the character undecided, the way of life uncertain, the ambition thick-sighted; thence proceeds mawkishness, and all the thousand bitters which those men I speak of must necessarily taste in going over the following pages."

Nothing can be more correct, more honest, or more beautifully expressed, than this. It exactly hits the cardinal fault of Keats' early poetry—viz., mawkishness. There is a desire for mere prettiness of diction, an intemperate use of ornament, a straining after verbal effect at the expense of thought, a weakness of touch, which were only too likely to offend the sense of critical readers. But there were also passages of such rare and visionary beauty, of such exquisite touch and diction, that the feeling man might well hesitate to inflict any very severe punishment upon a genius of such unusual promise. There are few men who have ever formed so correct an estimate of their own power as Keats; whatever were the confessions of present immaturity, he had a clear sense of his own capacity, and never doubted his ability to free himself from his early errors, and achieve really noble and memorable work.

In another part of this same preface he says that while *Endymion* may dwindle into obscurity he will be plotting and fitting himself for verses fit to live. He said on one

occasion, " I think I shall be remembered with the poets
when I am dead," and no bitterness of rebuke on the
part of a venal press ever dulled this clear perception of
the scope and promise of his own genius. *Endymion* is
a confusion of beauties and weaknesses, a tangled jungle
of rich foliage, but in it are some of the loveliest flowers
and fruits of English poetry. Its famous opening lines
should have arrested attention and regard :

> A thing of beauty is a joy forever :
> Its loveliness increases ; it will never
> Pass into nothingness ; but still will keep
> A bower quiet for us, and a sleep
> Full of sweet dreams, and health, and quiet breathing.

The touching modesty of its preface should have saved
it from the harsh handling of a careless or hostile criticism.
But neither of these results followed. The poem was
universally ridiculed, and Keats' first offering of beauty
was contemptuously flung back in his face.

Like Shelley, the rapidity with which Keats' genius
matured is astonishing. Destiny seemed anxious to
atone for the brevity of the time for work by hastening
its advance. In the later poems of Keats there is no
trace of the confusion of *Endymion*. *Hyperion* is a fragment only, but it is second in sublimity and massiveness
only to the work of Milton. In *Lamia, Isabella*, and
the *Eve of St. Agnes* we have workmanship which is so
excellent that it is vain to hope that it can be excelled,
and in the half-a-dozen great *Odes* which Keats has written we have work which the greatest of poets might
have been proud to claim. In the subtle magic of suggestive phrase, such as

> Magic casements, opening on the foam
> Of perilous seas, in faery lands forlorn,

Keats has no master. There is a veritable enchantment
about these *Odes*. They, indeed, surprise us by " a fine
excess," and intoxicate the imagination with their beauty.
They frequently reveal also a patient observation of
nature, and an accuracy in describing her, which is akin
to Wordsworth. Some of his phrases, in the delicacy
and intensity of their imagination, fairly rival Shakespeare. They fix themselves instantly in the memory,
and cannot be shaken off. And in all there is a sense of
romantic youth which is in itself fascinating. They are
the poems of adolescence, and, if they lack the firm
vigour of manly completeness, they excell in the fire and
passion of young delight. Nothing can be truer or finer
than the closing sentence of Mr. Michael Rossetti's brief
biography : " By his early death Keats was doomed to be
the poet of youthfulness ; by being the poet of youthfulness he was privileged to become and to remain endur-
ingly the poet of rapt expectation and passionate delight."

The later biographers of Keats have made it abundantly clear that the *Quarterly* criticism had nothing
whatever to do with his death. That impression is due
to Shelley's matchless dirge, *Adonais*, and to Byron's al-
lusion in *Don Juan* —

> 'Tis strange the mind, that very fiery particle,
> Should let itself be snuffed out by an article.

The fact is, Keats bore his rejection with quiet dignity
and manliness. The breakdown of his health was due to
other causes. It began with a walking-tour to Scotland,
during which his over-exertion, and exposure to bad
weather, ripened the first seeds of disease which he had
inherited from his mother. Then came his brother

Tom's death of consumption, and then his most unfortunate love affair.   Love with John Keats was a passion of singular intensity, and the fire consumed him.   He was in a constant fever of thought and desire, fascinated and repelled, torn by empty jealousies and ashamed of them, living in a constant whirlwind of excited passion, and it was more than his overtaxed strength could endure. He lived two years after the publication of *Endymion*, but they were years of labour and sorrow.   One night he coughed, and then called his friend Brown to bring him the candle.   " I know the colour of that blood," said he : " it is arterial blood.   I shall die."   There were temporary rallies, but the mischief was too deep-seated for cure.   He lived to write some of the noblest poems in the English language, and never had the flame of genius burned so brilliantly in him as in those last brief months of disease.   As a last resource he went to Rome, and there he died in the arms of his friend Severn.   " I am dying.   I shall die easy ; don't be frightened ; be firm, and thank God it has come," said he.   They were his last words.   He passed quietly away in his twenty-seventh year, and his remains were laid in the beautiful cemetery at Rome, where, seventeen months later, all of Shelley that could be rescued from the funeral fire at Spezzia was laid beside him.   He said his epitaph should be, " Here lies one whose name was writ in water."   The truer epitaph is, " Here lies one whose name is graven in adamant."   Or perhaps we may accept the fanciful transformation of his own imagery which Shelley made, when he wrote :

> Here lieth one whose name was writ in water;
> But, ere the breath that could erase it blew,
> Death, in remorse for that fell slaughter,—

Death, the immortalizing winter, flew
Athwart the stream, and time's mouthless torrent grew
A scroll of crystal, emblazoning the name
Of Adonais.

His influence upon the poets of his century has been unique and abiding : there is scarcely a poet, from his own day to the days of Tennyson and Rossetti, with the solitary exception of Wordsworth, who does not exhibit some trace of that influence. " John Keats is the greatest of us all," said Tennyson : and certainly in the work of this unhappy youth, whose sun went down while it was yet day, there is more of Shakespeare's magic, more of Milton's gravity of vision, than in any other poet of our literature.

VII

SIR WALTER SCOTT

Born in Edinburgh, " mine own romantic town," August 15, 1771. First original poem, The Lay of the Last Minstrel, published 1805. Died at Abbotsford, 21 September, 1832.

AMONG the men who did most to direct the course of literature in the beginning of the nineteenth century the most colossal figure is that of Walter Scott. At the time when Wordsworth had finally renounced the world, and turned northward to the calm retreats of Grasmere, Scott was girding himself for his work. Scott was the lifelong friend of Wordsworth, and there was much in their natures that was akin. We have seen how the disruptive force of the French Revolution acted on Southey and Coleridge, driving the one to fierce reaction, and the other to the maze of philosophic speculation. We have seen that it produced no effect whatever on Keats, and that the only two great spirits who remained true to its daring ideals were Shelley and Byron. Wordsworth turned from its Titanic confusion to the study of nature; Scott to the study of the romantic past. Indeed, it can scarcely be said that Scott even turned from it in the sense in which Wordsworth did, for there is no evidence that he was ever fascinated by it. All that wild outburst, which filled even so calm a nature as Wordsworth's with enthusiasm, and which made every chord of the world's heart vibrate with its intolerable stress and passion, passed over him and left him unmoved. Scott shared with Wordsworth

70

his intense delight in nature, but not his enthusiasm for humanity. It was the splendour of the past rather than the thrilling struggles of the present which fascinated his imagination. There was a sobriety of temperament about Scott which unfitted him for any active sympathy with the great movements of the time in which his lot was cast. Nevertheless, however unconsciously, the strong tide that was flowing did affect him, and the impulse of his age was on him. The result of that impulse of the age working on a nature so deep and sober as his is seen in a species of poetry, which was a magnificent innovation, and a long line of glorious fictions, which have made him the true father of the romantic novel.

We have seen also that of all the great writers of the dawn of the century, only two made their voices heard in Europe, and achieved a cosmopolitan fame. Those two, dissimilar in almost every respect, were Scott and Byron. Yet few men of really great genius have been so curiously limited in nature as Scott.

It was in the year 1805—the year in which Nelson died in the cockpit of the *Victory;* in which Austerlitz was fought, and Napoleon was crowned King of Italy, amid all the wild storm of trampling hosts and falling kingdoms—that Scott put forth his first poem, *The Lay of the Last Minstrel.* As it was something of an accident that led Scott to write novels, so it was what seemed a mere happy chance that produced the celebrated *Lay.* Lady Dalkeith had requested Scott to write a metrical sketch of a certain old legend which clung to the district in which she lived. Nothing could have suited the young Sheriff-depute of Selkirkshire better. From childhood his memory had been stored with fantastic relics of a legendary past. Old snatches of ballad-poetry, curious stories of second-sight, all the odds and ends which the literary antiquary loves and cherishes, were the natural heritage of Scott.   The grotesque, the heroic, the romantic were the diet upon which his imagination had been fed. Upon the impulse of this request, Scott set to work and composed a spirited sketch of a scene of feudal festivity in the hall of Branksome, disturbed by some pranks of a nondescript goblin.   The sketch pleased him so well that there flashed across his mind the idea of extending his simple outline so as to embrace a vivid panorama of that old border-life of war and tumult, and all earnest passions, with which his researches in minstrelsy had by degrees fed his imagination.   Gradually the sketch grew until it had expanded into a poem of six cantos.   From his friends it won little favour : from the great Scotch critics open rebuke.   The subject seemed to them too local to win general attention, and the octosyllabic verse which the poet had employed entirely unsuitable for narrative verse.   Both in theme and metre Scott was attempting a daring innovation, and innovations are rarely popular with critics.   As regards the metre, Scott pointed out later that it was the one metre perfectly adapted for narrative poetry.   He took, as an example, the opening lines of Pope's *Iliad* :—

> Achilles' wrath, to Greece the *direful* spring
> Of woes unnumbered, *heavenly* goddess, sing.
> The wrath which sent to Pluto's *gloomy* reign
> The souls of *mighty* chiefs in battle slain,
> Whose bones unburied on the *desert* shore,
> Devouring dogs and *hungry* vultures tore ;

and contended that the underlined adjectives were mere expletives, and that the verse would be much stronger and more expressive without them.   This is immediately apparent by comparison, and if we want further proof of the adaptability of octosyllabic metre to the most vivacious, terse, and resonant narrative-poetry, we have it in Scott's own work. According to Byron's verdict, Scott had completely triumphed over " the fatal facility of octosyllabic verse," and Byron in his subsequent poems was not slow to profit by the lesson. But Scott had done more than that. He had invented a new style of poetry, and had interested the world in an entirely new theme. The old stories of knight and lady, monastery and castle, tournament and chivalry, had wholly dropped out of view, and amid the immense drama of Europe as it was in 1805 men might well suppose there was no room for their revival.

Scott again rekindled the love of chivalry, the old admiration of the troubadour, in the English heart. He brought precisely the gifts needed for his work. He had no philosophic meditativeness, but he knew how to tell a story. He also knew how to paint a picture. The force of his verse lies in its simplicity and vivid directness of phrase. His imagery is seldom very original, but it is always spontaneous, and very frequently is striking. The idea of the wounded day bleeding in the sky, for instance, is not novel in poetry. Alexander Smith speaks of " bright bleeding day " ; Shakespeare impressively paints the red dawn of the battle of Shrewsbury when he says,

> How bloodily the sun begins to peer
> Above yond' bosky hill! the day looks pale
> At his distemperature.

But Scott has surpassed both in concentration of effect when he paints the setting sun in *Rokeby ;—*

With disc like battle-target red
He rushes to his burning bed,
Dyes the wild wave with bloody light,
Then sinks at once, and all is night.

Mr. Ruskin has testified how true was Scott's sense of colour, and with what fidelity he describes the scenery which was familiar to him. In this quality his outdoor life was the secret of his power. He had himself ridden over the hills his heroes scale in mad flight or pursuit. By birth, by natural impulse and character, he was precisely fitted to interpret all this. And he did interpret it, to the immeasurable delight of his readers, in the early days of the nineteenth century. The freshness and vivacity of his style, the newness of his theme, his obvious enthusiasm for his subject, won for him instant attention and fame. Fox and Pitt both read the *Lay* with intense interest, and Pitt said that the picture it presented was " a sort of thing which he might have expected in painting, but could never have fancied capable of being given in poetry." Before 1805 had ended Scott was universally recognized as the first poet of his day.

It is needless for us here to follow the subsequent poems of Scott with minute description. In essential respects there is little difference. In each there is the same romantic interest, the same steady hand producing sound and excellent work, the same freshness and wholesomeness of imagination and sentiment. Never was a poet so entirely free from the slightest trace of the morbid. His verse is like his own Scotch rivers : clear, full, and pleasant, suggestive of the mountains and the open sky, and filling the ear with simple music. But there Scott's power as a poet ends. There were other and deeper things working in men's hearts which he had no power to interpret. There was an intense feeling abroad that it was the present and not the past which was of supreme import : the natural feeling of men standing in a new age, and filled with a passionate hatred of its limitations, and an equally passionate belief in its enormous promises. It needed Byron to interpret this ; and when Byron began to lift up his voice of mingled cynicism and rage, his wild cry of despairing bitterness drew men's thoughts away from the old chivalrous lays of Scott. The sense of the time was profoundly right. Poetry which is a reproduction of the past must always bow before poetry which throbs with the actuality of the present. Men felt that the true romance and chivalry of life was at their doors, and that it was in the present the real knight must ride to the redress of wrong, and the real hero bow in his solitary vigil. " The burden of this unintelligible world " was being felt anew ; the pressure of social and theological problems was increasing, and men wanted other singers than Scott to move their hearts and dominate their thoughts.

It is characteristic of Scott that he knew perfectly well than when Byron began to write *his* day was over. He quietly said Byron had " bet him," and he never sang again. Without a touch of jealousy, with simple manliness, Scott admitted that a greater poet than himself had come, and instead of waging a losing battle for his lost supremacy, he praised his rival, and then left the arena with all the honours of war. There are few men who could have done this. That Scott did it, and did it easily, is at once a proof of the sturdy manliness of his nature, and of the robust common sense and generosity which marked his character.

Scott left the field of poetry with honour and dignity but it was only to open a new chapter in a great career. He was too ambitious and too full of energy to rest content under his defeat. In 1805 he had commenced a story which dealt with the history of Jacobite Scotland. In 1814 he took up the old MS., and thought sufficiently well of it to complete it. Lockhart has given a vivid and memorable account of how Scott wrote it, and Lockhart's narrative has become a classic quotation. Scott wrote at white-heat, and with scarcely a pause. Lockhart was assisting at a party held in a house which exactly faced the room where Scott was writing. One of the company suddenly rose from his chair and said he could " endure it no longer." What he had been enduring was the shadow of a hand, moving hour after hour, with rhythmic regularity, behind the opposite window, and piling up as it wrote sheet after sheet of MS. " I have been watching it," he said. " It fascinates the eye. It never stops. Page after page is thrown on that heap of MS. and still it goes on unwearied; and so it will be till the candles are brought in, and God knows how long after that. It is the same every night." Lockhart suggested that it was probably some stupid engrossing clerk. " No," said the host; " I well know what hand it is. It is Walter Scott's." It was thus *Waverley* was written, and a long series of immortal fictions, called the *Waverley Novels*, commenced.

To describe the *Waverley Novels* is now needless. Their characteristics are well known wherever the English language is spoken. There is a confident ease in Scott's way of telling his story, which no other writer of English fiction has ever possessed in anything like the same degree. He has made history live, and generally

speaking, his historic portraits are correct. At all events
they live, and bear the impress of reality. His characters
are as truly creations of imaginative art as Shakespeare's.
Scott never strains after effect; he accomplishes his greatest results by the use of the simplest means, in a manner
surpassed only by Shakespeare, and rivalled only by
Goethe. It is this simplicity of the *Waverley Novels*
which make them so unique. In almost every case they
were rapidly written. *Woodstock* was the work of three
weeks. *The Bride of Lammermoor* was dictated during
the intervals of agonizing pain. Apart from the felicity
or interest of the subject, there is little difference in the
quality of the work. Sometimes Scott chooses a subject
more suitable to his genius than at other times, but with
the exception of the two novels written after he had become a paralytic there is little difference in the genius
and power displayed. It is a full, rich stream, flowing on
with no sense of effort, with quiet strength and majesty,
sinking at will into a placid current, or swelling into an
overwhelming torrent. Until the shadow of death fell
upon Scott he never knew what it was to wait upon inspiration. He was always ready to write, and wrote with
a keen sense of vigour and enjoyment which made the
work a pastime and delight rather than a labour to him.[1]

If one were asked to put into a sentence what is the
total impression Scott himself produces upon us through
his writings, we should probably reply, the impression of
a thoroughly sound and wholesome nature. There is a
genial and withal sober manliness about him which is
very noticeable. Since his day we have had many varieties of novels, but in this quality of a genial humanity

[1] For detailed criticism of Scott's works in fiction, see *The Makers of
English Fiction.*

Scott still stands unrivalled.   He has none of the analytic power of George Eliot, the subtle irony of Thackeray, the grotesque exaggeration of Dickens, or the base sensationalism and tendency towards the unclean which some of our latest writers have displayed.   The native chivalry of his character works out a high and chivalrous ideal of womanhood; his genial healthfulness preserves in him a cordial and sympathetic view of life.   He is free alike from the taint of scepticism and the disease of sensationalism.   He does not seek bizarre effects; he does not in his effort to be impressive or original become grotesque. Of how few can so much as this be said?   Who has not almost tittered at Dumas and Victor Hugo when they have sought to be most impressive, and revolted from the pictures in which the horrible has been expected to do the work of the sublime?   And even in the exquisite analysis of George Eliot, full of compassion as it is, who has not felt sometimes a sense of intolerable pain, a feeling that the scalpel goes too deeply, and does its work too mercilessly?   Scott has dealt with every form of human tragedy, but he has done so with the large and tolerant spirit of a great master.   There is a massiveness about his work, a completeness, a large-hearted power; he deals with his subject with a sort of gigantic ease and wholeness of view, which is never unconscious of its acute points of interest, but which subordinates the points where George Eliot or Thackeray would have paused, and to which they would have devoted all their powers, to the interest of the whole.   Above all he is a great humorist.   He is quick to see the fun of a situation, and his laughter is Homeric.   It is this element of health in which Scott stands supreme, and it is precisely this quality which we most need to-day in our contemporary fiction and poetry.

Had not disaster overtaken Scott in the fulness of his fame, and shattered his fortunes in the very moment of their completion, it is questionable whether the world would ever have known his true greatness. His works had revealed the greatness of his genius; adversity revealed the greatness of his character. Destiny, which had so far apportioned him nothing but prosperous days, with troops of friends and golden opinions from all sorts of men, suddenly adjusted the balance, and made sorrow the familiar of the last period of his life. The spirit in which Scott faced adversity was admirable. He bore his calamity with the stoicism of a hero. He sat down with broken powers to pay with the earnings of his pen the enormous debt of £117,000, which the mismanagement of others had entailed upon him. He never murmured. He wrote his cousin, Humphry Davy, that he defied that direful chemist, Ill-luck, to overcome him. And he was true to his boast. The last scenes in the life of Scott are unsurpassed by anything in literature for grandeur and pathos. They still live before the student of literature, and they serve to reveal the genuine nobility of the man. The picture of Scott fighting down decay, and dying fighting, is a memorable and unforgettable one. He met his end with perfect calmness. His last words to his children were tinged with the spirit of a true and noble piety. So, amid the mourning of the world, Scott passed away, having fought a good fight, and won the victory. He left behind him a splendid fame, a stainless reputation, above all a great legacy of imperishable genius; and in the thousands of pages he had written there was not one that he might wish were blotted out when he lay upon his death-bed.

VIII

COLERIDGE

Born at Ottery St. Mary, Devon, October 20, 1772. Poems first published 1796. Died at Highgate, July 25, 1814.

IF the greatness of a man could be measured by the estimate of his contemporaries, there is no man who loomed before his age with a larger majesty of outline than Coleridge. Wordsworth described him as the most wonderful man he had ever known; De Quincey, as the man of most spacious intellect; Hazlitt, as the one man who completely fulfilled his idea of genius. Carlyle's striking description of Coleridge in his last days is likely to become as immortal as Lamb's description of "the inspired charity-schoolboy," who filled him with wonder and astonishment, when he wrote, " Come back into memory like as thou wert in the dayspring of thy fancies, with hope like a fiery column before thee—the dark pillar not yet turned,—Samuel Taylor Coleridge, logician, metaphysician, bard!" Rarely has a man of genius received such a perfect consensus of admiration from his contemporaries as Coleridge. There was, indeed, about him something of that " ocean-mindedness " which he finely attributes to Shakespeare; and, apart from the fascination of his eloquence, and the spell of an alluring individuality, what most impressed all who knew Coleridge was the comprehensiveness of his vision, and the profundity of his thought.

The noble friendship which existed between Lamb and

Coleridge, and the less intimate but equally beautiful intimacy of Coleridge with Southey and Wordsworth, are among the brightest chapters of literary history. Coleridge first met Lamb at Christ's Hospital, and the schoolboy friendship then formed lasted a lifetime. His acquaintance with Wordsworth and Southey came later, and sprang rather out of literary comradeship than spiritual fellowship. In one essential respect Coleridge differed entirely from his great contemporaries. From first to last there was a certain romantic charm about his character. He was an idealist of the purest type, and never seemed at home in the rough commerce of the world. Lamb humbly submitted himself to the yoke of drudgery, and made his literary work the luxury and solace of a life of uncomplaining suffering heroically borne. He once jokingly remarked that his real " works " were to be found in the ponderous ledgers of the East India Office, and there is something to us infinitely pathetic in the spectacle of so rare a spirit as Lamb's chained to the galley-oar of lifelong toil in a London office. Wordsworth, with all his real and noble unworldliness, had a certain shrewdness of character, which served him well in the ultimate disposition of his life. Southey, when once the fervour of youth, with its unconsidered hopes and unfulfilled ambitions, settled down, became one of the most industrious of men, toiling with a pertinacious energy in every walk of literature, and often in ways that gave little scope for the exercise of his true literary gift. But Coleridge ended as he began, an idealist, careless of worldly fame, and unable to master the merest rudiments of worldly success. He had none of that natural discernment which takes a correct measurement of life, and none of that natural pride which preserves men from the insolence and

imposition of the men of this world who have their portion in this life.   When he left Christ's he actually asked
to be apprenticed to a shoemaker ; and later on, when he
left Cambridge, he enlisted as a soldier.   With an un-
limited faith in human nature, a curious childlikeness of
spirit, an imagination that clothed at will the most prosaic
prospects with alluring brilliance, he found himself in the
great streets of the crowded world, as virtually a stranger
to the common order of human life as though he had
been born upon another planet.   He walked in a world
of dreams, and never bartered them for the sordid gross-
ness of reality.   If we can imagine some angelic child,
or some simple shepherd of Grecian myth and poetry,
suddenly set down in the "central roar" of London,
ignorant of every custom of the complex civilization
of to-day, and heedless of its forces, we have a tolerably
accurate picture of Coleridge, as he stepped into the whirl
of the million-peopled life of ordinary men.   He had
every sense save common sense, every faculty save the
faculty of worldly shrewdness.   He was like some
splendid galleon, laden with a precious argosy, from
whose decks there rose the unearthly melodies of singing-
men and singing-women, and harpers harping with their
harps, but at whose helm no one stood, to whose course
upon the widening waters none paid heed.   He never
learned to adjust himself to his environment.   He drew
from his lofty idealism a mystic joy, which seemed ample
compensation for the loss of worldly honour, and ignorance of the paths of worldly victory.   Had the days of
patronage still existed, Coleridge was precisely the poet who
would have gained most from the protection they afforded
against the rude buffetings of an unsympathetic world.
When he left Cambridge, he was thrown upon the world,

with genius indeed, with intellectual riches incomparable and unique, with infinite literary enthusiasm and aptitude, but with none of those equipments which enable lesser men of all grades to secure advancement and success in life.

To yoke the idealist to the tasks of common life is a difficult and almost impossible task, and the worldly failure of Coleridge's life is mainly attributable to this cause. It is only fair, however, to remember that in his early career at least Coleridge did what in him lay to harness his genius to the lowliest literary labours. He sought drudgery as though he loved it, and never complained of its degradations or penurious rewards. A dreamer of dreams he might be, but a selfish idler he was not. He never lost a chance of work ; the fact is, he seldom had a chance. And yet this statement needs modification, for while it is true that he eagerly seized on every opportunity of casual literary employment, when the one great opportunity of competence in journalism came to him he at once refused it. At the age of twenty-eight an offer was made to him of half-shares in the *Courier* and *Post*, on condition that he devoted himself entirely to these journals. To most young men this would have been a sufficiently brilliant offer, for it meant not less than £2,000 per annum. Coleridge rejected it, and has given us his reasons for rejecting it. He would not give up the country for the town, he would not spend the strength of his brains on journalism, and, moreover, he avowed his opinion that any income beyond £350 per annum was a real evil, and one which he dared not incur. Yet at this period he was able to make only a modest income from journalism, and whatever mere worldly prudence may suggest, there is surely something very noble in Coleridge's refusal of a munificent income which, according

to his view of things, entailed wealth which he did not
desire, at the sacrifice of higher aims which he could not
renounce.   Long afterwards, in the troubled close of life,
he said that poetry had been for him its " own exceeding
great reward."   And we cannot doubt that Coleridge
chose wisely, with a just and perfect apprehension of his
own powers, when he renounçed journalism for literature.
It was the same temptation which in later days was presented to Carlyle, and was refused with the same noble
promptitude and decision.   To both men ephemeral and
anonymous success, attended by whatsoever munificence
of present reward, seemed odious, compared with the
more remote and uncertain gain of literary fame.   So
each turned calmly to the steep ways of renunciation in
which genius has always found its training, and prepared
to do the one thing which he was born to do.   This
action of Coleridge's is significant of the sincerity of his
nature, and reveals to us a strength of manly fibre and
courage not usually associated with his name.

The cardinal defect in Coleridge's life was in one accursed habit—opium-taking.   The first half of his life is
without flaw or serious blemish.   He is poor, but noble
thoughts console him, noble work enchants him, and true
love sweetens all his lot, and casts above his hours of
drudgery its rainbow bridge of hope.   Coleridge had
great animal spirits, unfailing buoyancy, and even " unusual physical energy."   He was amiable to a fault, and,
indeed, his one cardinal fault of irresolution sprang from
the sensitive tenderness of his nature.   At twenty-one
he had " done the day's work of a giant " ; he had won
reputation, he had fought the world at great odds, and
not altogether unsuccessfully.   Then all changes, and
what Lamb pathetically calls the " dark pillar " begins to

cast its gloom on Coleridge, and the brightness of the
fiery column of hope begins slowly to revolve, and pass
away.   Coleridge's first taking of opium was accidental.
He was recommended to take for his rheumatic pains—the
Keswick Black Drop.   It acted like the distillation of an
alchemist; instantly his pain fled as by magic.   In a few
weeks the habit had become a despotism; in six months
Coleridge was a shattered man.   He was degraded, and
he knew it: his power of free-will was paralyzed.   From
that moment the life of Coleridge becomes a tragedy.
His power of thought was broken, his strength for toil
impaired, his joy in life poisoned, his domestic peace
shattered: his old bright buoyancy departed, leaving
only unutterable despair, the agony of impotence, the
spasmodic struggles of a will that knows itself infirm, and
which after each attempt at freedom sinks lower in its
corrupting bondage.

There is good reason for thinking that in the end
Coleridge broke his bondage, but it was not till the
treasuries of domestic love were closed to him, and he
had lost power to open those further doors of the treasuries of wisdom to which his youthful genius had led
him.   It has indeed been stupidly alleged that the habit
of opium-taking gave fineness and ethereal brilliancy to
the poetry of Coleridge, but this is wholly false.   The
noblest work of Coleridge was done before he acquired
the fatal habit.   From that moment the fountain of his
genius became intermittent in flow, and deficient in
quality.   No one knew it, no one felt it, more keenly
than he.   Years after, when he again met Wordsworth
in the zenith of his powers, and thought of his own lost
opportunities, he wrote those pathetic lines in which we
seem to hear the sighings of a breaking heart:

O great Bard!
Ere yet that last strain dying awed the air,
With steadfast eye I viewed thee in the choir
Of ever-enduring men.
Ah! as I listened with a heart forlorn,
The pulses of my being beat anew!

Of De Quincey's famous *Confessions* he says: " Oh,
may the God to whom I look for mercy through Christ,
show mercy on the author of *The Confessions of an
Opium-eater* if, as I have too strong reason to believe,
his book has been the occasion of seducing others into
the withering vice through wantonness. From this
aggravation I have, I humbly trust, been free. Even to
the author of that work I pleaded with flowing tears, and
with an agony of forewarning." There is no mistaking
the meaning of these pathetic words. If the later life of
Coleridge stands out in painful contrast to the earlier; if
it appear desultory, aimless, brilliant only with an intermittent splendour, the fiery pillar only at rare intervals
turning its Divine radiance towards him, there is one explanation for it all—sad, tragic, and sufficient—" the
accursed drug."

What of the works of Coleridge? It may be said
briefly that it is upon his poetry that the fame of Coleridge is built. His *Friend* is full of the ripest wisdom;
his *Biographia Literaria* of isolated passages of great
beauty; his lectures on Shakespeare have long held their
place as masterpieces of critical insight; but it is, after
all, by his poetry that future generations will know him.
The *Ancient Mariner* and *Christabel* stand alone in English literature. Coleridge has an extraordinary power of
interpreting the supernatural, the night-side of Nature,
that weird, subtle, spiritual undercurrent of life which in-

vests with mysterious significance this hard outer world. In doing this he has done superbly what no other has attempted with more than partial success. He possesses force of imagination and felicity of epithet, and each in an extraordinary degree. His words are music, and his power of producing on the ear the effect of fine music merely by the assonance of words is unrivalled. No great poet has written less, but the best of what he has written is so perfect of its kind that there can be no mistaking the superscription of immortality with which it is stamped.

The real wealth of Coleridge's mind, however, was poured out in his conversations, and of these we have but scanty examples. Yet these are enough to indicate that the man was greater than anything he achieved. Coleridge's conversation was an overpowering stream: wise, witty, profound, embracing all subjects, astonishing all hearers. He once asked Lamb if he had ever heard him preach. " I have never heard you do anything else," said Lamb. It was a perfectly just description of Coleridge's conversations. Any subject gave him a text, and, once started, he would maintain for hours a sort of inspired monologue, often mystical, occasionally incomprehensible, but always most impressively eloquent. He needed a Boswell, and no man since Johnson would have so well repaid the assiduity of that prince of eavesdroppers. The few specimens of table-talk which are ours are not less marked by their incisiveness than by their luminous and sorrowful wisdom. In all Coleridge's later utterances the accent of suffering is very pronounced. We feel that, like Dante, he is " a man who has been in hell." He inspires in us a tenderness and sympathy which arrest judgment, and hush the voice of censure, for

which there was but too much ground of justification.
It is impossible to think of Coleridge without a mingled
sense of pity and affection, and we may say of him, as
Mrs. Browning said of Napoleon, but with greater truth :

> I do not praise him : but since he had
> The genius to be loved, why let him have
> The justice to be honoured in his grave.

He himself has appealed yet more effectually to our sympathy in his own pathetic epitaph :

> Stop, Christian passer-by ; stop, child of God,
> And read with gentle breast.   Beneath this sod
> A poet lies, or that which once seemed he.
> O lift one thought in prayer for S. T. C.,
> That he who many a year with toil of breath
> Found death in life, may here find life in death,
> Mercy for praise,—to be forgiven for fame,—
> He asked and hoped through Christ.   Do thou the same.

The faults of Coleridge's style are its occasional tur-
gidity and diffuseness.   This, however, is most apparent
in his political poems, and is probably attributable to the
fact that Coleridge found the theme uncongenial.   It
was in the world of pure imagination he was most at
home, and it was there he attained his highest literary
excellence.   In delicate and airy fancy, not less than in
imaginative intensity, he has few rivals.   Such a poem
as *Kubla Khan,*—a mere dream within a dream, may
illustrate the one, and the *Ancient Mariner* the other.
His force as a thinker and metaphysician is a waning
force, but his poetic fame has never stood so high as
now.   This result was accurately perceived immediately
on his death by the review that had persistently ridiculed
him for many years when it wrote : " Coleridge, of all

men who ever lived, was always a poet,—in all his moods,
and they were many, inspired." It is so the best poems
of Coleridge still impress us, and when the logician and
the metaphysician weary us, we turn with ever fresh delight to the bard. The pity of it is that Coleridge was
so seldom the bard, and so often the metaphysician; for
who would not give all the prose writings of Coleridge
for another twenty pages of poetry like the *Ancient
Mariner?*

IX

ROBERT SOUTHEY

Born at Bristol, August 12, 1774. Became Poet-Laureate, 1813. Died at Greta Hall, Keswick, March 21, 1843.

WHEN we speak of those who have wrought most nobly in the field of modern English, it is impossible altogether to ignore Robert Southey. That there should be any temptation to do so may seem somewhat strange. But the reasons are not far to seek. Southey belongs to the great brotherhood of the Lake Poets by force of friendship, but scarcely by force of genius. To write of Wordsworth and Coleridge, and say nothing of Southey, would be invidious and unjust, yet his claims as an English master are not to be mentioned in the same breath as theirs. The man who was the friend of Lamb, the true and faithful counsellor of Coleridge in his difficult life, and his most efficient helper, the first man of his time to recognize at its proper worth the transcendent genius of Wordsworth, and to maintain his cause through evil and through good report, and in like manner the generous critic of Scott, at least deserves a record among those who have done so much to render the literature of their time illustrious. But the point of divergence between these men and Southey is that, while he was the more perfect specimen of the man of letters, and has produced the most various work, they were his superiors in all that constitutes real genius. Indeed it may be well doubted if Southey possessed genius at all.

He possessed great talents, and he used them with wonderful aptitude and industry. He always wrote well, but
rarely with that supreme touch and inspiration which
give immortality to literature. He presented to his age
a noble spectacle of a life of unsurpassed literary industry,
dominated by admirable purposes, and free from faults
of conduct such as disfigure the fame of some of his great
contemporaries. Byron has used all the resources of his
wicked wit in holding Southey up to ridicule, but even
Byron recognized his true character when he said, " He
is the only existing entire man of letters." There is
nothing in burlesque poetry more bitter in its humour
than the picture Byron draws of Southey, in the *Vision
of Judgment*, offering to write the life of Satan since he
had written the life of Wesley, and describing how he
would publish it —

> In two octavo volumes nicely bound,
> With notes and preface, all that most allures
> The pious purchaser ; and there's no ground
> For fear, for I can choose my own reviewers.

And it must be confessed that the political changes of
Southey gave an unscrupulous antagonist like Byron
only too good ground for the still bitterer stanzas —

> He had written praises of a regicide ;
> He had written praises of all kings whatever ;
> He had written for republics far and wide,
> And then against them bitterer than ever ;
> For pantisocracy he once had cried
> Aloud—a scheme less moral than 'twas clever ;
> Then grew a hearty anti-Jacobin,
> Had turned his coat—and would have turned his skin.

When Byron took to controversy any weapons were

good enough : there was no man more adroit in throw-
ing mud, or more careful to select the most unfragrant
qualities of that peculiarly unwelcome missile.   The
result of Byron's attacks on Southey is that, for vast
numbers of readers, Southey is only known through the
medium of Byron's burlesque.   They see the mud-spat-
tered renegade of Byron's verse: they do not know the
loyal friend of Coleridge, and the perfect biographer of
Nelson.

It was as a poet Southey first challenged the attention
of his countrymen, and he died wearing the bays of
laureateship.   How is it then that his poetry has so
wholly fallen into desuetude to-day?   The main cause
lies in the fact that his poetry has no true relation to
human life and experience.   The qualities which give
permanence to poetry are various.   Poems may be ex-
positions of nature, summaries of experience, lessons in
philosophy, vivid and ardent pictures of human emotion,
the quintessence of passionate hopes or still more
passionate sorrows.   Or, even if they can hardly be
ranked under one or other of these heads, they may
still live by some curious felicity of phrase which lin-
gers in the memory and stimulates the fancy or imagination.   Southey's poetry has none of these qualities.   He has no power of phrase, none of those concentrated and intense epithets which cannot easily be forgotten.   He has no true insight into Nature ; he does not
know her at first hand, and is therefore unable to depict
her with fidelity—a curious lack in the writings of a man
who was the close friend of Wordsworth, and who knew
how to recognize at its proper worth Wordsworth's
power of revealing Nature when most of his contemporaries saw nothing in his poems but idiotic simplicity and

unrestrained egoism. Nor does Southey strike any true
vibrating chord of deep human experience. There is no
passion in his voice ; or, if there be, it is histrionic passion—shallow, stagey, and simulated. He teaches nothing, he reveals nothing. His whole theory of poetry was
hopelessly wrong. His themes, for the most part, are
utterly remote from human life, and his method was a
loose, rambling, rhymeless metrical arrangement ; occasionally, indeed, striking a note of real melody, but for the
most part little better than poor prose run mad. When
he would be impressive he becomes bombastic ; when he
aims at description he attains only diffuseness. He
pours out an immense stream of descriptive and semi-
descriptive verse, as in such a poem as *Thalaba*, in which
there is scarcely one striking epithet, one gleam of real
imagination, one note of true poetic power. In later life
Coleridge read again, at the request of Thomas Hood,
Southey's *Joan of Arc*, and this is the crushing verdict
which he pronounces on a poem for some of whose lines
at least he himself was responsible. " I was really astonished," says Coleridge, " (1) at the schoolboy, wretched,
allegoric machinery ; (2) at the transmogrification of the
fanatic virago into a modern novel-pawing proselyte of
the *Age of Reason*, a Tom Paine in petticoats, but ' so
lovely and in love more dear,' ' on her rubied cheek hung
pity's crystal gem '; (3) at the utter want of all rhythm in
its verse, the monotony and dead plumb of its pauses,
and the absence of all bone, muscle, and sinew in the
single lines." The latter clause of this criticism may be
fairly applied to all the more ambitious poems of
Southey. There is no virility in them. We read them
with an overwhelming sense of wonder at their former
popularity, and we have no desire to re-read or

possess them.   We cheerfully acquiesce in the fate
that has consigned them to oblivion, and we feel that no
worse disservice could be done to Southey's memory than
to disinter them.   However much we may regret the
spirit of Bryon's brilliant invective, we cannot help agree-
ing with him in the criticism which writes down as trash
the gouty hexameters, the "spavined dactyls," and the
"foundered verse" of Southey's multitudinous attempts
in poetry.

The chief interest of Southey's poetry, from a literary
point of view, is that with all its novelties of rhythm it is
a survival of the past.   It is a curious example of poetry
which is modern in form, but is wholly at variance with
the modern spirit.   It is an interruption, the interpola-
tion of a worn-out ideal, in the full current of new
thoughts, and new ideals of poetry, which marked the
beginning   of   the   century.   Southey received the
Laureateship on the death of Pye in 1813, and although
in all that concerns mere form there could not be greater
variance than between Pye and Southey, yet essentially
the poetic traditions of Pye are reproduced in Southey.
It was not altogether a stroke of malicious satire, it was
a genuine critical instinct, that led Byron to identify
Southey with Pye, and exclaim —

Pye come again?   No more—no more of that.

There is the same lack of depth and freshness, the same
barren platitude, the same stereotyped way of treating
Nature, and entire deficiency of any real instinct for her
interpretation.   To Southey Nature is once more a mere
collection of properties for the adornment of his verse.
He is always on the lookout for grandiose effects.   If an

immense collection of adjectives could interpret Nature, Southey might be her interpreter, but he entirely lacks that largeness of touch which makes his verbal pictures impressive.   It is said that Southey regarded the rise of the ornate school of poetry as a vice in art, and condemned it unsparingly.   We can well believe this when we remember that the two chief distinctions of the ornate school—of which Tennyson is the undisputed master— are felicity of epithet, and exquisite fidelity in the depiction of natural phenomena.   Keats set the example of the one, and Wordsworth of the other.   But to the lessons of both Southey was strikingly indifferent.   Perhaps the real reason of this indifference and lack of insight is to be found in the character of Southey's life. He did not give himself time to be a poet.   He was an intensely busy man :

> He had written much blank verse, and blanker prose,
> And more of both than anybody knows.

There was no touch of brooding contemplation about him, no time in his laborious life for meditative calm. He took up poetry in a thoroughly businesslike way, and applied himself to it as he would to the writing of a review article, and with much the same results.   He writes, for instance, to one of his friends : " Last night I began the preface [to *Specimens of English Poets*].   And now, Grosvenor, let me tell you what I have to do.   I am writing (1) *The History of Portugal*, (2) *The Chronicle of the Cid*, (3) *The Curse of Kehama*, (4) *Espriella's Letters*.   Look you, all these I *am* writing.   I can't afford to do one thing at a time—no, nor two neither ; and it is only by doing many things that I contrive to do so much."   Much of the explanation of Southey's failure as

a poet lies in this confession. Poetry was not the solitary purpose of his life; it was the recreation rather than
the business of his intellect. And poetry, more than
any other art, demands the entire surrender of its votaries,
and the complete dedication of their powers. Southey
was unable to make that surrender. It could not but
happen, therefore, that he should fall back on trite ideas
and effete models; that he should fail in the accurate
depiction of Nature; that he should resent the rise of a
school of poetry which spends infinite patience on the
perfection of its form; and that, finally, his own poetry
should become one of the most remarkable anomalies of
modern literature, and should utterly fail in securing anything beyond the most ephemeral and imperfect fame.

We are chiefly concerned here with Southey's claims
as a poet, but it will be convenient to include in our
survey his numerous prose contributions to literature.
And here, again, it may be said, Southey suffers from
the excess of his industry. At the best, the stream of
his genius was not copious: concentrated within narrow
bounds, it might have worn a permanent channel for
itself; but Southey committed the error of diffusing it
over an immense area, where its best qualities are dissipated. He certainly wrote far more " than anybody
knows." Too much of his work was really a superior
sort of hack-work, done to order, and therefore deficient
in charm and spontaneity. Who has read his *History of
Brazil?* Yet it is a work of great labour, and possesses
many passages of real eloquence and force. That im-
partial process of natural selection which goes on in
literature has by this time definitely rejected almost all
Southey's more ambitious works, and has left us two only
of his slighter works as candidates for immortality—his

Life of Wesley and his *Life of Nelson.*   Even the first of
these has not the hold upon the public mind it once
had; perhaps it now owes its fame mainly to the confession of Coleridge, that it was the favourite of his
library among many favourites, that he had read it twenty
times, and could read it when he could read nothing
else.   But his *Life of Nelson* still remains as the most
perfect piece of biography, on a small scale, which
modern literature possesses.   Even Byron could find
nothing but praise for so admirable an essay of literary
art.   Its charm lies in its perfect lucidity, directness, and
simplicity of style.   The narrative moves with quiet
power, with the ease of complete mastery, never once
becoming dull, never surprising us by unexpected and
evanescent excellences, but never failing to fill the ear
with pleasant music, or to keep the attention at a steady
poise of interest.   What praise can be higher than to
say that Southey has risen without effort to the height
of the most splendid story of modern heroism, and has
reared a fitting monument to the noblest of modern
patriots ?   In no other work of Southey's is there so
much that reveals the noble qualities of his mind or of
his style.   He writes with a sense of inspiration and
enthusiasm which makes his story an epic.   The real
poetry of his soul, never fitly expressed in his verse, is
uttered here.   There are few nobler passages in the English language than the last pages of this brief biography,
and especially its conclusion, so laudatory and yet so
just, so measured and yet so triumphant, that it thrills us
still like a peal of trumpets, or the last notes of some
majestic organ requiem : " Yet he cannot be said to have
fallen prematurely whose work was done ; nor ought he
to be lamented who died so full of honours, and at the

height of human fame. The most triumphant death is
that of the martyr; the most awful, that of the martyred
patriot; the most splendid, that of the hero in the hour
of victory ; and if the chariots and horses of fire had been
vouchsafed for Nelson's translation, he could scarcely
have departed in a brighter blaze of glory."   Prose like
this is worth many reams of Thalabas and Curses of
Kehama; and long after the meretricious glitter of
Southey's poetry is forgotten, his *Life of Nelson* will
remain as one of the few absolutely perfect specimens
of biography which we possess.

It might also be justly added that Southey's own life
will remain as an admirable example of a career devoted
to the service of literature, and characterized throughout
by magnanimity of mind and purity of conduct. " Is
Southey magnanimous ? " asked Byron of Rogers when
he desired to meet him in 1813.   Rogers replied that he
could guarantee the magnanimity of Southey, and the
two poets met.   It is true that the meeting formed no
real basis for future friendship.   *Don Juan* was soon to
see the light, and much as Southey valued the friendship
of Byron, he dared not let that poem pass without a protest against the degradation of great powers and the
profanation of poetry which it displayed.   Friendship
between two men so alien was virtually impossible.
There was a side of Southey's character which Byron
was incapable of appreciating, but which for us constitutes its dignity and nobleness.   He knew how to repress
himself, how to be patient under the limitations of his
lot, how to practice without murmur daily self-sacrifice
and industry for the sake of those he loved.   He knew
also how to appreciate qualities he did not possess ; and
nothing is more beautifully conspicuous in his life than

this delight in the fame of others.   He was always ready
to help with pen or purse any literary aspirant, and his
geniality of temperament in this respect added no incon-
siderable burden to the labour of his life.   He was not a
great man, not one of those rare men who impress us by
the amplitude of their powers and the splendour of their
achievements.   But if not a great man, he was a good
man, with a sincere and unostentatious goodness, whose
outward expression was found in a life of genial sympathies, of unremitting industry, of strenuous purpose.
Faults of temper we may charge him with, but, as Froude
says of Carlyle, in all the graver matters of the law he is
blameless.   He set a noble example of what the life of
the man of letters should be ; and if we cannot wholly
endorse the eulogy of Landor when he says,

> No firmer breast than thine hath Heaven
> To poet, sage, or hero given,

we may at least agree that the pious excellence of his life
justifies Landor's concluding lines, that he was one who
shall at the last,

> .   .   .   with soul elate,
> Rise up before the Eternal Throne,
> And hear, in God's own voice, " Well done ! "

X

WILLIAM WORDSWORTH

Born at Cockermouth, April 7, 1770. Poems first published, 1798. Became Poet-Laureate, 1843. Died at Rydal Mount, April 23, 1850.

WE now come to the consideration of the character, work, and influence of William Wordsworth. In many respects, and those the most essential, Wordsworth's influence is the most powerful and abiding poetic influence of the Victorian period. During his lifetime his fame was comparatively restricted, and during the greater part of his career his very claim to be a poet was eagerly disputed, and widely and vehemently denied. Lord Jeffrey's verdict that he was a drivelling idiot, and wouldn't do, has become historical, and is a memorable example of the ineptitude and virulence of that criticism which prevailed in the palmy days of the *Edinburgh Review.* By a curious chastisement of Fate, the ancient criticism is chiefly remembered to-day by its contemptuous hostility to Byron, its brutal attack on Keats, and its undiscerning violence of hatred for Wordsworth. Sydney Smith said he would be glad to be as sure of anything as Macaulay was of everything, and the dogmatical criticism of Macaulay was typical of the criticism of the time. It possessed neither justice nor urbanity; its weapons were the bludgeon and the tomahawk; and it knew no mean between extravagant laudation and merciless abuse. Some one has spoken of

Macaulay as " stamping " through the fields of literature, and the phrase admirably pictures the energetic Philistinism of the critical dogmatist. It was in this spirit that England first received the poetry of a man who has been, and is, one of the noblest voices in the literary life of the century. The critics simply " stamped " upon his writings; and not merely howled derision on them, but taught his countrymen everywhere to receive his name with guffaws of brutal ridicule.

In considering the works and influence of Wordsworth, we are bound to take full cognizance of the peculiarities of his own character, and the events of his own life. With all poets it is necessary to do this, but with Wordsworth most of all, because everything he has written is deeply coloured with his own individuality. He has written little that is impersonal; across almost every page there is projected the huge shadow of his own peculiar personality. While other poets have gone to history or mythology for their themes, Wordsworth found his within himself, or in the simple surroundings of one of the simplest and most uneventful of lives. He brooded over the " abysmal deeps of personality," and from them he drew the inspiration of his noblest poetry. Sometimes this superb egotism of Wordsworth is irritating, and often he becomes tedious by attaching enormous importance to the very slightest influences which have helped to form his mind, or the most trivial incidents which have composed its record. *The Prelude*, which is one of his longest poems, describes the growth of an individual mind, and among many passages of profound thought and beauty, contains others that are both tedious and trivial, and are tedious because they are trivial. It is because Wordsworth always found the impulse of poetry within himself that it is impossible to understand his writings without a clear understanding of the significance of his life.   He boldly declared that he must be taken as a teacher or as nothing.   He was no fitful singer of an idle day ; he believed he had a message to deliver, as truly as ever ancient seer or prophet had.   For this reason Wordsworth fulfills, more perfectly than any other modern poet, the ideal conception of the Bard.   According to some philologists, " minister " and " minstrel " spring from the same root, and convey the same idea.   The true poet is the bard, the seer, the minister; he has a Divine ordination, and is sacred by a Divine anointing; he is a consecrated spirit, selected and commissioned for the performance of a Divine behest.   This was Wordsworth's view of the function of the poet, and he endeavoured to fulfill it.   This is what he meant when he said that vows were made for him, and that he must be considered as a teacher or nothing.   This is the secret of that prophetic force which throbs in his best verses, and which gives them a subtle and enduring charm.   They are the expression of an austere and separated soul, of a spirit who dwells amid inaccessible heights of devout vision, and speaks with the accent of one who knows the peace of lofty and satisfying purposes.

This claim of Wordsworth's—to be considered as a teacher or as nothing—was a new claim to the critics of fifty years ago, and was undoubtedly one cause, and perhaps the main cause, of their prolonged and bitter hostility.   We shall see, hereafter, precisely what Wordsworth meant by the claim, and how he has built up a philosophy which is its justification.   But, in the first instance the claim was based almost as much upon the literary form of his work as on its philosophic qualities,

and upon a theory of literary composition which he himself has stated and developed in his prefaces with great
fullness. What was that theory? Briefly put, it
amounted to this: Wordsworth complained that the
commonly accepted theory of poetry was both false and
vicious. It had practically invented a dialect of its own,
which was as far as possible removed from the ordinary
dialect of the common people. It was artificial and
stilted—the cant of a coterie and not the language of
ordinary life. Its spirit also was wholly wrong and mistaken: it had lost hold on common life, and scorned it
as low and mean; it had lost hold on Nature, because it
did not know how to speak of her except in ancient
rhetorical phrases, which were the bronze coinage of
poetry, defaced by use, and whatever might once have
been true or just about them was now depraved and
mutilated by unthinking use. Wordsworth held that
there was sufficient interest in common life to inspire the
noblest achievements of the poet, and that Nature must
be observed with unflinching fidelity if she was to be
described with truth or freshness. He asks why should
poetry be

> A history only of departed things,
> Or a mere fiction of what never was?
> For the discerning intellect of Man,
> When wedded to this goodly universe
> In love and holy passion, shall find these
> A simple produce of the common day.
> I, long before the blissful hour arrives,
> Would chant, in lonely peace, the spousal hour
> Of this great consummation :—and, by words
> *Which speak of nothing more than what we are,*
> Would I arouse the sensual from their sleep
> Of Death, and win the vacant and the vain

To noble raptures ; while my voice proclaims
How exquisitely the individual mind
(And the progressive powers perhaps no less
Of the whole species) to the external world
Is fitted :—and how exquisitely too —
Theme this but little heard of among men —
The external world is fitted to the mind.

In this noble passage from the *Recluse*, the gist of Wordsworth's peculiar view of poetry is to be found. He announces a return to simplicity, to simple themes and simple language, and teaches that in the simplest sights of life and Nature there is sufficient inspiration for the true poet. He speaks of nothing more than what we are, and is prepared to write nothing that is not justified by the actual truth of things. He sets himself against that species of poetry which finds its impulse and its public in theatrical passion and morbid or exaggerated sentiment. To him the " meanest flower that blows can give thoughts that do often lie too deep for tears," and by preserving his soul in austere simplicity he aims at producing a species of poetry which will affect men by its truth rather than its passion, and will effect even the lowliest of men, because it is expressed in the plain and unadorned language of common life.

How truly Wordsworth adhered to the great principles here enunciated his life and work declare, but it will also be apparent that his theory of *poetic expression* hopelessly broke down after a short trial. It may be said, indeed, that occasionally even his theory of poetry itself breaks down. In the attempt to be simple he becomes childish, and in his selection of the commonest themes he more than once has selected themes which no human genius could make poetic. In the main, however, the principles of *thought* which he enunciated he strictly observed throughout a long life, and his noblest effects have been produced within the limitations he invented, and which he was contented to obey. But when we consider the question of his literary *expression*, we at once perceive that he does not use the language of common life, nor was it possible that he should. The vocabulary of the educated man is far wider than the vocabulary of the illiterate, and the vocabulary of the great poet is usually the fullest of all. Wordsworth simply could not help himself when he used forms of expression which the plowman and pedlar could never have used. It was in vain that he said : " I have proposed to myself to imitate, and, as far as is possible, to adopt the very language of men. I have taken as much pains to avoid what is usually called poetic diction as others ordinarily take to produce it." In poems like *The Idiot Boy*, or *The Thorn*, he certainly fulfills this purpose : he has so entirely succeeded in avoiding poetic diction than he has produced verses which by no stretch of literary charity could be called poetry at all. Wordsworth's noblest poetry is noble in direct contravention of his own theory of poetry, and is a pertinent illustration of the futility of all such theories to bind men of real genius. His theory is that true poetry should be merely " the language really spoken by men, with metre superadded," and he asks us, " What other distinction from prose would we have ? " We reply that from the true poet we expect melody and magic of phrase—the gift of musical expression which can make words a power equal to music, in producing exquisite sensations on the ear, and which is a still higher power than music, because it can directly produce noble thoughts and passions in the soul. If Wordsworth had only given us the language of prose with metre superadded, we should not be reading his pages to-day with ever-fresh delight. It is because he discards his own theory of poetic expression, and has given us many verses written in language unmatched for purity and melody of phrase, and wholly different from the " language really spoken by men," that we have judged him a great poet.

When we consider the vehemence of that ridicule with which Wordsworth was greeted, and the virulence of that criticism with which he was pursued for nearly half a century, it is necessary, therefore, to bear in mind how absurd this theory of poetic expression is, and how doubly absurd it must have seemed to those who were the critical authorities of his day. And it must also be recollected that Wordsworth pressed his theory in season and out of season. The temper of mind which made him attach an overweening importance to the slightest incidents in his own intellectual development made him also blind to the relative values of his poems. He deliberately chose poems like *The Idiot Boy*— which were written in his worst style—and solemnly insisted on their significance as illustrative of his theory. If he had had any sense of humour, he would have perceived how absurd this was ; but in humour Wordsworth was singularly deficient. There was a stiffness of controversial temper about him which refused any parley with the enemy. The consequence was that the more strenuously Wordsworth insisted on the value of his worst poems, the more blind men became to the supreme excellence of his best. They accepted his worst poems as typical of his genius, and it was easy to turn them into ridicule. If poetry were, indeed, only prose with metre superadded, it was obvious that any prose man could become a poet at will ; and the facile retort rose to the lips that Wordsworth had justified his theory by writing prose under the delusion that it was poetry. The astonishing thing is that men of genuine critical ability were so slow to recognize that among many poems which were little better than prose cut up into metrical lengths, there were other poems of great and enduring excellence, which the greatest poets of all time might be proud to claim. However, a truce has long since been called to such contentions. No one cares much to-day what particular poetic fads Wordsworth may have advocated : the fact that has gradually grown clear and clearer to the world is that in Wordsworth we possess a poet of profound originality and of supreme genius, and his greatness is generally recognized. It is also generally recognized that, more than any other modern poet, Wordsworth has expressed in his poems a noble philosophy ; and it is to the study of that philosophy that I invite those who would read Wordsworth with a seeing eye and an understanding heart.

XI

THE CONNECTION BETWEEN WORDS-WORTH'S LIFE AND HIS POETRY

I HAVE already said that with Wordsworth, more than with most poets, the life of the poet must be considered in connection with his poetry. Let us now look at this subject a little more closely. Wordsworth was born on the borders of that Lake Country which he loved so well, at Cockermouth, on April 7th, 1770. From his boyhood he was familiar with English mountain scenery, and the subduing spirit of its beauty touched his earliest life. He himself tells us —

> Nothing at that time
> So welcome, no temptation half so dear
> As that which urged me to a daring feat.
> Deep pools, tall trees, black chasms and dizzy crags,
> And tottering towers: I loved to stand and read
> Their looks forbidding, read and disobey.

It is a vivid picture of the wild child of Nature, awed and yet exhilarated in her presence, which Wordsworth paints in these lines. The boyish Wordsworth described in the *Recluse* is a true boy, touched more perhaps than a boy should be with a sense of mystery in Nature, but not distinguished by any unwholesome precocity or unnatural meditativeness. The awe of Nature seems to have been a feeling early developed in him, and it never left him. He tells us how one day while nutting he penetrated into a distant solitude of the wood, where the silence and sense of sacredness were so profound, that he

108

hastily retreated, with the feeling that he had invaded a
sanctuary. But in other passages, such as the above, the
idea left upon the mind is of a sturdy youth, rejoicing in
his strength of limb and sureness of foot, and taking a
thoroughly healthy delight in outdoor life. He has the
wholesome blood of the Cumberland dalesman in his
veins, and loves the mountains as only those love them
whose life has thriven beneath their shadows; but even
as a boy he learned to feel something of that healing
serenity which Nature breathes into the soul that loves
her. He felt that " whatever of highest he can hope, it
is hers to promise ; all that is dark in him she must purge
into purity ; all that is failing in him she must strengthen
into truth ; in her, through all the world's warfare, he
must find his peace " ; or, to quote his own memorable
words :

> But me hath Nature tamed, and bade to seek
> For other agitations, or be calm ;
> Hath dealt with me as with a turbulent stream,
> Some nursling of the mountains, which she leads
> Through quiet meadows, after he has learnt
> His strength, and had his triumph and his joy,
> His desperate course of tumult and of glee.

The first noticeable thing, therefore, is that Wordsworth was a true " nursling of the mountains," and the
influence of natural beauty and pastoral life was one of
the earliest influences which shaped his mind. He had
no love of cities, and knew little of them. When he spoke
of them it was with reluctance and compassion; he
brooded

> Above the fierce confederate storm
> Of sorrow, barricadoed ever more
> Within the walls of cities,

for it seemed to him that cities were the natural homes
of sorrow, and the open fields the true abodes of peace.
He had a passionate love for an outdoor life, and his mind
naturally lent itself to that deep meditativeness which is
a common characteristic of those who spend many hours
of every day in the loneliness of Nature.   Strangely
enough, in one who is known to fame as a man of letters,
it was nevertheless true that the three things most difficult for him to do, to the very end of his life, were reading, writing, and the toil of literary composition.   When
he is a young man of thirty-three, he writes to Sir George
Beaumont that he never has a pen in his hand for five
minutes without becoming a bundle of uneasiness, and
experiencing an insufferable oppression.   " Nine-tenths
of my verses," he writes forty years later, " have been
murmured out in the open air."   When a visitor at
Rydal Mount asked to see Wordsworth's study, the reply
was that he could see his " library, where he keeps his
books, but his study is out of doors."   The peculiarities
thus described are the typical peculiarities of the sturdy
dalesman, and such in many respects Wordsworth was
to the end of his days.   When he described the peasants
and farmers of the mountains, it was no fanciful love that
attracted him to them : he spoke of men whom he thoroughly understood, because he was physically akin to
them.   The sturdy fibre of his mind, his intellectual honesty, his independence, his power of contemplation, his
sufficiency—not the coarse sufficiency of the vulgar egoist,
but the habitual sufficiency of a well-poised and self-re-
liant nature—all these were the distinguishing characteristics of his neighbours, but touched in him with a loftier
spirit, and put to higher purposes.   Even in his face and
figure—in the ruggedness of the one and the firmness and

sturdiness of the other—much of this was discernible.   It
was a figure that showed worst in drawing-rooms, as
though consciously alien to them; a face that seemed
almost vacant to the nimble-minded dwellers in cities, but
which glowed with true illumination and nobility among
the sounds and visions of his native countryside.   The
mould in which Wordsworth was cast was a strong one.
His nature was slow, and deep, and steadfast: what he
was at thirty he practically was at seventy, save that there
had been an inevitable stiffening of ideas, and an equally
inevitable growth of self reliant sufficiency.

Let any one try to picture to himself the leading characteristics of the life of a Cumbrian dalesman, and, if he
pleases, let him go to the poems of Wordsworth himself
for materials, and he will find that the life so outlined
will be, above all things, independent, self-respecting,
and self-sufficient, frugal without parsimony, pious without formality, and simple without boorishness.   It is a
wholesome life of humble industries and simple pleasures,
and such a life was not merely to Wordsworth the ideal
life, but it was an ideal which he himself perfectly fulfilled.
And let any one think again of the sort of life which
found favour with the poets of his day, and the sort of
life they themselves lived—Byron with his bitter mis-
anthropy, Shelley with his outraged sensitiveness, Keats
with his recoil from a sordid world to the ideal paradise
of Greek mythology, Moore with his cockney glitter,
Coleridge with his remote and visionary splendour—let
him think of this, and he will see how strange a thing it
was to such a world, that a Cumbrian dalesman's life
should have been thrust before it as an ideal human life,
and that, too, by a man of rare intellectual powers who
had himself chosen such a life for himself, and had found

in it tranquillity and satisfaction. In that age there were only two poets who had shown any genuine love of Nature in her daily and common manifestations, and had written verses which might have " been murmured out in the open air." These were Burns and Scott, and it is noticeable that for both Wordsworth felt a deep attraction. In both there is a supreme healthfulness, a sense of robust enjoyment in fresh air and simple sights. When Scott describes Nature it is always with a true eye for colour, and Burns's poems touch us by their artless rusticity not less than by their artistic beauty. Wordsworth himself has told us how " admirably has Burns given way to these impulses of Nature, both with reference to himself and in describing the condition of others " ; and it was the simple humanness of the Ayrshire farmer that endeared him to a poet who valued more than anything else simplicity and virtue in human nature. But where Wordsworth differed from all other poets of his day was that he had a conscious ideal of what human life might be made, through simplicity of desire and communion with Nature, and he resolutely set himself to the fulfillment of his ideal. Especially was the dalesman's independence and self-sufficiency marked in him. He knew what it was to be a law unto himself, and found in his own nature the true impulses of action. And so he writes : " These two things, contradictory as they seem, must go together, manly dependence and manly independence, manly reliance, and manly self-reliance." And again : " Let the poet first consult his own heart, as I have done, and leave the rest to posterity—to, I hope, an improving posterity. I have not written down to the level of superficial observers or unthinking minds." The spirit of these words reveals the man, and the man so revealed could only have thriven in a region where simplicity, and manliness, and rugged honesty were the prime virtues and common heritage of daily life.

The great turning-point in the life of Wordsworth was the year 1795, when his sister Dora joined him, and became henceforth the chosen comrade of his intellectual life, not less than the confidant of his emotions. The period preceding had been spent somewhat aimlessly, and is memorable only for the foreign travel Wordsworth had indulged in, his hopes of France, and his subsequent disillusionment and despair. Like every poet of his day, save Keats and Scott, he was violently affected by the French Revolution, and was caught within the whirl of its frantic fascination. But with the Reign of Terror his hopes of world-wide regeneration perished, and a sullen and impenetrable despair fell upon him. He was indeed slow to give up hope, and when England declared war upon France he flamed out in indignant denunciation of what seemed to him a disgraceful outrage. The effect of these events on his poetry we shall best see when we come to consider his patriotic poems. In the meantime, what we have to observe is that in 1795 Wordsworth was as unsettled as man could well be, and was without any true aim or work in life. He was, to quote Mr. F. W. Myers, " a rough and somewhat stubborn young man, who, in nearly thirty years of life, had seemed alternately to idle without grace and to study without advantage, and it might well have seemed incredible that he could have anything new or valuable to communicate to mankind." It was from this state of lethargic aimlessness that Dora Wordsworth redeemed him. She revealed to him the true bent of his nature, and discovered to him his true powers. She led him back to the healing solitude of Nature, where alone, as she justly perceived, his mind could find a fit environment, and his powers could ripen into greatness. She understood him better than he understood himself. She knew that he was unfitted for public life, or the conduct of affairs, but that there was in him that which might be of infinite service to the world, if fitting opportunity were given for its development. And she judged that nowhere so well as in the beloved environment of his native mountains would that spark of ethereal fire which possessed him be kindled into a living and animating flame. Some years were yet to elapse before he finally settled at Grasmere, but they were years passed in seclusion, during which he gradually gave himself up to that appointed task of poetic toil, to which he felt himself divinely consecrated. It meant for him a practical renunciation of the world. He had but the scantiest means of subsistence, and knew well that such a life as he now contemplated must be almost a peasant's life, lived upon a peasant's frugal fare and in a peasant's mean surroundings. When he turned his back upon great cities, and steadfastly set his face towards the English mountains, he resolutely shut the door upon all hopes of brilliant worldly success, upon all the natural hopes of advancement in life, which a man of culture and education may legitimately entertain.

His only guide in this most difficult hour was the need and impulse of his own nature. He felt that in the solitude of Nature there was peace, and there only was a life of plain living and high thinking possible. All he knew was that the common ideals of life did not satisfy him, and he scornfully exclaimed —

The wealthiest man amongst us is the best ;
No grandeur now in nature or in book
Delights us.

He had learned the great lesson of living, not for things temporal, but for things eternal ; he had set himself above all to be true to his own self, and he had the rare daring of being absolutely faithful to the voice of this supreme conviction. Any greatness which attaches to Wordsworth's character directly springs from this spiritual honesty of purpose. The noblest qualities of his poetry, all the qualities indeed which differentiate and distinguish it, and give it a lofty isolation in English literature, were the natural result of this temper of spirit and method of life. There, far from the fevered life of cities, where the free winds blew, and the spacious silence taught serenity ; there, in the daily contemplation of simple life and natural beauty among his own mountains, the bonds of custom fell from Wordsworth's spirit, and he became enfranchised with a glorious liberty. Strength returned to him, clearness and resoluteness of spirit, sanity and joy of mind. The great lesson which he was consecrated to expound was the nobleness of unworldly and simple life, and such a lesson could only be learned, much less taught, by a life which was itself infinitely removed from the vulgar scramble for wealth, and the insane thirst for social power. It is not too much to say that it is to Dora Wordsworth that England owes the precious gift of her brother's genius. She recognized it when he himself was dubious ; she taught him how to collect his powers and develop them ; she encouraged him when almost every other voice was hostile ; and, finally, she taught him that serene confidence in himself, and in his mission, which made him say to his few friends, when the public contempt and apathy of his time seemed universal and unbearable: "Make yourselves at rest respecting me; I speak the truths the world must feel at last."

XII

SOME CHARACTERISTICS OF WORDS-
WORTH'S POETRY

WE have seen how Wordsworth began his poetic career with certain clearly defined and original views on the art of poetic expression. If he had been a less self-contained and self-confident man, he would hardly have dared to put forth these views with such perfect indifference to the current of popular taste which prevailed in the beginning of the century. But the truth is that Wordsworth was not a student of books. De Quincey says that his library did not exceed three hundred volumes, and many of these were in a very incomplete condition. He was imperfectly acquainted with English literature as a whole, and almost entirely ignorant of the poets of his own day. He was acquainted with the poetry of Scott and Southey, but he thought little of it. At a moment when Byron was dazzling society, and his poems were selling by thousands, Wordsworth had scarcely glanced at them ; nor is there any sign that the tragic force of Byron stirred so much as a ripple in the calm of Wordsworth's mind. He certainly knew little of Shelley, and nothing of Keats. The only poet of his time who had anything to do with the shaping of his taste was Coleridge. From Coleridge he may have learned something of the spell of melody, for a greater master of lyrical melody than Coleridge never lived. But in the main it may be said that Wordsworth stood alone.   He had no mentors—he copied no models. With the solitary exceptions of *Laodamia*, which was inspired by a re-perusal of Virgil in middle life, and the *Ode on Intimations of Immortality*, which owes its suggestion, perhaps, to certain beautiful lines of Henry Vaughan, the Silurist, it is impossible to trace the origin of any considerable poem of Wordsworth's to literary sources.   The effects of this limitation of literary culture in Wordsworth are twofold: we find that both the great qualities and the great defects of his genius are liberally displayed in his writings.   A solitary man possessed by a theory is sure to exaggerate the importance of his theory, and to write many things which he would not have written had his views been corrected by a more generous commerce with the world.   Nothing else can account for the almost ludicrous complacency with which he calls our attention to such a poem as *The Idiot Boy*, and tells us he never " wrote anything with so much glee."   On the other hand, the best poems of Wordsworth could only have been written by a man nourished in solitary contemplation, and indifferent to the literary standards of his time.   Because he owes his inspiration not to literature but to Nature, he is able to rise into a region of profound thought and emotion, to which the greatest of literary guides could not have conducted him ; and, for the same reason, all that he has written has its own distinctive note, and bears the stamp of a dominant individuality.

When we endeavour to ascertain the characteristics of a poet's work, what we really mean is the characteristics of his style, and his peculiar moral and emotional interest. Turning first, then, to the style of Wordsworth, it seems to be generally admitted that the period in which his really memorable work was done may be limited to about twenty years (1798–1818). For what Wordsworth overlooked, and what all inventors of poetic theories and formulæ have always overlooked, is that the art of poetic expression is an indefinable gift, which can neither be obtained by obedience to any rules of composition, nor obscured by any defects of literary culture. It is something in the poet which is spontaneous and natural, which the world can neither give nor take away. The absolute fullness of the gift makes itself felt at once in the verses of an imperfectly educated rustic like Burns; and the limitation and frequent absence of the gift is equally apparent in the brilliant lines of a thoroughly cultured poet like Pope. When we speak of the inspiration of the poet we use no vain phrase; for that indefinable charm which dwells in the poetry of a true poet is something that the poet cannot produce at will, nor retain according to his pleasure. It is a gift of illumination and power, an inspiration which visits him irregularly, a sort of diviner soul which possesses him and purges him, and which is as independent even of character as it is of culture or knowledge. The poet may, indeed, seek to fit himself for the high tasks of the muse, as both Milton and Wordsworth did; but even then it by no means follows that when the lamp is cleansed and trimmed the sacred flame will kindle. And in no poet is the truth of these remarks more obvious than in Wordsworth. During these twenty years the genius of Wordsworth was in its prime. He is so far true to his theory of poetry that he uses the simplest words, and often chooses the homeliest subjects; but his words have a compactness, a melody, a subtle charm of emotion, which make them enter into the secret places of the human spirit, and cling to the

memory like an enduring fragrance. It is hard to say
where the charm lies ; indeed, we do not know.   But we
feel its inspiration, we thrill before its power.   The very
simplicity of the words, the sincerity and noble gravity
of the spirit which is revealed through them, fascinate
and attract us.   But apart from all the moral influences
of such poems, we cannot but notice that the style of
Wordsworth is, during these twenty years, at its best.
It is direct, nervous, cogent, full of undesigned felicities,
and often full of lovely melody.   During these twenty
years the genius of Wordsworth poured itself out like a
clear unfailing fountain, and it is almost possible to say
exactly where the culminating point is reached.   His last
really great verses, in which the peculiar felicities of his
style are at their height, are the lines " composed upon
an evening of extraordinary splendour and beauty " in
the autumn of 1818.   The peace and splendour of the
sunset pervade them.   He says :

> No sound is uttered, but a deep
> And solemn harmony pervades
> The hollow vale from steep to steep,
> And penetrates the glades.
>
> *   *   *   *   *   *
>
> And if there be whom broken ties
> Afflict, or injuries assail,
> Yon hazy ridges to their eyes
> Present a glorious scale,
> Climbing suffused with sunny air,
> To stop—no record hath told where !
> And tempting fancy to ascend,
> And with immortal spirits blend ;
> Wings at my shoulders seem to play ;
> But rooted here, I stand and gaze
> On those bright steps that heavenward raise
> Their practicable way.

Wordsworth lived long and wrote much after this memorable evening, but his magic wand was broken. Occasionally some bright gleam of that "light which never was on sea or shore" falls upon his later poems; but it is intermittent and transient. He still teaches and instructs us, but too often a didactic dryness has succeeded the old charm of manner, and he touches the old string without the old music. When the sun sank that night over Rydal water, all unknown to himself the "glory of his prime" was past. The light that so long had lightened him had once more flamed up into a Divine brilliance, and there was something pathetically prophetic of his own future in the concluding lines of the poem —

> 'Tis past; the visionary splendour fades,
> And Night approaches with her shades.

When we ask what are the moral characteristics of Wordsworth's poetry, the same difficulty of a complete and sufficing answer presents itself. He excites in us many emotions, but they are always pure and ennobling emotions. Those who seek for coarse and violent excitement must not come to Wordsworth; they must go to Byron. The Rev. F. W. Robertson has truly observed that "in reading Wordsworth the sensation is as the sensation of the pure water drinker, whose palate is so refined that he can distinguish between rill and rill, river and river, fountain and fountain, as compared with the obtuser sensations of him who has destroyed the delicacy of his palate by grosser libations, and who can distinguish no difference between water and water, because to him all pure things are equally insipid." There is a gravity and sweetness in Wordsworth's poems which could only spring from a noble nature, ruled by the daily vigilance of duty, and dedicated to the daily contemplation of lofty purposes. He makes us feel his entire remoteness from all sordid aims and debasing passions, and he calls us to a higher, a simpler, a serener life. He preaches to an age corrupted with sensationalism the joy that lies in natural emotions; to an age stung with the hunger for impossible ideals the attainable valour and nobility of homely life; to an age tormented by insatiable thirst for riches the old Divine lesson that " a man's life consisteth not in the abundance of things which he possesseth." To the worldly he speaks of unworldliness; to the perplexed, of trust; to the victims of vain perturbation and disquiet, of peace. There is an ineffable, and almost saintly charm about the voice that reaches us from these green solitudes of lake and mountain. He breathes consolation and encouragement into tired hearts and failing spirits. He is the apostle of peace, the minister of cleansing to his time. He has nothing new or startling to say: he sings of love and duty, of disciplined desires and purged and regulated passions, but he speaks as one who has attained and knows the secret of perpetual content. He speaks

> With heart as calm as lakes that sleep,
>   In frosty moonlight glistening,
> Or mountain-torrents, where they creep
> Along a channel smooth and deep,
>   To their own far-off murmurs listening.

Well does Mr. F. W. Myers say, " What touch has given to these lines their impress of an unfathomable peace? For there speaks from them a tranquillity which seems to overcome one's soul; which makes us feel in the midst of toil and passion that we are disquieting ourselves in vain; that we are travelling to a region where these things shall not be; that ' so shall immoderate fear leave us, and inordinate love shall die.' " We cannot explain the touch, but there it is : an unearthly and profoundly religious charm which breathes upon us in all the best poems of Wordsworth. It is, in truth, the voice of a great prophet, who speaks words which are for the healing of the nations.

We might illustrate these observations by copious quotations from the poetry of Wordsworth, but perhaps a better mode of proof is to quote the words in which others, and those the foremost leaders of our time, have described the power of Wordsworth over them. Ruskin has said that Wordsworth is " the keenest-eyed of all modern poets for what is deep and essential in Nature." John Stuart Mill has written in his *Autobiography :* " What made his poems a medicine for my state of mind was that they expressed not mere outward beauty, but states of feeling and thought coloured by feeling, under the excitement of beauty. I needed to be made to feel that there was real permanent happiness in tranquil contemplation. Wordsworth taught me this, not only without turning away from, but with greatly increased interest in, the common feelings and common destiny of human beings." George Eliot read the *Prelude* with ever-fresh delight, and declared : " I never before met so many of my own feelings expressed just as I should like them." It is true, indeed, as Matthew Arnold has said, that

> Wordsworth's eyes avert their ken
> From half of human fate,

but that is simply saying that Wordsworth's poetry has the defects of its qualities. He does not plumb the depths of the more debasing and tragic passions of humanity. His realism is not the new-fangled realism which is fascinated only by corrupt things, but the realism that dwells upon the valours and homely pieties of common life. And when Matthew Arnold would embody in a phrase the secret of Wordsworth's power, he also bears the same testimony as Mill and George Eliot, when he speaks of Wordsworth's " healing power." " He contests," says Mr. R. H. Hutton, " the ground inch by inch with all despondent and indolent humours, and often, too, with movements of inconsiderate and wasteful joy ; " for there is something more than the steadfastness of tranquillity in Wordsworth : there is the steadfastness of strength. He rouses us from languor, because, with all his calm, there is mixed a strenuous and eager spirit, conscious of a Divine mission, and bent on its fulfillment. It is this moral pre-eminence of Wordsworth which is the secret of his mastery over such very different minds as Mill's and Ruskin's, George Eliot's and Arnold's. It is largely also his moral fervour which has given him a species of priesthood in literature, and has surrounded his memory with a sort of sacred halo. To the passionate heart of youth Wordsworth does not appeal ; but as life goes on, and its first fervid glow fades, men find more and more how deep a well of consolation there is in the writings of a poet who sang of nothing more than what we are, and the long-neglected voice of Wordsworth reaches us in mid-life, and haunts us with its mild persistence, and cheers us with its friendly hope.

To some natures, of course Wordsworth will never appeal. Macaulay could find nothing in him but an " endless wilderness of twaddle," and Swinburne can discern little save pompous dullness. Three great writers of his own day, and only three, knew him for what he was: Scott honoured him, Coleridge loved him, and Southey praised him in the famous words that there never was, and never will be, a greater poet. We cannot accept this brotherly exaggeration as wholly true, but clearly Southey is far nearer the truth than Swinburne or Macaulay. And the more Wordsworth's writings are read, the more distinctly is it felt that if he is not the greatest of poets, there is no poet who has given us a body of thought and emotion more humanizing, more wholesome, more inspiring in its tendency. That, at least, is the aim that Wordsworth set before himself in his memorable criticism of his poems written to Lady Beaumont in 1807. " Trouble not yourself," he says, " about their present reception ; of what moment is that compared with what I trust is their destiny? To console the afflicted; to add sunshine to daylight, by making the happy happier ; to teach the young and the gracious of every age to see, to think, and feel, and therefore to become more actively and securely virtuous,—this is their office, which I trust they will faithfully perform, long after we (that is, all that is mortal of us) are mouldered in our graves." Never have the essential moral characteristics of Wordsworth's poetry been set forth with truer insight and completeness than in this prophetic passage, written in the days when no indication of fame had reached him, and when, with some few honourable exceptions, signal contempt was awarded him by the blind and undiscerning critics who attempted to direct the taste and culture of their age.

XIII

WORDSWORTH'S VIEW OF NATURE AND MAN

I HAVE spoken of Wordsworth as having a new and original philosophy to unfold, a new and individual view of Nature to expound: what then, was that view? The love of Nature is to be found in all the English poets, from Chaucer downward. In Wordsworth's own day both Byron and Shelley were writing poems thoroughly impregnated with the love of Nature. If we eliminated from English poetry all the passages which deal with the charm and glory of Nature, we should have destroyed all that is sweetest, freshest, and most characteristic in it. What is there, then, in Wordsworth's treatment of Nature which differs from the poetry of those who have gone before him? It is perilous to be too positive where many fine and delicate distinctions are involved; but, speaking generally, it may be said that Wordsworth differs from all other poets in the stress he puts upon the moral influences of Nature. To Byron, Nature was the great consoler in the hour of his revolt against the folly of man, and he found in her, not merely hospitality, but a certain exhilaration which fed the fierce defiance of his heart, and armed him with new strength for the fight. To Shelley, Nature is more of a personality than to Byron, but it is an ethereal and lovely presence, a veiled splendour, kindling sweet ardour in the heart, and exercising an intoxicating magic on the mind. But

126

with Wordsworth the idea of the living personality of
Nature is a definite reality.   He loves her as he might
love a mistress, and communes with her as mind may
commune with mind.   To him she is a vast embodied
Thought, a Presence not merely capable of inspiring delightful ardour, but of elevating man by noble discipline.
Take, for instance, his *Sonnet on Calais Beach:*

> It is a beauteous evening, calm and free;
> The holy time is quiet as a nun
> Breathless with adoration; the broad sun
> Is sinking down in its tranquillity;
> The gentleness of heaven is on the sea:
> Listen! the Mighty Being is awake,
> And doth with His eternal motion make
> A sound like thunder—everlastingly.

Or take his conception of human life in the presence of
the everlastingness of Nature:

> Our noisy years seem moments in the being
> Of the eternal silence.

Or ponder the spirit of the well-known verses:

> The outward shows of sky and earth,
> Of hill and valley he has viewed;
> And impulses of deeper birth
> Have come to him in solitude.
>
> In common things that round us lie
> Some random truths can he impart —
> The harvest of a quiet eye
> That broods and sleeps on his own heart.

Or mark how he replies to the restlessness of life which
is divorced from habitual intercourse with Nature:

Think you, 'mid all this mighty sum
    Of things forever speaking,
That nothing of itself will come,
    But we must still be seeking?

Nor less I deem that there are powers
    Which of themselves our minds impress;
That we can feed this mind of ours
    Into a wise passiveness.

And hark! how blithe the throstle sings;
    He, too, is no mean preacher;
Come forth into the light of things,—
    Let Nature be your teacher.

One impulse of a vernal wood
    May teach you more of man,
Of moral evil and of good,
    Than all the sages can.

In these verses what most strikes us is the vividness of
Wordsworth's conception of Nature as endowed with personality—"the mighty Being," and the emphasis with
which he declares that Nature is a teacher whose wisdom
we can learn if we will, and without which any human
life is vain and incomplete.

An artist, who is also a teacher of art, has laid down
the rule that in painting landscape what we want is not
the catalogue of the landscape, but the emotion of the
artist in painting it.   This is the artistic theory of the
Impressionist school, and it may be said that in this
sense Wordsworth was an impressionist.   Such a poet as
Thomson gives us in his *Seasons* the mere catalogue of
Nature, and as a catalogue it is excellent.   If the effects
of Nature were to be put up to auction, no catalogue
could serve us better than Thomson's *Seasons*.   But
what Thomson cannot give us, and what Wordsworth
does give us, is the impression which Nature produces

on his own spirit.   He teaches us that between man and
Nature there is mutual consciousness and mystic intercourse.   It is not for nothing God has set man in
this world of sound and vision: it is in the power of
Nature to penetrate his spirit, to reveal him to himself,
to communicate to him Divine instruction, to lift him
into spiritual life and ecstasy.   The poem of *The Daffodils*
is simply a piece of lovely word-painting till we reach
the lines —

> They flash upon the inward eye,
> Which is the bliss of solitude ;

and it is in those lines the real spirit of the poem speaks.
There was something in that sight of the daffodils, dancing in jocund glee, that kindled a joy, an intuition, a
hope in the poet's mind, and through the vision an undy-
ing impulse of delight and illumination reached him.
Wordsworth does not indulge in the " pathetic fallacy."
He does not take his mood to Nature and persuade himself that she reflects it ; but he goes to Nature with an
open mind, and leaves her to create the mood in him.
He does not ask her to echo him ; but he stands docile in
her presence, and asks to be taught of her.   To persuade
ourselves that Nature mirrors our mood, giving gray
skies to our grief, and the piping of glad birds in answer
to the joy-bells of our hope, is not to take a genuine delight in Nature.   It is to make her our accomplice rather
than our instructress ; our mimic, not our mistress.
Many poets have done this, and nothing is commoner in
current poetry.   The originality of Wordsworth is that
he never thinks of Nature in any other way than as a
Mighty Presence, before whom he stands silent, like a
faithful high-priest, who waits in solemn expectation for
the whisper of enlightenment and wisdom.

Let us turn to one of his earliest poems, the *Lines Composed at Tintern Abbey*, July 13, 1798, and we shall see how clearly defined in Wordsworth's mind this conception of Nature was, even at the commencement of his career.   Wordsworth was not yet thirty, and had not yet recognized his true vocation in life; but, nevertheless, all that he afterwards said about Nature is uttered in outline in these memorable lines.   He speaks of the " tranquil restoration," the sensations sweet, " felt in the blood, and felt along the heart," which Nature had already wrought in him.   He has peace,

> While with an eye made quiet by the powe
> Of harmony, and the deep power of song,
> We see into the life of things.

The mere boyish love of Nature, when the sounding cataract haunted him like a passion, he characterizes as one of the " glad animal movements " of the boy ; now he has perceived how Nature not merely works delight in the blood, but flashes illumination on the soul.

> For I have learned
> To look on Nature, not as in the hours
> Of thoughtless youth, but hearing oftentimes
> The still, sad music of humanity,
> Nor harsh nor grating, though of ample power
> To chasten and subdue.   And I have felt
> A presence that disturbs me with the joy
> Of elevated thoughts ; a sense sublime
> Of something far more deeply interfused,
> Whose dwelling is the light of setting suns,
> And the round ocean, and the living air,
> And the blue sky, and in the mind of man ;
> A motion and a spirit, that impels
> All thinking things, all objects of all thought,
> And rolls through all things.   Therefore am I still

A lover of the meadows and the woods,
And mountains ; and of all that we behold
From this round earth ; and of all the mighty world
Of eye and ear, both what they half create
And what perceive ; well pleased to recognize
In Nature and the language of the sense,
The anchor of my purest thoughts, the nurse,
The guide, the guardian of my heart, and soul,
Of all my moral being.

We have only to compare this passage with such poems as Byron's address to the Ocean, or Shelley's *Ode to the West Wind*, to see how great is the difference between Wordsworth's view of Nature and theirs, and how profoundly original Wordsworth's view is.   There is a subtle power in Wordsworth's verses which seems to breathe the very spirit of Nature, and to interpret her. We entirely lose sight of the revealer in the revelation ; we pass out of the sphere of Wordsworth's mood into the very mood and heart of Nature ; we feel the presence of something deeply interfused through all the inanimate world.   The world indeed is no longer dead to us, but animate, and we feel the spirit and motion of Nature like the actual contact of a living and a larger soul.   Wordsworth is thus not so much the poet as the high-priest of Nature, and the feeling he creates in us is not so much delight as worship.

One effect of this ardent love of Nature in Wordsworth is that he excels all other poets in the fidelity of his descriptions, the minute accuracy of his observation of natural beauty.   His eye for nature is always fresh and true, and what he sees he describes with an admirable realism.   His sense of form and colour is also perfect, and in nothing is he so great an artist as in his power of conveying in a phrase the exact truth of the things he

sees. When he speaks of the voice of the stock-dove as
" buried among trees," he uses the only word that could
completely convey to us the idea of seclusion, the remote
depth of greenwood in which the dove loves to hide
herself. The star-shaped shadow of the daisy cast upon
the stone is noted also with the same loving accuracy,
and can only be the result of direct observation. Nothing escaped his vigilance, and his sense of sound was as
perfect as his power of vision. The wild wind-swept
summit of a mountain-pass could hardly be better
painted than in this word-picture :

> The single sheep, and that one blasted tree,
> And the bleak music of that old stone wall.

We hear, as we read these lines, the wind whistling
through the crevices of the stone walls of Westmoreland,
and by the magic of this single phrase we feel at once
the desolation of the scene, and we catch its spirit. For,
after all, it is not in the power of the most accurate description of itself to create emotion in us ; it is the emotion
of the poet we need to interpret for us the spirit of
what he sees, and this is just what Wordsworth does for
us. He scorned what he called taking an inventory of
Nature, and said that Nature did not permit it. His
comment on a brilliant poet was : " He should have left
his pencil and note-book at home, fixed his eye as he
walked with a reverent attention on all that surrounded
him, and taken all into a heart that could understand
and enjoy. He would have discovered that while much
of what he had admired was preserved to him, much was
also most wisely obliterated ; that which remained—the
picture surviving in his mind—would have presented the
ideal and essential truth of the scene, and done so in a

large part by discarding much which, though in itself striking, was not characteristic." This was Wordsworth's own method. Though unsurpassed in the fidelity of his observation, he never relies on observation alone for his interpretation of Nature. When he has observed he allows the picture of what he has seen to sink quietly into the memory, and he broods above it in silent joy. The result is that when the hour comes to combine his materials in a poem, they are already sifted for us, and are saturated with sentiment. Many of the noblest passages in Wordsworth might be thus described as observation touched with emotion; unusually accurate observation touched with the finest and purest emotion.

Another direct effect of Wordsworth's view of Nature is his view of man. He began life with the most ardent hopes for the moral regeneration of mankind, and it was only with bitter reluctance he renounced them, in the frantic recoil which the excesses of the French Revolution produced. From the bitterness of that trouble, as we have seen, he was rescued by his sister Dora, and, going back to the calm of Nature, he found a truer view of mankind. He believed that he had put his finger on the real secret of the unsatisfied passions and misery of mankind when he taught that man, divorced from living intercourse with Nature, could not but be restless and unhappy. Man was set in this world of Nature because the world of Nature was necessary to his well-being, nor were spiritual sanity and delight possible without contact with Nature. In this view he was confirmed when he found that in the remote dales of the English Lake District human life attained a robust virtue denied to the dwellers in great cities. He saw that the essentials of a really lofty and happy life were few, and that they were

found in the greatest profusion where life was simplest
and contact with Nature was habitual.   His faith in man
kind returned, and man again became

> An object of delight,
> Of pure imagination and of love.

Set in his proper environment of Nature, breathing
clear air, looking on refreshing visions of glory and delight, Wordsworth saw that man was at his best, and he
regarded him with genuine reverence.   His panacea for
the healing of his country was a return to Nature, and it
was in pathetic reproach he wrote:

> The world is too much with us; late and soon,
>   Getting and spending, we lay waste our powers ;
>   Little we see in Nature that is ours !
> We have given away our hearts, a sordid boon!

There is no poet who shows so great a reverence for
man, *as man*.   Lowliness and poverty cannot hide from
him the great qualities of heart and character, which the
selfish and unthinking never see.   He sings the homely
sanctities and virtues of the poor.   Human nature is to
him a sacred thing, and even in its frailest and humblest
forms is regarded with gentleness and sympathy.   And
the real source of Wordsworth's reverence for man lies
in his reverence for Nature.   It is the constant and purg-
ing vision of Nature which enables him to perceive how
mean are the cares with which those who are rich burden
themselves, and how noble, and even joyous, men can be
under the stress of penury and labour, if they let Nature
lead them and exalt them.

The spirit of this teaching is nowhere more happily
expressed than in the lovely lines which occur in the
conclusion of the *Song at the Feast of Brougham Castle*,

Love had he found in huts where poor men lie ;
His daily teachers had been woods and rills,
The silence which is in the starry sky,
The sleep that is among the lonely hills.

These were the agencies which had softened, soothed,
and tamed the fiery heart of Clifford, and it was by the
same simple ministration he himself had been led into
settled peace.

It may, indeed, be doubted whether it is possible to
understand the full significance of Wordsworth's poetry
in any other environment than that in which it was produced. So at least thought James Macdonell, when he
wrote : " What blasts of heavenly sunshine, as if blown
direct from the gates of some austerely Puritan Paradise !
What gusts of air, touched with the cold rigour of the
mountain peak ! What depth of moralizing, touched
with the hues of a masculine gloom ! What felicity of
diction, clothing in immortal brevity of phrase the deepest aspirations of the brave ! Never did I read Wordsworth with such full delight, because never had I so
charged my mind with the spirit of the mountains which
were the food of his soul."

What Burns did for the Scotch peasant, Wordsworth
has done for the shepherds and the husbandmen of England. But he has done more than illustrate the virtues
of a class : from the study of peasant life, set amid the
splendour, and vivified by the influence of Nature, he attained a profound faith in man himself, and a reverent
understanding of the inherent grandeur of all human life.

XIV

WORDSWORTH'S PATRIOTIC AND POLITICAL POEMS

AN excellent and eloquent critic, Professor Dowden, has spoken of Wordsworth's " uncourageous elder years," and has founded the phrase upon this sentence of Wordsworth's : " Years have deprived me of courage, in the sense which the word bears when applied by Chaucer to the animation of birds in spring-time." A little reflection will, I think, show that this confession of the poet hardly justifies the phrase of the critic. Nevertheless, it is a general impression that Wordsworth began life an ardent Radical, and ended it as a staunch Conservative. If this were all, the phrase might be allowed to pass, but the impression such a phrase creates is that Wordsworth not merely renounced his early hopes and creed, but grew apathetic towards the great human causes which stirred his blood in youth. Browning's fine poem of the *Lost Leader* has often been applied to Wordsworth, and it has been assumed in many quarters, with what degree of truth we do not know, that Browning had Wordsworth in his mind when he wrote that powerful and pathetic indictment. However this may be, nothing is commoner than the assumption that one result of Wordsworth's remote seclusion from the stress of life was that he lost interest in public affairs, and cared little for the great movements of his day. Than this assumption nothing can be falser. To say nothing of the prose writings of Wordsworth, few poets have given us a larger body of patriotic poetry, and poetry impregnated with politics, than Wordsworth.   Perhaps it is because the finest poems of Wordsworth are those that deal with the emotions of man in the presence of Nature, that comparatively little interest attaches to his patriotic poetry. Such poetry, however, Wordsworth wrote throughout his life, and if he was not altogether a political force, it is quite certain that he never ceased to take a keen interest in politics.   He had national aims, and was full of the most ardent love of country.   It may be well to recall to the minds of my readers this aspect of Wordsworth's life and influence.

As regards the earlier part of his life, Wordsworth has left an abundant record of his thoughts in his prose writings.   No poet, save Milton, has written with so large a touch upon national affairs, and has displayed so lofty a spirit.   His prose does not indeed glow with so intense a passion, nor is it so gorgeous as Milton's, but it is animated and inspired by the same spirit.   And in its more passionate passages something of Milton's pomp of style is discernible—something of his overwhelming force of language and cogency of thought.   Wordsworth's tract on the *Convention of Cintra* belongs to the same class of writings as Milton's *Areopagitica*, and while not its equal in sustained splendour of diction, it is distinguished by the same breadth of view and eager patriotism.   Wordsworth has himself defined excellence of writing as the conjunction of reason and passion, and, judged by this test, Wordsworth's occasional utterances on politics attain a rare excellence.   It would have been singular in such an age if any man who possessed emotion enough to be a poet had nothing to say upon the great events which were altering the map of Europe.   Wordsworth from the first never concealed his opinions on these subjects. He went as far as he could in apologizing for the errors of the French Revolution, when he said truly that " Revolution is not the season of true liberty." The austerity which characterized his whole life characterizes the very temper of his apology for the excesses of the Revolution.   He shed no tears over the execution of Louis.   He laments a larger public calamity, " that any combination of circumstances should have rendered it necessary or advisable to veil for a moment the statutes of the laws, and that by such emergency the cause of twenty-five millions of people, I may say of the whole human race, should have been so materially injured. Any other sorrow for the death of Louis is irrational and weak."   He is even ardent Republican enough to argue for equality, and to say that in the perfect state " no distinctions are to be admitted but such as have evidently for their object the general good."   This last sentence strikes the key-note in much of the philosophy of Wordsworth.   " Simplification was," as John Morley has observed, " the key-note of the revolutionary time."   That lesson Wordsworth thoroughly learned, and never forgot. It is the very essence of the democratic spirit to pierce beneath the artificial distinctions of a time, and grasp the essential ; to take man for what he is, not for what he seems to be ; to reverence man wherever he is found, and to reverence not least the man who toils in the lowliest walks of life.   If this be the spirit of democracy then Wordsworth kept the democratic faith whole and undefiled.   So far from repudiating the political creed of his life, he spiritualized it, and lived in obedience to its essential elements all his life.   That in later life he manifested an incapacity for the rapid assimilation of new ideas; that his notions stiffened, and his perceptions failed; that he opposed Catholic Emancipation and the Reform Bill, is merely to say, in other words, that Wordsworth grew old. It is a rare spectacle, perhaps the rarest, to see a great mind resist the stiffening of age, and retain its versatility and freshness of outlook in the last decades of life. Wordsworth was never a versatile man, and never had any marked capacity for the assimilation of new ideas. But how very far Wordsworth was from ever being a fossilized Tory we may judge by his own saying in later life: " I have no respect whatever for Whigs, but I have a good deal of the Chartist in me." However his political insight may have failed him in his apprehension of the party measures of his later life, it cannot be seriously questioned that Wordsworth always remained true at heart to the cause of the people, and never swerved in his real reverence for man as man.

The urgency of the political passion in Wordsworth can be felt all through the days of the great war, and perhaps the noblest record of that period is in the long series of sonnets which Wordsworth wrote between the years 1803 and 1816. In the year 1809 he wrote scarcely anything that was not related to the life of nations. It was then that he apostrophized Saragossa, and lamented over the submission of the Tyrolese. And if few poets have written so largely on the current events of their day, it may certainly be added that no poet has showed a more cosmopolitan spirit. It was indeed a time when England was in closer touch with the struggling nationalities of the Continent than ever before. A common calamity had drawn together all the peoples of Europe who still loved liberty. England had never breathed the spirit of so large a life as in those troublous days. She had never known a period of such intense suspense and united enthusiasm. The beacon-fire was built on every hill; every village-green resounded to the clang of martial drill; every port had its eager watchers, who swept the waste fields of sea with restless scrutiny. Children were sent to bed with all their clothes neatly packed beside them, in case the alarm of war should break the midnight silence; and invasion was for months an hourly fear. It was one of those moments of supreme peril and passion which come rarely in the life of nations : one of those great regenerating moments when factions perish, and a nation rises into nobler life; and the stress of that great period is felt in every line that Wordsworth wrote. His patriotism was of that diviner kind which founds itself on principles of universal truth and right-eousness. It was no splendid prejudice, no insularity of thought, no mere sentimental love of country : it gath-ered in its embrace the passions of Europe, and pleaded in its strenuous eloquence the cause of the oppressed throughout the world. This breadth of view which char-acterized Wordsworth's patriotism is its noblest charac-teristic. It is a catholic love of liberty which gives him spiritual comradeship with every man who has toiled or suffered for his country. And this spirit can find no fuller exemplification than in his noble sonnet, written in 1802,

TO TOUSSAINT L'OUVERTURE

Toussaint, the most unhappy man of men !
Whether the whistling Rustic tend his plow
Within thy hearing, or thy head be now
Pillowed in some dark dungeon's earless den ;
O miserable Chieftain ! where and when

Wilt thou find patience?   Yet die not! do thou
Wear rather in thy bonds a cheerful brow ;
Though fallen thyself, never to rise again,
Live, and take comfort!   Thou hast left behind
Powers that will work for thee ; air, earth, and skies;
There's not a breathing of the common wind
That will forget thee.   Thou hast great allies;
Thy friends are exaltations, agonies,
And love, and man's unconquerable mind.

But catholic as Wordsworth's patriotic sympathies were, the noblest expressions of his patriotism are his addresses and appeals to his own countrymen.   If in later life he did not discern the true spirit of his times, and unconsciously resisted the august spirit of progress, it was in part because his honest pride of country grew with his growth and strengthened with his age.   He was loth to admit faults and flaws in a form of government which seemed to meet every just demand of liberty and order. Besides, the great hindrance to democratic development was to Wordsworth not discoverable in any error or defect of government, but in the defective method of life which his countrymen adopted.   When he is called upon to judge the political measures of his day, his touch is not sure, nor his discrimination wise ; but when he estimates the tendencies of the social life of England he is always clear, cogent, and convincing.   His social grasp is always surer than his political, and his finest sonnets are those in which he combines his social insight with patriotic passion.   Such a sonnet is this :

When I have borne in memory what has tamed
   Great nations, how ennobling thoughts depart
   When men change swords for ledgers, and desert
The student's bower for gold, some fear, unnamed
I had, my country!—am I to be blamed ?

> Now when I think of thee, and what thou art,
>   Verily in the bottom of my heart
> Of those unfilial fears I am ashamed.
>   For dearly must we prize thee ; we who find
> In thee a bulwark for the cause of men ;
>   And I by my affection was beguiled.
> What wonder if a poet now and then,
>   Among the many movements of his mind,
> Felt for thee as a lover or a child ?

And this is a note which is struck again and again. In the hour of peril his countrymen rose to the supreme daring of the occasion. What he fears is that the relaxation of that intense moral strain may mean that national life may lose its saving salt of lofty purpose, and sink into carnal contentment and repose. " Getting and spending we lay waste our powers " is the thought that frequently recurs in his later poems. He fears the enervation of prosperity more than the buffeting of adversity. When nations are surfeited with victory and peace, they are too apt to lose the Spartan temper of austere devotion to their country which made them great in warlike days. And why Wordsworth so often recurs to this thought, is that his pride in his country has no bounds. For the nation which has saved the liberties of Europe to fall into inglorious self-indulgence would be the last calamity in the possible tragedy of nations. It is in the hour when such fears beset him, that he appeals to " Sidney, Marvel, Harrington," who

> Knew how genuine glory is put on,
> Taught us how rightfully a nation shone
> In splendour, what strength was that would not bend
> But in magnanimous meekness.

It is then also he thinks of Milton, whose " soul was as

a star and dwelt apart," and invokes that mighty shade
which haunts the Puritan past of England —

> We are selfish men ;
> O raise us up, return to us again,
> And give us manners, virtue, freedom, power.

And it is when the memory of that heroic past of England is most vivid to his mind that he touches his highest
note of dignified and haughty pride, and scorns the
thought

> That this most famous stream in bogs and sands
> Should perish ! and to evil and to good
> Be lost forever.   In our halls is hung
>   Armoury of the invincible knights of old ;
> We must be free or die, who speak the tongue
>   That Shakespeare spake : the faith and morals hold
> Which Milton held.   In everything we are sprung
>   Of earth's first blood ; have titles manifold.

The patriotism of Wordsworth is not violent or
frenzied; it is comparatively restrained; but, for that
very reason, in the moments of its highest utterance there
is a depth and force in it such as few writers display.
When habitually calm men break the barriers of reserve,
there is something strangely impressive in their passion.
There is nothing more impressive in Wordsworth, as indicative of the strength of his emotions, than these occasional bursts of exalted patriotism, and their force is
heightened by the contrast they furnish to his habitual
serenity of temper.

There is one poem of Wordsworth's which stands out
in particular prominence as the greatest of all his poems
which express the spirit of patriotism : that is the
Happy Warrior.   This poem was written in the year

1806, and was inspired by the death of Nelson. It was in the autumn of the previous year that Nelson had fallen on the deck of the *Victory*, and the shock of sorrow and consternation which passed over England has never been equalled by any similar public calamity. Certainly the death of no individual has ever called forth so spontaneous and general a lamentation. Nelson was to the England of his day the very incarnation of manly courage and heroiç virtue. The fascination of his name affected every class of society. He seemed to sum up in himself that reverence for duty which is so characteristic a feature of the English race. Between Nelson and Wordsworth there could be little in common, save this bond of ardent patriotism, but that was sufficient to call forth from Wordsworth one of his finest poems. Just as we can specify certain poems which constitute the high-water mark of Wordsworth's genius in philosophic or lyric poetry, so we can confidently take this poem as his maturest word in patriotic poetry. It breathes the very spirit of consecrated heroism. Some points of the poem were suggested by a more private sorrow—the loss at sea of his brother John; but it was out of the larger emotion occasioned by the death of Nelson that the poem originated. It is the idealized Nelson who stands before us in these verses :

> But who, if he be called upon to face
> Some awful moment, to which Heaven has joined
> Great issues, good or bad for human kind,
> Is happy as a Lover, and attired
> With sudden brightness, like a Man inspired :
> And, through the heat of conflict, keeps the law
> In calmness made, and sees what he foresaw ;

> Or if an unexpected call succeed,
> Come when it will, is equal to the need.
> He who, though thus endued as with a sense
> And faculty for storm and turbulence,
> Is yet a Soul whose master-bias leans
> To homefelt pleasures, and to gentler scenes.
> This is the Happy Warrior, this is He
> That every man in arms should wish to be.

When we read these words we are reminded of a passage in the *Recluse*, in which Wordsworth tells us he could never read of two great war-ships grappling without a thrill of emulation, more ardent than wise men should know.   It is a passage which throws a new light upon the nature of Wordsworth.   If he was serene, it was not because he was lethargic; if he urged the blessedness of regulated passions, it was not because his own heart was cold : he, too, had a passionate nature and heroic fibre in him, and that courageous and soldierly temper is fitly vindicated and expressed in the lofty spirit of his patriotic poems.

XV

WORDSWORTH'S PERSONAL CHAR-
ACTERISTICS

W HEN we put down the works of a poet, we are naturally inclined to ask what the poet himself was like in actual life, and to seek some authentic presentment of him as he moved among men. In the case of Wordsworth we have many partial portraits, but it can hardly be said that we have any true and finished picture. The seclusion of Wordsworth's life saved him from the scrutiny of that social world where every little trait of character is indelibly photographed on some retentive memory, and the trifles of unconsidered conversation are gathered up, and often reproduced after many days in diaries and reminiscences. Considering the literary force which Wordsworth was, few men have had such scanty dealings with the literary circles of their time. If Wordsworth had died at fifty, it is pretty certain that beyond the reminiscences of personal friends, like Coleridge and Southey, there would have been little to guide us to a true understanding of his person and character. Gradually, however, as the tide set in his favour, the quiet house at Rydal Mount became more and more a place of pilgrimage, and few visitors of eminence came away without noting down certain impressions, more or less instructive, of the great Lake Poet.

First of all there come naturally the testimonies of

those men of letters who formed a little colony beside the English Lakes, and whose names are inseparably associated with Wordsworth's.   Southey's sense of Wordsworth's powers may be measured by his enthusiastic verdict, that there never was and never would be a greater poet.   Coleridge conveys his impression of Wordsworth's strength of character, not less than of his genius, in the pathetic lines written in the days of his own eclipse and sorrow, and already quoted:

> O great Bard!
> Ere yet that last strain dying awed the air,
> With steadfast eye I viewed thee in the choir
> Of *ever-enduring men.*
> Ah! as I listen with a heart forlorn,
> The pulses of my being beat anew.

The quality in Wordsworth which struck Coleridge most was naturally the quality in which he himself was most deficient—the robustness and sufficiency of the poet's nature.   De Quincey, in his sketch, observes the same characteristic, and probably this was the first and deepest impression which Wordsworth created.   He struck all who knew him as a solid, indomitable man, somewhat taciturn, save when the theme inspired him and the company was fitting; a man who knew in what he had believed, and knew how to stand true to himself and his convictions, amid evil report and good report. That there should be something of childlike vanity and harmless egotism about him, was perhaps the natural consequence of his lack of humour and his secluded life. When Emerson visited him he was much amused to see Wordsworth solemnly prepare himself for action, and then declaim like a schoolboy his latest sonnet on Fingal's

Cave. If Wordsworth had had any of the elements of humour in him, he himself would have been too conscious of the ludicrous side of the proceeding to have indulged in it. But Wordsworth united in himself philosophic seriousness and childlike simplicity, and was singularly insensible to humour. His neighbours said they never heard him laugh, and remarked that you could tell from his face there was no laughter in his poetry. He took life seriously, and, to quote Mrs. Browning's fine phrase, poetry was to him " as serious as life." He once told Sir George Beaumont that in his opinion " a man of letters, and indeed all public men of every pursuit, should be severely frugal." The Puritan discipline which he applied to his life moulded his character, and a constant life of plain living and high thinking left little room for the casual graces of persiflage and banter. Of mere cleverness, the airy agility of shallow brains and ready tongues, he was destitute. He was not suave, not fascinating, scarcely prepossessing. But if he was calm it was not with any natural coldness of temperament; his calm was the fruit of long discipline and fortitude. One acute observer speaks of the fearful intensity of his feelings and affections, and says that if his intellect had been less strong they would have destroyed him long ago. De Quincey in like manner noted his look of permature age,[1] " the furrowed and rugged countenance, the brooding intensity of the eye, the bursts of anger at the report of evil doings "—the signs of the passionate forces which worked within him. He himself in his many self-revelations conveys the same impression of a nature hard to govern, of violent

[1] De Quincey says that when Wordsworth was thirty-nine his age was guessed at over sixty.

passions disciplined with difficulty, of wild and tumultuous desires only conquered by incessant vigilance. He
bore upon himself the marks of a difficult life : and it
was a touch of genuine insight which led Coleridge to
describe him by the brief and pregnant phrase—an
" ever-enduring man."

The picture which Harriet Martineau gives of Wordsworth as she knew him in his old age does not err on the
side of adulation, but it cannot conceal the essential
nobleness of his character. Harriet Martineau thought
little of his writings, and says so with caustic frankness.
According to her view—the view be it remembered of an
incessantly busy woman—Wordsworth suffered from having nothing to do ; and he suffered yet more in his old
age from the adulation of the crowd of visitors who
poured towards Rydal Mount during the tourist season.
To each of these idle visitors, and they averaged five
hundred a season, Wordsworth behaved much in the same
way. He politely showed them round his grounds, explained at what particular spot certain poems were written, and then politely bowed them out. He had no reticence either in reciting his poems or talking of them ;
indeed, he often spoke of them in an impersonal sort of
way, as though they had no relation to himself, and he
criticised them as freely as though some one else had
written them. Thus, he told Harriet Martineau that the
Happy Warrior did not " best fulfill the conditions of
poetry, but it was a chain of extremely *valooable*
thoughts," a criticism which Miss Martineau endorses as
" eminently just." In these, and in many similar pro-
ceedings, we recognize the naive simplicity of the man.
He solemnly advised Miss Martineau to give nothing but
tea to her visitors, and if they wanted meat let them pay

for it themselves, that having been his own method of proceeding in his early days of penury at Grasmere. That this frugal suggestion did not spring from any inhospitable meanness is abundantly evident from the larger generosities of Wordsworth's life. His treatment of poor Hartley Coleridge is above praise. Miss Martineau only met Hartley five times, and on each occasion he was drunk. Wordsworth treated him as an erring son, and when all hope of reclaiming him was over, paid for his lodgings, cared for his wants, and smoothed his passage to the grave. There are few more touching pictures than that of the old poet standing bareheaded by the grave of Hartley, on the bleak winter morning when all that was mortal of that unhappy genius was laid to rest in the quiet God's acre which was soon to receive the dust of Wordsworth.

An equally beautiful picture is painted by Miss Martineau of the poet as she often met him, " attended perhaps by half-a-score of cottagers' children, the youngest pulling at his cloak or holding by his trousers, while he cut ash switches out of the hedge for them." This little touch of nature may be paired off with Mr. Rawnsley's story, of how a pastor in a faraway parish was asked by a very refined, handsome-looking woman on her deathbed to read over to her and to her husband the poem of *The Pet Lamb*, and how she had said at the end, " That was written about me ; Mr. Wordsworth often spoke to me, and patted my head when a child," and had added with a sigh, " Eh, but he was such a dear kind old man ! " Miss Martineau also strongly confirms the impression of Wordsworth's isolation from the main streams of life, the solitary self-containedness of his character, when she says that his life was " self-enclosed," and that he had scarcely any intercourse with other minds, in books or conversation.

Another source of information about Wordsworth is found in the reminiscences of him among the peasantry, which have been so excellently collated by Mr. Rawnsley. These have a unique value as the only record we possess of the impression which Wordsworth created, not on cultivated minds, but on the minds of the simple dales-people whose virtues he so strenuously sang. The northern mind has two distinguishing qualities—a certain quickness of imagination which finds expression in the use of singularly vivid phrases, and a certain shrewd touch of humour which delights in exaggerative travesty. Making allowance for these conditions, we may construct a remarkably lifelike portrait from these observations of Wordsworth's humble neighbours. We are face to face with Wordsworth in the prime of his power and force, when, we are told, he was " a plainish-faaced man, but a fine man, leish (active), and almost always upon the road. He wasn't a man of many words, would walk by you times enuff wi'out sayin' owt, specially when he was in study. He was always a-studying, and you might see his lips a-goin' as he went along the road." Another speaks of him as " a vara practical-eyed man, a man as seemed to see aw that was stirrin'." He walked in later days with " a bit of a stoop," which somewhat diminished the sense of his real height, which was about six feet. When he was making a poem, " he would set his head a bit forward, and put his hands behint his back. And then he would start a-bumming, and it was bum, bum, bum, stop ; and then he'd set down, and git a bit o' paper out, and write a bit. However, his lips were always goan' whoale time he was upon gress walk. He was a kind mon,

there's no two words about that ; if any one was sick i'
the plaace, he wad be off to see til' 'em." His only rec-
reations were walking and skating. He was first upon
the ice, and

> Wheeled about
> Proud and exulting like an untired horse,
> That cares not for his home.

He had very little care for personal appearance. He
usually wore a wide-awake and old blue cloak: " niver
seed him in a boxer in my life," says one witness with
pathetic reproach. He had even been known to ride in a
dung-cart upon his longer excursions : " just a dung-cart,
wi' a seat-board in front, and bit o' bracken in t' bottom,
comfortable as owt." He had a deep bass voice, and when
he was " bumming " away in some remote part at night-
fall, the casual passenger was almost terrified. He constituted himself by common consent general custodian of
the beauties of the district, and prevented many a copse
from being cut down, and superintended the building of
many a cottage. Not a companionable man, however.
A remoteness about him which awed men rather than attracted them. Indeed, their one complaint about him was
that he had no convivial tendencies, like Hartley Coleridge, who came very much nearer the rustic ideal of a
poet than the solitary of Rydal Mount. He was " a des-
olate-minded man ; as for his habits, he had noan ; niver
knew him with a pot i' his hand, or a pipe i' his mouth."
He " was not lovable in the faace, by noa means "—the
face was too rugged and austere to be fascinating. So
one rustic observer after another bears his witness, the net
result being a sufficiently luminous picture of a strong
and somewhat taciturn man, buried in his own thoughts,

passing up and down among his fellows with a certain
awe-inspiring unapproachableness, and yet a man of
warm heart and quick sympathy ; not a cheerful man, but
a man who, after long battle, has won the secret of
peace, and walks a solitary path, clothed with silence, and
winning from others the reverence due to the hermit and
the sage.

Stiff and awkward as Wordsworth often was in conversation, yet there were times when he created a sincere
admiration by his talk.   Haydon says, " Never did any
man so beguile the time as Wordsworth.   His purity of
heart, his kindness, his soundness of principle, his information, his knowledge, and the intense and eager feelings
with which he pours forth all he knows, affect, interest, and
enchant one."   But among all the various literary portraits
which we possess of Wordsworth, there is none so subtle
and so potent as Carlyle's.   Carlyle thought little of
Wordsworth's writings, but after he had met him he says :
" He talked well in his way ; with veracity, easy brevity,
and force.   His voice was good, frank, sonorous ; though
practically clear, distinct, forcible, rather than melodious ;
the tone of him businesslike, sedately confident, no dis-
courtesy, yet no anxiety about being courteous ; a fine
wholesome rusticity, fresh as his mountain-breezes, sat
well on the stalwart veteran, and on all he said and did.
You would have said he was a usually taciturn man, glad
to unlock himself, to audience sympathetic and intelligent, when such offered itself.   His face bore marks of
much, not always peaceful, meditation ; the look of it not
bland or benevolent so much as close, impregnable, and
hard ; a man *multa tacere loquive paratus*, in a world where
he had experienced no lack of contradictions as he strode
along.   The eyes were not very brilliant, but they had a

quiet clearness; there was enough of brow, and well-shaped. He was large-boned, lean, but still firm-knit, tall, and strong-looking when he stood; a right good old steel-gray figure, with a fine rustic simplicity and dignity about him, and a veracious *strength* looking through him, which might have suited one of those old steel-gray *Markgrafs*, whom Henry the Fowler set up to ward the marches, and do battle with the intrusive heathen in a stalwart and judicious manner." The last phrase recalls to us Wordsworth's confession in the *Prelude* to his early love of battle-histories, and thirst for a life of heroic action. A man who had not had something of the fighter in him could never have defied the world as he defied it. His imaginative faculty made him a poet; but under all his intellectual life there throbbed the difficult pulse of a valorous restlessness, and he had in him the pith and sinew of the hero. Poets have too often been the victims of their own sensitiveness, but Wordsworth stands among them as a man of stubborn strength, an altogether sturdy and unsubduable man. " Out of this sense of loneliness," a friend once wrote to Harriet Martineau, " shall grow your strength, as the oak, standing alone, grows and strengthens with the storm; whilst the ivy, clinging for protection to the old temple-wall, has no power of self-support." Doubtless the loneliness of Wordsworth's life fed his strength, and no finer image than that of the oak could be found to describe the resolute vigour of Wordsworth's character. He certainly was no weak spray of ivy clinging to a temple wall; but he never forgot the temple and its sanctities notwithstanding; and if he were an oak, it was an oak that had its roots in sacred soil, and cast the shadow of its branches on the doorways of the sanctuary.

XVI

WILLIAM WORDSWORTH—CONCLUDING SURVEY

IT is evident to the reader who has followed this imperfect study of Wordsworth with any degree of care that his merits and defects are alike great, and in concluding our survey it is well to recapitulate them. In few poets are the profound and trivial found in such close proximity, and this is his chief defect. Like Browning, for many years Wordsworth had few readers, and consequently wrote more for his own pleasure than with the artistic restraint and carefulness which the sense of public praise and criticism impose. Such criticism as he received was little better than insane or spiteful vituperation, and its only effect was to increase in a man of Wordsworth's temperament a stubborn dependence on himself. It is hard to say which acts with worse effect upon a poet, the adulation of an undiscerning or the apathy of an indifferent public. It seems likely, however, that if Wordsworth had received any public encouragement early in life, it would have acted beneficially, in leading him to perceive his own faults of style, and perhaps to correct them. There are various passages in Wordsworth's letters which prove that, while he braced himself to endure public hostility with uncomplaining stoicism, yet he would not the less have valued public encouragement. But as years wore away, and his circle of readers still continued to be of the narrowest, he cared less

and less to write with any definite attempt to gain the public ear. He wrote for his own delectation, and, as we have
seen, often attached false values to his poems. He failed,
as every solitary writer must fail, to discriminate between
the perfect and imperfect work of his genius. The result
is that to-day the perfect work of Wordsworth is ham-
pered by its association with the imperfect. His readers
often fail to take a just measurement of the noble qualities
of his genius, because it is so easy for them to pass from
his greatest poems to passages of verse-writing which are
dull, trivial, bald and in every way unworthy of him. This
fact has been amply recognized by Matthew Arnold, and
he has endeavoured to remedy the defect by his admirable selection from the works of Wordsworth. Few poets
bear the process of selection so well, and certainly none
have so much to gain by it.

There is something of pathos, indeed, in the recollection of the relation which Wordsworth bore to the literature of his day. He came in the wake of Byron, and
uttered a note so different that it is scarcely surprising
that the multitude who read Byron had no ear for Wordsworth. For every thousand who bought *Childe Harold*,
there was perhaps one who bought the *Lyrical Ballads*.
When contempt and hostility had slowly passed into
grateful recognition his fame was menaced from another
quarter. By that time Tennyson was making himself
heard, and Tennyson soon passed Wordsworth in the
race for fame. Wordsworth never knew the joy of
unrivalled and indisputable preëminence. His star rose
unperceived in the firmament where Byron reigned in
splendour, and before the fading afterglow of Byron had
left a space for his modest light to spread, it was again
eclipsed by the growing beams of Tennyson. The one

poet had the vehement personality, and the other the rich and ornate style, which Wordsworth lacked. Each appealed to the popular ear as he did not; the one with a more masterful, the other with a more musical, note. It seemed part of the irony of fate that Wordsworth should nurture his heart in solitary endurance to the end, and should never know what it was to reap the full harvest of his toils. Perhaps also there is a law of compensation at work which has ensured to Wordsworth a more solid fame than Byron seems likely to enjoy, or Tennyson is likely to attain. The sureness which we usually associate with slowness has certainly marked the growth of Wordsworth's fame; and it may be confidently said that at no period since the appearance of the *Lyrical Ballads* has Wordsworth been so widely read as now. Can as much be said of Byron? Will as much be said in a hundred years of Tennyson? Of Byron at least it is true that he has decreased while Wordsworth has increased. While the star of Byron has gradually receded, the star of Wordsworth has risen into dominance, and burns with an enduring and immitigable flame.

There are, of course, some dissentients to this judgment, but one hardly pays much attention nowadays to the erratic criticisms of Swinburne, and still less to Mr. Andrew Lang, when he is good enough to inform us that he does not care " very much for Mr. William Wordsworth." The latter is merely the small impertinence of criticism, meant to excite laughter, but likelier to inspire contempt, and in no case worthy of any serious resentment. Nor can one quarrel seriously with so genial a humourist as Edward Fitzgerald, when he is provoked by the almost irritating respectability of Wordsworth to write of him as " my daddy." It is more to the purpose

to recollect that Coleridge placed Wordsworth " nearest
of all modern writers to Shakespeare and Milton, yet in
a kind perfectly unborrowed and his own." If this be
regarded as the unconsidered praise of enthusiastic
friendship, we have also to recollect that Matthew
Arnold, who was always frugal in his praise, and never
guilty of untempered adulation, has practically endorsed
this verdict. With Shakespeare and Milton he will not
compare him, but next to these august names he ranks
Wordsworth as the man who has contributed most to
the permanent wealth of English poetry since the
Elizabethan age. Nor does John Morley, one of the
most judicial critics of Wordsworth, contest the justice of
this criticism. He cannot grant him Shakespeare's
vastness of compass, nor Milton's sublimity, nor Dante's
" ardent force of vision," but he admits Wordsworth's
right to comparison, and admirably states Wordsworth's
peculiar gift when he says, " What Wordsworth does is
to assuage, to reconcile, to fortify. Wordsworth, at any
rate, by his secret of bringing the infinite into common
life, as he invokes it out of common life, has the skill to
lead us, so long as we yield ourselves to his influence,
into inner moods of settled peace ; to touch ' the depth
and not the tumult of the soul ' ; to give us quietness,
strength, steadfastness, and purpose, whether to do or to
endure." He would be a daring man who contested a
verdict endorsed by the three most eminent names of
modern criticism, and it is pretty safe to assume that on
all the main issues this verdict is decisive, and is not
likely to be seriously impugned.

Any final survey of Wordsworth's work would be
incomplete without mention of what may, after all, be
taken as his noblest single poem, the *Ode on Intimations*

of Immortality from Recollections of Early Childhood.
This poem was written when Wordsworth was at the
prime of his powers (1803-6), and is rich in his peculiar
excellences.   It also sums up much that is most characteristic in his philosophy.   The starting-point of his
philosophy is that man has in himself all the elements of
perfect life, if he will but learn how to adjust himself to
the environment in which he finds himself:

> The Child is father of the Man,
> I could wish my days to be
> Bound each to each in natural piety.

The evils of life spring from the perverse disregard of
his true instincts, to which man is prone.   The child
loves Nature, and is happiest in contact with Nature, and
it is for that reason Wordsworth urges the absolute need
for communion with Nature in the perfect human life.
In the natural instincts of the child's heart we have, if we
only knew it, the true indications of the highest possible
development of human nature.   They are the pointer-
stars by which we can measure the firmament of human
life, and ascertain the true bearings and infinite courses
of human destiny.   But behind this assumption another
question lies : we ask, What is there to prove to us that
these instincts are right, and from whence do they
spring ?   The answer to this question Wordsworth gives
in this great ode.   As usual, he probes the mystic depths
of his own experiences, and from that depth rescues the
clue which interprets to him the whole mystery and cir-
cumference of human destiny.   He tells us that as a
child he had no notion of death, nor could he bring
himself to realize it as a state applicable to his own being.
He felt within himself the movements of a spirit that

knew nothing of decay or death. He even felt it difficult to realize the fact of an external world, so absorbed
was he in the rapture of idealism. " Many times," he
says, " while going to school, have I grasped at a wall or
tree to recall myself from this abyss of idealism to the
reality. At that time I was afraid of such processes.
In later periods of life I have deplored, as we have all
reason to do, a subjugation of an opposite character, and
have rejoiced over the remembrances, as is expressed in
the lines :

> Obstinate questionings
> Of sense and outward things,
> Fallings from us, vanishings,
> Blank misgivings of a Creature,
> Moving about in worlds not recognized,
> High instincts, before which our mortal nature
> Did tremble like a guilty Thing surprised.

He recalls the " dream-like vividness and splendour which
invests objects of sight in childhood," and then asks :
What is the interpretation of this sense of wonder and
strangeness which is the earliest recollection of childhood
in the presence of external nature ? His reply is that in
the child's spiritual aloofness from the world, in his sense
of the foreignness of life as he finds it, is the intimation
of his previous existence in the purer realms of spirit, and
of his ultimate return to a spiritual existence. He is a
spirit clothed with fleshy apparel for a moment, but immortal in himself, and moving through the darkened
ways of mortality with the primal fire of immortality
burning in his heart, and trembling upwards to the source
from which it sprang. The world is his prison-house,
and the great end of life is not to be reconciled to the
prison-house, but to retain and strengthen the Divine

desires which haunt him with the sense of something lost,
and something higher. Mere shadowy recollections they
may be, and yet they are

> The fountain-light of all our day,
> Are yet a master-light of all our seeing ;
> Uphold us, cherish, and have power to make
> Our noisy years seem moments in the being
> Of the eternal silence ; truths that wake
>   To perish never ;
>   Which neither listlessness, nor mad endeavour,
>   Nor Man nor Boy,
> Nor all that is at enmity with joy
> Can utterly abolish or destroy !

This poem is the noblest of all testimony to the profound
religiousness of Wordsworth's spirit. It breathes something more than the peace, it trembles with the rapture
of the loftiest piety. It purges, it transforms, it exalts
us. We catch a spiritual glow as we listen, we see before
us the unfolding vision of glory beyond glory, such as he
saw who stood on Patmos and beheld the heavens opened,
and the infinite cycles of immeasurable Divine purposes
fulfilling themselves. Prisoners though we be, stifled in a
world of sense, weighed upon with fetters of ignoble
custom, yet as we climb the solitary peak of contemplation where Wordsworth stands like a seer lost in vision —

> Our souls have sight of that immortal sea
>   Which brought us thither,
>   Can in a moment travel hither,
> And see the children sport upon the shore,
> And hear the mighty waters rolling evermore.

And last, it may be noted, that in literary finish and
pregnancy of phrase Wordsworth never surpassed this

poem.   It marks the complete culmination of his power.
Phrase after phrase, such as

> Faith that looks through death,
> In years that bring the philosophic mind ;

or,

> Our birth is but a sleep and a forgetting ;

or,

> To me the meanest flower that blows can give
> Thoughts that do often lie too deep for tears,

has passed into the currency of literature unnoticed, by
reason of some unforgettable quality of thought or expression, which stamps itself upon the universal memory.
Longer poems, full of passages of memorable insight or
emotion, Wordsworth has written, but his great qualities
find no nobler display than in this poem.   Nowhere does
he more nearly approach to " Milton's sublime and unflagging strength, and Dante's severe, vivid, ardent force
of vision."   It is, in fact, one of the few great odes of
English literature, and is in itself sufficient to give Wordsworth rank among the few greatest poets who stand secure above the transience of human taste,—

> the great of old,
> The dead but sceptred sov'reigns, who still rule
> Our spirits from their urns.

Finally, we note that Wordsworth is not the poet of
youth, but of maturity.   There is poetry, as there is art,
which does not dazzle us with wealth of colour, but which
deals in cool and silvery grays, unnoticed by the taste
which seeks startling and sensational effects, but infinitely
refreshing to tired eyes which have long since turned

from the sensational in resentment and something of disgust. Perhaps it is not until we have been surfeited with gaudy art that we learn fully to appreciate this very different art. Then is the time for the cool gray : then it is that these softer and soberer tones of colour soothe the eye and satisfy the brain. It is, in the same way, precisely when the poets of our youth cease to allure us that the charm of Wordsworth begins to be most keenly felt. To the mature man, who has wearied of the theatrical glitter of Byron or the cloying sweetness of Keats, Wordsworth comes like the presence of Nature herself. He does not captivate the taste with casual brilliance, but he subdues it with a sense of infinite tranquillity and refreshment. He satisfies the heart, he inspires and stimulates the thought. We read him not once, but many times, and as life advances we find that he is one of the few poets we need not cast aside. He ennobles and invigourates us. He advances with us as we pass into those shadows which lie about the doorways of mortality, and his voice never falters in its encouragement and pious hope. He becomes to us more than a poet—he is our guide, philosopher, and friend; and when many other guides of youth are shaken off, the mature mind grows more and more sympathetic to Wordsworth, and finds in him a spiritual comradeship such as no other poet has it in his power to give.

XVII

THE HUMANITARIAN MOVEMENT IN POETRY—THOMAS HOOD AND MRS. BROWNING

Thomas Hood, born in London, 1798. Wrote the Song of the Shirt, 1843. Died in London, May, 1845.—Mrs. Browning, born in London, March 4, 1809. Died in Florence, June 29, 1861.

ANY survey of the poets would be incomplete which did not take into account the beginnings of a movement in modern literature which we may call the Humanitarian Movement. If we cared to go back far enough in the search for its beginnings, we should clearly have to touch again upon the work of Crabbe, who is in many respects the father of humanitarian realism in poetry. Crabbe had no delicacy of touch and little refinement of mind, but he knew how to paint his pictures of the suffering poor in a broad and effective fashion, which secured him both attention and fame in his day. The weak point in Crabbe's work is a certain vitiating touch of coarseness. He sometimes excites repulsion where he means to stimulate pity. Between pity and repulsion the line of demarcation is often slender, and Crabbe's power of discernment was not sensitive and subtle enough always to observe it. There is a certain air of deliberation about his realism, and sometimes a tedious accumulation of detail in his method, which hide from us the genuine, honest sympathy of his nature. In a word,

Crabbe lacks passion.   His nature is too slow and solid
to kindle into white-heat, or to kindle others.   It was re-
served for two later poets, Thomas Hood and Mrs.
Browning, to take up the work which he began, and to
do it with such vehemence and passion that their writings
constitute a new era in modern poetry.

Dissimilar as Thomas Hood and Mrs. Browning were in
many respects, yet their lives bear a close resemblance in
familiarity with misfortune.   Hood's life was a story of
hard work faithfully done; of frequent sorrows borne
with brave endurance and buoyant trust.   His first verses
appeared in a Dundee newspaper, and like many other
men he slid into literature rather by force of circumstances
than by intention and deliberate dedication.   Like many
others, he also found that literature was an excellent
crutch but a bad support.   His knowledge of engraving
and his comic genius brought him bread, but the means
of living were often sorely scanty.   At one time he was
virtually expatriated by commercial losses, and took up
his residence in Germany.   With weak health, often
broken by periods of acute suffering, with a family which
increased with embarrassing rapidity, with constant
pecuniary difficulties to depress and harass him, Hood
never bated a jot of heart or hope ; and for those who can
discern the true nobleness of such a struggle as this Hood
will wear something of the lustre of the true hero.   It
was not the Byronic heroism which mouths its part upon
the stage, and invites the public to share its secrets, but
the heroism of reticence, which endures and is quiet.
Hood obeyed Carlyle's doctrine : he consumed his own
smoke.   He wrote no bitter, petulant, or complaining
poems.   To the public his mouth was always full of jests,
and his kindly face always lit with smiles.   The crowd ap·

plauded his jests, but little knew how heavy was the heart of the jester.   Hood was not the man to let them know. Perhaps with him, as with Abraham Lincoln, " laughter was his vent for sorrow " : if he had not laughed he would have died of a broken heart or frenzied brain. He so habitually practiced the art of jesting at his sorrows that his son tells us that even when the shadow of death had fallen on him, and a sinapism of more than usual potency was applied to his wasted chest, he said, smilingly, " It seems a great deal of mustard for so very little meat." And this lifelong sorrow of Hood, this daily-enacted tragedy of " despairing hope," did not make him selfish, but sympathetic, and led him to look with passionate insight and pity on the sorrows of others.   Perhaps it needs a sufferer to interpret suffering, and only a man who had found how hard it was to work for bread in London could have written the *Song of the Shirt.*

The same story of personal suffering occupies more than half of the life of Mrs. Browning.   She indeed was opulent enough to be above the bitter fight for bread, but her troubles came in another way.   Her first volume was published in her seventeenth year, and bore the ambitious title *An Essay on Mind.*   This was followed by a translation of the *Prometheus Bound,* of Æschylus, in 1833, and this again by two volumes of original poems in 1838-9. It was at this period that the shadow of calamity was projected over the life of the young poet.   She burst a blood vessel, and was removed in a state of extreme debility to Torquay.   While there her brother and two other young men were drowned by the capsizing of a sailing boat. This tragic event completed the prostration of the sufferer. From that hour, and for many years to come, she lived the life of a confirmed invalid—a life that hung trembling on the borders of the invisible land, and which was never lifted out of the solemn shadows of eternal things. The bloom of her youth was gone, and her thoughts naturally took a deeper and a devotional tone. The inactivity of her body seemed to stimulate her mind to redoubled exertion. Her close friend, Miss Mitford, has given us in a sentence a picture of the isolated and yet intense life which Miss Barrett—as she then was—spent for many years. She was " confined to a darkened chamber, to which only her own family and a few devoted friends were admitted; reading meanwhile almost every book worth reading in almost every language, and studying with ever-fresh delight the great classic authors in the original." For Mrs. Browning was one of the few women who have attained to ripe and exact classical scholarship, and in her day that was an attainment far rarer than it is in ours. In that darkened chamber the great minds of all ages held converse with her, and they alone were friends who never wearied, who never came too early, never stayed too long and never were denied an audience. And in that life of languor and suffering her feelings were liberated, and her sympathies educated into an almost painful sensitiveness. The contact of the world's sorrow was for her like a burning iron laid upon a raw place. It was impossible for her to speak of it save with an accent of pathos so deep as to be almost agonized. Her power of pathos pervaded everything she wrote. Her verses often seem to quiver and throb with the passionate sympathy out of which they sprang. We hear the weeping in them, we feel the yearning. There is a sort of heart-searching power in Mrs. Browning, which no other poet of our times has had. She is wholly possessed with her subject, and her intensity possesses and overcomes her readers. It is impossible to doubt that with her, as with Hood, suffering was an education. The acquaintance with grief taught her the secret of comfort, the mystery of pain the secret of trust, and the loneliness of life the secret of insight. It was that prolonged comradeship with sorrow which instructed her how to touch the springs of human sympathy with so sure a hand, and led her through the avenues of her own suffering into a sacrificial comradeship in the sufferings of society.

At this point, however, an essential difference between Hood and Mrs. Browning is evident. To Mrs. Browning poetry was not so much a purpose as a passion, whereas Hood's serious poetry was the rare counterfoil to his comic genius. Mrs. Browning said of her life-work, " Poetry has been as serious to me as life itself, and life has been very serious. I never mistook pleasure for the final cause of poetry, nor leisure for the hour of the poet. I have done my work so far as work; not as mere hand and head work apart from the personal being, but as the completest exposition of that being to which I could attain, and as work I offer it to the public, feeling its shortcomings more deeply than any of my readers, because measured by the height of my aspiration." It is feared that poor Hood never had time to make poetry his life-work. His son said that nothing would have surprised him more than to have witnessed the publication of his *Serious Poems*. How finely Hood could write, when the pressure of life left him a brief leisure for the higher exercise of his powers, is seen in such poems as the *Haunted House, Eugene Aram*, and in such sweet, bird-like notes of lyric pathos and melody as *It was the Time of Roses* and *I remember*. Hood possessed a strong imagination, together with great nobleness of feeling and purity of diction. The *Haunted House* is one of the most masterly studies in horror which any literature can show. The slow, deliberate piling-up of the imagery of horror, the association of all that superstition can invent or cowardice can dread, of all that past tragedy can accomplish or bequeath, the gradual culmination of gloom and horror as the poem passes to its conclusion, make it in its way an extraordinary production, such as only an artist of first-rate excellence could have perfected. In the hands of any one but a master the reiteration and multiplication of images of fear would have become absurd or monotonous, but with Hood they produce the effect of thickening gloom, and it is an unbearable and doomful voice which utters the hoarse refrain,

> O'er all there hung the shadow of a fear,
> A sense of mystery the spirit daunted,
> And said, as plain as whisper in the ear,
> The place is haunted !

We have need to turn to poems like these to form a true estimate of Hood's poems. In ardour of thought and intensity of imagination he falls very far behind Mrs. Browning, but we should not forget that while Mrs. Browning had every opportunity for the development of her genius, Hood's noblest powers were stifled by the sordid needs of life. The kinship between them was not intellectual, but moral. And at one point in the development of these widely different lives they touched and mingled, and for both poetry became as serious as life, and was not so much a purpose as a passion. That point of accord was the humanitarian sympathy which wrung from the solitary student of Greek poetry and mediæval romance the *Cry of the Children*, and from the sickly journalist who must needs jest for bread the *Bridge of Sighs* and the *Song of the Shirt*.

Another thing worthy of notice is that it was in the writings, and through the influence, of Thomas Hood and Mrs. Browning, that the city in its tragic social aspects became definitely annexed to the realm of English poetry. The poetry of the country is easily perceived: it needed a more discerning eye to recognize the strange and moving poetry of the city. Both these poets were Londoners, and so thoroughly was Hood a child of the city that he might have said with a later poet:

> City! I am true child of thine!
> Ne'er dwelt I where great mornings shine
>   Around the bleating pens;
> Ne'er by the rivulets I strayed,
> And ne'er upon my childhood weighed
>   The silence of the glens;
> Instead of shores where ocean beats,
> I hear the ebb and flow of streets.

Hood knew the " tragic heart of towns," and was almost the first of our poets to recognize in poetry the social problems of great cities. Until Hood wrote it may even be said that English poets had little or nothing to say about cities. Poetry had haunted the quiet dales of Westmoreland and the sunny heights of Italy, the happy places of flowers and feasting, the solemn places of tragic gloom where world-wide histories had been shaped, but it had shown no appreciation of the tragic miseries of great cities. Wordsworth saw no vision from Westminster Bridge but the vision of the dawn adding splendour and majesty to the long lines of houses and the broad sweep

of flashing river. Even Shelley, with all his sympathy
for suffering, wrote no poem directly dealing with the
slow martyrdom of the obscure and half-famished toilers
of London. He did once say, bitterly enough, that hell
must be a city very like London—but that was all. He
was the child of dreams, and in his lifelong dream of
social reconstruction was too absorbed in the splendours
of hope to take minute note of the sorrows of reality.
But Hood lived in London, and saw day by day the
open secret of its misery. He lived at the beginning of
a new social age which was fast blotting out the hamlets
of England, and replacing them by an empire of cities.
He was face to face with the social problems which over-
shadowed the nineteenth century ; and what wonder is
it that behind the woven tapestry of city splendour, the
outward glory and sustained dignity of metropolitan life,
he pierced to the silent tragedy of its multitudinous lives
spent in unvictorious struggle, in famished drudgery, and
reluctant shame ? Hood recalled men from the vision of
Nature to the vision of man ; from the vision of man in
rustic innocence to the vision of man among the sordid
degradations of vast cities. It is now generally admitted
that deterioration is the Nemesis of city life, and perhaps
not merely deterioration of physique, but of sympathy,
which is a far more serious matter. Possibly Hood
would not have gone so far as to say that a great city is
a great calamity, but when he cried,

> Alas ! for the rarity
> Of Christian charity
> Under the sun !

he meant his rebuke to be specially applied to that callous indifference to others which cities inevitably breed,

and his words struck the first note of a new movement which is fast socializing poetry, and changing not merely its themes but its spirit.

In the same spirit, if not in the same degree, Mrs. Browning is also the poet of cities. She can paint with Turneresque breadth and vigour the sun pushing its way through a London fog, and can delight in

> Fair fantastic Paris! who wears trees
> Like plumes, as if man made them, spire and tower,
> As if they had grown by nature ; tossing up
> Her fountains in the sunshine of her squares,
> As if in beauty's game she tossed the dice,
> Or blew the silver down-balls of her dreams
> To sow futurity with seeds of thought.

And if in her later poetry Mrs. Browning sings of cities, it is clearly not because she has lost her fresh and vigorous delight in Nature. Who has ever spoken of Nature with more rapt intensity of joy ? She loves rural England so well that she says it is

> As if God's finger touched but did not press
> In making England, such an up and down
> Of verdure ; nothing too much up or down ;
> A ripple of land, such little hills, the sky
> Can stoop to tenderly, and the wheat-fields climb ;
> Such nooks of valleys lined with orchises,
> Fed full of noises by invisible streams.

And how exquisitely she speaks of

> Spring's delicious trouble in the ground,
> Tormented by the quickened blood of roots,
> And softly pricked by golden crocus-sheaves.

And how perfectly she speaks also of herself, in that young green world, " singing at a work apart,"

> As sings the lark when sucked up out of sight
> In vortices of glory and blue air.

So lost is she in a world of symbolism, that she tells us

> Every natural flower which grows on earth
> Implies a flower upon the spiritual side ;

and withal there is about her a spiritual imaginativeness, to which the whole mystery of earth and heaven lies naked and open, which is almost unmatched for purity and intensity among our poets. Such a woman, had she lived all her life in the home of violets, might have sung only of the fragrance and delight of Nature, and she had done well. But she also lived in London, and London weighed upon her soul. She could not rid herself of its ghastly presences, and so the hand that wrote these lovely passages, which seem almost to exhale the very odour of the spring, wrote also of the social evil which

> Slurs our cruel streets from end to end
> With eighty thousand women in one smile,
> Who only smile at night beneath the gas.

What it costs for a woman of such delicate sensitiveness and womanly purity as Mrs. Browning to write such lines as these we cannot know, but we can measure by them the depth of that impression which the horror of cities had made upon her spirit. And we can understand also how the spectacle of wronged and martyred child-life in great cities moved her not less deeply, and we realize the fierce tension of almost prophetic malediction which hurled against our vaunted civilization the reproach of our

> Ragged children, with bare feet,
> Whom the angels in white raiment
> Know the names of to repeat
> When they come on us for payment.

With Mrs. Browning, as with Hood, it was the force of an intense sympathy which urged her to the contemplation of social wrongs, and wrung from her a song of poignant sorrow, indignation, and reproach.

And again, of Hood and Mrs. Browning it must be added that each is a Christian humanitarian. Bitter as is the indictment which they bring against society, yet neither is hopeless. Mrs. Browning sometimes writes as one who "at the cross of hope with hopeless hand is clinging," and tells us —

> I was heavy then,
> And stupid, and distracted with the cries
> Of tortured prisoners in the polished brass
> Of that Phalarian bull, Society —
> I beheld the world
> As one great famishing carnivorous mouth,
> An open mouth, a gross want, bread to fill the lips
> No more ——

but she also hastens to add that her despair was because she

> heard the cries
> Too close ; I could not hear the angels lift
> A fold of rustling air, nor what they said
> To help my pity.

Despair springs from want of imagination, and Mrs. Browning had far too vivid a vision of eternal things to be pessimistic. A Divine trust, a tender resignation, a clear hope in a beyond, both for the individual and society, fill her writings, and Christ is in all her thoughts of men, and all her hopes for the future of man.

In her essay on *The Great Christian Poets* she has said : " We want the touch of Christ's hand upon our literature as it touched other dead things ; we want the

sense of the saturation of Christ's blood upon the souls
of our poets, that it may cry through them in answer to
the ceaseless wail of the Sphinx of our humanity, ex-
pounding agony into renovation. Something of this has
always been perceived in art when its glory was at the
fullest." Something of this—a hopefulness in the final
triumph of humanity—is always to be perceived in Mrs.
Browning's poetry. The agony of the world weighs
heavily upon her. The wail of its pain and desolation
vibrates incessantly upon her heart. She not merely
hears it and feels it, but actually shares it. By force of exquisite sensitiveness, she seems to appropriate the sum of
the world's agony to herself, till it is the agony of one
who not only sees and sympathizes with sorrow, but
whose own heart is literally pierced and bleeding with
the rankling barbs. There are poems of Mrs. Browning's
which could only have been written in a flood of tears,
and which cannot be read without tears. The intensity
of her yearning, her tenderness, her compassion, is almost
painful. But she always knows how to expound agony
into renovation. She sees the brightness of a great hope
falling across the world like the slanting beams of a growing sunrise, and she ever points towards the dawn. And
although Hood's work in humanitarian poetry is limited
to two powerful poems, and he has nothing of Mrs.
Browning's prophetic force and vision, yet it is clear also
that while he attacks society he is not unhopeful of it.
The Christian faith which enabled him to bear his hard
lot without murmur, and to say when he was dying,
" Lord, say, Arise, take up thy Cross and follow Me," enabled him also to believe that through the charity and
sacrifice of which the Cross is a type, and through that
alone, the healing of society would come. For in the

true social gospel there must always be something more than vehemence, and something better than violence: there must be the message and counsel of reconstruction, and the hope of final triumph and millennium.

Perhaps it is a large claim to make for the writer of the *Song of the Shirt* that he was unconsciously a great voice in inaugurating a new movement in poetry; but we have to remember that single poems have more than once proved epoch-making in literature. But it is certainly a valid contention in any case, that the poet is frequently the secret force from which national tendencies and purposes are born.

> It takes a soul
> To move a body; it takes a high-souled man
> To move the masses even to a cleaner stye;
> It takes the ideal to blow an inch aside
> The dust of the actual; and your Fouriers failed,
> Because not poets enough to understand
> That life develops from within.

It is the humanitarian passion of poets like Hood and Mrs. Browning that do far more than we think to soften life with charity, and inspire it with sacrifice and compassion. Of course both Hood and Mrs. Browning were not humanitarian poets alone. Mrs. Browning is the uncontested queen of English song, and her work is various and wonderful. The strength of her affections, the ardour of her thought, the devoutness of her spirit, are qualities quite as marked as the tenderness and breadth of her sympathies. But when we come to estimate the most enduring force in her poetry, we find it to be its humanitarian passion. It was that which inspired not only her *Cry of the Children* and the *Song for Ragged Schools*, but the greatest, if the most unequal, of all her poems, *Aurora*

Leigh. Had Hood not written the *Song of the Shirt,* he could have claimed no place among the chief literary forces of our time. As it is, we have to estimate the rare quality of his genius as much by its intimations as its accomplishments. But if Mrs. Browning had never written *Aurora Leigh* she would still have been a great poet; she would not have been so great a poet, however, and she would certainly have missed the greater portion of her fame. For it is in the power of sympathy that Mrs. Browning stands supreme, and the noblest outbursts of her sympathy were caused by social inequalities, sorrows, and martyrdoms. It is for this reason that, passing over a hundred other things which might be said about her genius and her poetry, we fix on this dominant aspect of her life-work, nor perhaps would she have wished it otherwise. The simple and sufficient epitaph which covers the dust of Hood is, " He sang the *Song of the Shirt,*" and to have written the *Cry of the Children* and *Aurora Leigh* is praise sufficient even for one of the most rarely-gifted writers who has ever enriched the world of English poetry.

XVIII

LORD TENNYSON. GENERAL CHARACTERISTICS

Born at Somersby, Lincolnshire, August 5, 1809. Poems by Two Brothers, published by J. Jackson, Louth, 1827. Poems, chiefly lyrical, published 1830. Poems, in two volumes (Moxon), 1842. The Princess, 1847. In Memoriam, 1850. Became Poet-Laureate in the same year. Maud, 1855. The Idylls of the King, 1859 : completed, 1885. Enoch Arden, 1864. Offered and accepted a Peerage, 1883. Died October 6, 1892. Buried in Westminster Abbey, October 12.

WHEN we come to the name of Tennyson we do well to pause, for in his many-sidedness he represents more fully than any other poet of our day the complex thought and activities of the century in which his lot has been cast. Seldom has a poet's fame grown more slowly or securely, and never has a poet's career been crowned with a larger degree of worldly success. It is now more than half a century since his first slender volume of poems appeared. At that date Christopher North, otherwise Professor Wilson, and the Edinburgh reviewers were in the full heyday of their power, and exercised a dominance in criticism which it is difficult for us to understand to-day. A new poet in those days had to fear ridicule more than indifference, a position which may now be said to be entirely reversed. By turning to that section of the complete works of Tennyson headed Juvenilia, we can ourselves judge what was the character of the claim which the young poet in 1830 made upon the public attention. The volume is not merely slender in bulk, but equally slight in quality. The influence of Keats is apparent everywhere. There is a femininity of tone and a sensuousness of word-painting which are in the exact manner of Keats. The triviality of Keats' worst style is as apparent as the magic phrasing of his best. Take, for instance, this stanza from *Claribel* —

> The slumbrous wave outwelleth,
> The babbling runnel crispeth,
> The hollow grot replieth,
> Where Claribel low-lieth.

This is weak with the peculiar weakness of Keats; the straining after effect by the use of uncommon and affected forms of speech.

There are, however, splendid indications of true and genuine power amid much that is weak and imitative. *Mariana* is a piece of powerful painting, done with excellent artistic taste, intention, and finish. Finer still is the *Recollections of the Arabian Nights.* It is rich, almost too rich indeed, in its colouring, but no one can fail to feel the charm of words in such lines as these : —

> At night my shallop rustling thro'
> The low and blooming foliage, drove
> The fragrant glistening deeps, and clove
> The citron-shadows in the blue :
> By garden-porches on the brim,
> The costly doors flung open wide,
> Gold glittering through lamplight dim,
> And broidered sofas on each side ;
> In sooth it was a goodly time,
> For it was in the golden prime
> Of good Haroun Alraschid.

But in fineness of workmanship and depth of feeling the *Deserted House*, the *Dying Swan*, and *Oriana* take an easy precedence.   In the second of these poems there is that which goes further to ensure a poet the attention of the public than anything else—there is distinctiveness and originality.   The *Dying Swan* was sufficient at once to stamp Tennyson as an original poet.   In its perfectly accurate depiction of Nature it may remind us somewhat of Wordsworth, but it is a mere suggestion, and the style is wholly different.   Wordsworth's has been described as the pure style in poetry ; Tennyson's as the ornate.   The bond of likeness is in the fidelity of each poet to the actual facts of Nature.   Wordsworth never drew a picture of mountain solitude, or lake scenery, more simply true to fact than the picture this young Lincolnshire poet gives of the great open spaces of the fen-country, with their breadth of sky and far-stretching solitude, which is almost desolation, and their gleaming watercourses fretting everywhere, like silver threads the waste of green.

> The plain was grassy, wild, and bare,
> Wide, wild, and open to the air,
> Which had built up everywhere
> An underroof of doleful gray.
>
> *   *   *   *   *
>
> Ever the weary wind went on,
> And took the reed-tops as it went.
>
> *   *   *   *   *
>
> One willow o'er the river wept
> And shook the wave as the wind did sigh ;
> Above in the wind was the swallow,
> Chasing itself at its own wild will,
> And far thro' the marish green, and still
> The tangled watercourses slept,
> Shot over with purple, and green, and yellow.

The sense of desolation is complete. It is not conveyed to the mind by a single vivid touch, in the manner
of Wordsworth, but by a series of cumulative effects,
which are equally striking. It is not wonderful that a
poem like this should arrest the attention of a mind like
Christopher North's. The first volume of a poet has
rarely contained anything so full of conscious strength,
and so complete in its mastery of the art of poetry, as
this pathetic picture of the *Dying Swan.*

Christopher North—" rusty, crusty Christopher "—as
Tennyson afterwards called him, was perhaps more conscious of the weakness of the young poet than of his
strength. In 1832, when the famous " Blackwood " criticism appeared, Wordsworth was still a rock of offence to
the critics, and gibes and insult had not yet ceased to follow him to his solitude at Grasmere. Seven years were
to elapse before Oxford was to recognize his greatness,
eleven years before the Laureateship was his. It was an
unpropitious hour for poets. There had come a great ebb
tide in poetry, perhaps a natural result of that extraordinary outburst of lyric splendour with which the names
of Shelley and Keats are associated. Robert Southey
was Laureate, and an age which had enthroned Southey as
Laureate might well turn a deaf ear to the voice of Tennyson. Upon the whole it is greatly to the credit of
Professor Wilson that he had discrimination enough to
see anything at all in the humble volume of poems by
Alfred Tennyson, which was sent him for review ; and he
took occasion to give the young poet some excellent
advice, for which he had the humility and discernment to
be thankful.

The cardinal error of these early poems Professor
Wilson was keen enough to discern at once. It was

what he called " puerility."   There was a sort of unwholesome sadness about them, a distasteful melancholy, a
mawkishness of tone and subject.   It may be added that
the note of restrained and tender melancholy has always
been one of the chief features of Tennyson's poetry.   It
is not obtrusive, but it is pervasive; it is rarely bitter or
cynical, but it is always there.   It is apparent in the
choice of subject, even in these early poems.   Death and
change strike the key-note of the volume.   Mariana " in
the moated grange " cries —

> I am aweary, aweary,
> Would God that I were dead !

One of the sweetest of the songs is —

> Of the mouldering flowers ;
>
> * * * * *
>
> The air is damp, and hushed, and close,
> As a sick man's room when he taketh repose
> An hour before death.

The fine ballad of *Oriana* is a ballad of death, and the
Dying Swan, although it rises into a voice of noble
music in its close, is nevertheless a poem of desolation
and sorrow.   And over and above all this, a large part of
the volume, no fewer than five poems indeed, are devoted
to the depiction of various types of womanhood.   Sweetness there is in the volume, but not strength ; and the
sweetness is cloying rather than piercing.   It is not the
voice of the strong and hopeful man, but of the poet
touched with an incurable melancholy of thought and
outlook.   Yet if melancholy strikes the key-note of the
whole, it is not less true that the melody is really new
and striking.   The first poem bears the under-title of *A*

Melody, and in the word Tennyson shows an exact appreciation of his own powers. Melodious he always is. No poet has ever had a profounder knowledge of the laws of metrical music. It is the melody of his phrase that carries it home to the memory, not less than its felicity. Any students of Tennyson can recall at will scores of lines which cling to the memory by the charm of their own exquisite music.

Take such examples as these :—

From *Tithonus*:

> While Ilion like a mist rose into towers.

From *Ulysses*:

> And drunk delight of battle with my peers
> Far on the ringing plains of windy Troy.

From the *Princess* :

> Myriads of rivulets hurrying thro' the lawn,
> The moan of doves in immemorial elms,
> And murmuring of innumerable bees.

In these last lines there is an overpowering imaginative charm, something almost magical in its bewitchment, which makes us think of the words of Keats, that to him a fine phrase was an intoxicating delight. It is melody, the finest and most magical melody of which words are capable. There is nothing in the early poems of Tennyson to match such exquisite phrasing as this, but there are nevertheless sure indications of where the real power of the poet lay. It was the advent of an intensely artistic mind, palpitatingly alive to the vision and power of beauty, touched with the artist's ecstasy, and with the artist's corresponding melancholy, keen, subtle, delicately-poised, possessing the secret of loveliness rather than of rude vigour; it was the advent of such a mind into the world of English poetry which was signalized by that slender volume of Poems by Alfred Tennyson, published in 1830.

But bright as were the indications of poetic genius in the earliest work of Tennyson, few could have dared to augur from them the height of excellence to which the poet subsequently attained. A yet severer critic than Wilson was Lockhart, who reviewed the poems in the *Quarterly Review*, and it is noticeable that almost every suggestion of Lockhart was hereafter adopted by Tennyson. He had the sense to take the advice of his critics, to rid himself of puerilities, to be patient, to dare to investigate and grapple with his own faults, to enter upon a course of arduous labour and invincible watchfulness, to practice not merely the earnest culture of art, but also to seek the self-restraint of art; and he has fully justified their presage that he had in him the making of a great poet. Poetry has not been to him a pastime, but the supreme passion and toil of life. Again and again he has polished and remoulded his earlier poems, not always, perhaps, to their advantage, but always with the intent of making them more perfect in metrical harmony, and more complete and concise in poetic workmanship. The melody has grown with the years; it has become more subtle, more penetrating, more magical. He has carried the art of metrical construction to a height of perfection never before attempted in English poetry. It is difficult to find a false rhyme, a slovenly stanza, or a halting metre in all the great bulk of his completed works. As an example of the infinite laboriousness of true poetic art there can be no finer example. And in variety

of subject he has but one rival. He has treated the
romantic, the antique, the domestic life of the world
with equal skill.   History and theology, art and science,
legendary lore and modern social problems find constant
reflection and presentment in his poetry.   Some of
his poems are so clearly hewn that they are like mighty
fragments of the antique ; some treat of English
peasant life; some of fairy lore, some of religious
fancy, some of social dreams and yearnings ; in some
the theme is slight, but the slightness of the theme is
forgotten in the excellence of the workmanship; in
some the theme is as solemn as life and death, and
touches issues which are as old as human thought.
" Rapt nuns," it has been said, "English ladies, peasant
girls, artists, lawyers, farmers,—in short, a tolerably
complete representation of the miscellaneous public
of the present day," jostle one another in his picture
galleries. True, the cosmopolitan note of Browning
is wanting ; but if Tennyson has not the catholic
sympathies of Browning, he has succeeded in touching
with the utmost felicity many aspects of English life
which his great rival has ignored.   And his mood and
style are as various as his themes.   In such poems as
Dora we have a Wordsworthian simplicity of diction, a
coolness and purity of colouring almost cold in its
severity.   In such poems as *Maud* and *Locksley Hall*
we have the utmost elaboration of ornate imagery and
effect.   He can be severely simple and chastely sensuous,
classic and grotesque, subtle and passionate, passing
with the ease of perfect mastery from love to dialectics,
from the wail of a sombre pessimism to the exaltation
and rapture of the triumphant lover.   He can even be
humorous, and excellently humorous too, as in such a

poem as the *Northern Farmer*. It is probably in this diversity of gifts that the great secret of Tennyson's wide popularity is to be found. He touches many classes of readers, many varieties of mind. Of his limitations, his peculiarities of view and outlook, his attitude to religion and politics, his pervading melancholy and the causes of it, we shall see more as we devote more particular attention to his works ; but enough has been said to explain why it is that he has won not merely wide but sound popularity ; and not merely popularity, but fame and success such as no other English poet has ever enjoyed in the brief period during which his work was actually being done, when the fruits of success were keenest to the taste, and most alluring to the ambition.

XIX

TENNYSON'S TREATMENT OF NATURE

THE variety of Tennyson's work makes the task of arranging it more than usually difficult. Certain portions of his work are directly philosophical, and are meant to be elucidations or solutions of some of the deepest problems of humanity. Others are surcharged with mournfulness, and might be called lamentations; dirges over dead hopes, lost glories of chivalry, or the bitter presage of future trouble travelling towards us in the development of social perils. Others are purely fanciful, lyrics finished with airy grace, or poems breathing the enchantment of fairy lore. But such a classification as this is incomplete, and fails to yield the result which a just criticism desires. Broadly speaking, there are certain great subjects on which all true poets have something to say. These subjects are nature, woman, life, politics, and religion. Nature needs no definition; under the head of woman we must include all that pertains to love and chivalry; under the head of life, the general view of human action and society which distinguishes a poet; under politics, the poet's view of progress and the future of the race; under religion, what the poet has to say about the devout longings of humanity, its sorrows and their solution, the future and its promises. It will be found that under this classification the works of all great poets can be readily placed. It is the view of Nature which is the distinguishing feature in Words-

187

worth ; it is the view of woman—gross, carnal, callous —which is the damning feature in Byron ; it is the view of religion which lends such paramount interest to the poetry of Arnold and Browning. Let us begin, then, by examining what Tennyson has to say about Nature.

We have already seen that to Shelley Nature was something more than an abstract phrase ; she was something alive, a radiant and potent spirit, a glorious power filling the mind with infinite delight, and drawing out the spirit of man in ecstatic communion.   The first thing we note about Tennyson is that Nature is not to him what she was to either Shelley or Wordsworth.   He nowhere regards Nature as a living presence.   He at no time listens for her voice as for the voice of God.   To Shelley Nature was Love ; to Wordsworth she was Thought ; to Tennyson she is neither.   He does not habitually regard Nature as the vesture of the Highest—the outward adumbration of the invisible God.   He does not even regard her with the purely sensuous delight of Keats.   And the reason for this lies in the fact that the sympathies of Tennyson are so various that there is no excess in any ; it is the full play of an exquisitely-balanced mind that we see, rather than the fine ecstasy of an enthusiastic artist.   To Words-worth Nature was everything, and on the solitary hills he worshipped before her altars, and in the voice of the winds and waters he heard her breathings, and caught the message of her wisdom.   Apart from men, in solemn loneliness, incurious about the crowded life of cities, or the vast movements of the troubled sea of human thought, he stood, silent and entranced, waiting for rev-elations of that Eternal Power, whose splendour glowed upon the hills at dawn, and whose mind uttered itself out of the starry spaces of the wind-swept heavens at night. But Tennyson has never professed himself incurious about the progress of human opinion, or indifferent to the life of cities. Wordsworth's was the priestly temperament, Tennyson's is the artistic. The great drama of human life has not been permitted to pass him un-noticed. He has found joy in the refinements of wealth, interest in the progress of society, passionate absorption in the theological controversies of his time. A certain dramatic interest has always drawn him towards the tragic realities of past history and of present life. He has the quick eye of the scientific observer, or of the artistic draughtsman, but little of the rapt contemplation of the seer. Thus it follows that, while Nature perpetually colours his writings, he has nothing new to say about her.

There is, however, one quality which distinguishes his view of Nature from that of other poets, viz., the scientific accuracy of his observation. Nature to him is neither Love nor Thought: she is Law. He is full of the modern scientific spirit. He sees everywhere the movement of law, and the fulfillment of vast purposes which are part of a universal order. He is under no delusion as to the meaning of Nature; so far from being Love, she is "red in tooth and claw with rapine." The conclusions of modern science Tennyson has accepted with unquestioning faith, and the only factor which preserves him from an unpoetical view of Nature is the religious faith, which makes him perceive Nature not as a mechanical engine of fate, but as a process of law leading to nobler life and larger being. That is the mission of law: not to slay, but to make alive; not to fulfill a blind course, but to work out a Divine purpose, and a diviner life for man, in those far-distant cycles which eye hath not seen, nor hath it entered into the heart of man to conceive.

> Then comes the statelier Eden back to men ;
> Then reign the world's great bridals, chaste, and calm ;
> Then springs the crowning race of human kind.

In other words, Tennyson sees Nature with the eye of the evolutionist, and traces through all her processes the fulfillment of a Divine wisdom, which means well towards man, and all that it has made —

> One God, one law, one element,
> And one far-off Divine event
> To which the whole creation moves.

On the other hand, because Tennyson says little that is new about Nature, it must not be assumed that he does not love her.   On the contrary, he has studied her with unwearied fidelity, for which his knowledge of science has probably given him sharpened instinct and patience.   It would be a curiously interesting study to mark the wide difference between even Shelley's broad generalizations of Nature, accurate as they are, and the minute patience which Tennyson has devoted to every little touch of depiction, in which clouds, or birds, or woods are represented to us.   Tennyson's mind is not merely exquisitely sensitive to natural beauty, but it is deeply tinged with the characteristics of that scenery in which his early manhood was passed.   The gray hillside, the " ridged wolds," the wattled sheepfold, the long plain, the misty mornings on the fens, the russet colouring of autumn— this is scenery such as England abounds in, and is especially characteristic of Lincolnshire.   Even more distinctly drawn from the fen scenery are such lines as these :

And the creeping mosses, and clambering weeds,
And the willow-branches, hoar and dank,
And the wavy swell of the soughing reeds,
And the silvery marish-flowers that throng
The desolate creeks and pools among
Were flooded over with eddying song.

In this single poem of the *Dying Swan*, as we have seen, there is an extraordinary accumulation of effects, drawn from the sadness of Nature, and used with perfect skill to enhance the pathos of the picture ; and the soughing of the wind in the Lincolnshire reeds is to be heard in many another poem with equal sadness and distinctness.

It is not without interest to remark that so great a poet as Tennyson is educated not amid the wonderful dawns and cloud scenery of the Lake district, but under the " doleful underroof of gray " built up everywhere above a flat country, where no doubt the tourist—if such, indeed, ever ventures into such solemn solitudes—would aver that there is nothing picturesque or striking. For a poet who was to express the sadness and satiety of the nineteenth century, however, it may be doubted if a more appropriate cradle-land could be discovered.

No doubt it is in part to these natural influences which surrounded his boyhood that the extraordinary fidelity of Tennyson's descriptions of Nature is to be attributed. Where there was little to describe it was natural that the power of observation should be trained to minute accuracy. Miss Thackeray tells us that he once asked her to notice whether the skylark did not come down *sideways* on the wing. This is extremely characteristic of Tennyson's habit in the observation of Nature. He never coins a false phrase about the humblest flower that blows, for the sake of the felicity of the phrase and at

the expense of the tints of the flower. He tells us precisely what he has *seen*. If he tells us that in the spring
" a fuller crimson comes upon the robin's breast," and a
" livelier iris changes on the burnished dove," we may be
quite sure that he has watched the robin and the dove,
and written with his eyes on them rather than on the
paper. The sidelong descent of the lark is a thing to be
noted, that when he comes to speak of it he may use a
phrase that even the scientific naturalist would approve.
The consequence of this fidelity to Nature is that Tennyson is constantly startling us with the vivid accuracy of
his descriptions. We say again and again, " That is so;
I have seen it," and the picture is ineffaceably stamped
upon the memory. Sometimes it is done with a single
phrase, or even a concentrated word. The writer will
not soon forget how throughout one autumn he was
haunted by the phrase, —

All in a death-dumb, autumn-dripping gloom.

Again and again, as he climbed the Dorsetshire hills, the
line met him at the summit: for there lay the death-
dumb land, the long plain with its dim wisps of fog
already beginning to rise, without voice or sound; the
stillness of the dying season like the silence of a death-
chamber; and just perceptible in the near hedgerow the
constant drip of the dew, like the falling of unavailing
tears. Let any one choose a very quiet, gray day in late
autumn, when there has been a previous night of fog, and
stand in a solitary place and listen, as the night begins to
fill the land, and he will feel how exquisite is the truth
of the description of Arthur coming home, and climbing
slowly to his castle —

All in a death-dumb, autumn-dripping gloom.

The same vivid pictorial power is illustrated in many other passages which will readily occur to the Tennysonian student. How admirable a touch of depiction is this : it is the hour of sunset on the marshes, when

> The lone hern forgets his melancholy,
> Lets down his other leg, and, stretching, dreams
> Of goodly supper in the distant pools.

" A full sea, glazed with muffled moonlight," is the perfect vignette of what he once saw at Torquay ; a waterfall " slow-dropping veils of thinnest lawn," a sketch taken on the Pyrenees ; " a great black cloud draw inward from the deep," an etching made upon the top of Snowdon. From boyhood he loved the sea, and studied it in all its moods, with the result that his sea-pictures are always exquisitely truthful. In those hours of " wise passiveness " he marked

> The curled white of the coming wave
> Glass'd in the slippery sand before it breaks,

and how

> The wild wave in the wide north-sea,
> Green-glimmering towards the summit, bears with all
> Its stormy crests *that smoke against the skies*
> Down on a bark, and overbears the bark
> And him that helms it.

It would be difficult for words to attain to higher pictorial art than this : these two verses are two perfect pictures of the summer and the winter sea.

The main point to observe, therefore, about Tennyson is, that in him we have the scientific observer and the artist, rather than the interpreter of Nature. Wordsworth interprets ; Tennyson describes. He is vivid,

pictorial, picturesque; but he has no fresh insight into
the soul of things, save such as his science furnishes him.
But if he has no new gospel to preach us from the book
of Nature, we may at least rejoice in the perfect finish
and enchantment of his pictures.

To this it may be added that these pictures are for the
most part essentially English in tone, atmosphere, and
subject.   Now and again, but with great rareness, he has
depicted foreign scenery, as in the *Daisy* : —

> How faintly-flushed, how phantom-fair,
> Was Monte Rosa, hanging there,
> A thousand shadowy pencilled valleys
> And snowy dells in a golden air.

And the picture is perfect both in glamour and fidelity.
But it is in English pictures he excels.   Who that has
seen the land of Kent does not recognize this? —

> The happy valleys, half in light, and half
> Far shadowing from the west, a land of peace;
> Gray halls alone among their massive groves;
> Trim hamlets : here and there a rustic tower
> Half lost in belts of hop and breadths of wheat;
> The shimmering glimpses of a stream; the seas;
> A red sail or a white; and far beyond,
> Imagined more than seen, the skirts of France.

Or who does not feel the truth of this touch of rural life
in England? —

> The golden autumn woodland reels
> Athwart the smoke of burning weeds.

Nor is it only such peaceful scenes as these that Tennyson
can invest with the magic of his art; he knows how to
grasp the larger effects of Nature, the mountain-gloom,

the cloud-grandeur, the dawn of day or night of tempest, and seize them with an imaginative skill and power of phrase which stamp them indelibly on the memory. For let him who has watched the pageant of the dying day say if any human art could more grandly fix in words the western cloud effects than this : —

> Yonder cloud,
> That rises upward, always higher,
> And topples round the dreary west,
> A looming bastion fringed with fire.

Or let him who has studied the warfare of wind and cloud and the wild upheaval and terror of gathering tempest say if this is not a picture such as Turner would have delighted to paint, and only he could have painted in all its stern magnificence : —

> The forest cracked, the waters curl'd,
> The cattle huddled on the lea ;
> And wildly dashed on tower and tree
> The sunbeam strikes along the world.

Nor could an angry morning after tempest be better painted than in this one pregnant line : —

> All in a fiery dawning, wild with wind.

Nor could the savage splendour of Alpine fastnesses, where precipice and glacier rise tier above tier, in shattered beauty and unvanquishable strength, be better brought home to the imagination than in this touch of solemn imagery : —

> The monstrous ledges slope, and spill
> Their thousand wreaths of dangling water-smoke
> That like a ruined purpose waste in air.

Nor has the breaking up of a stormy sky, when the clouds suddenly lift as though withdrawn upon invisible pulleys, and there is light at eventide, ever been represented better than in one of the earliest of all these poems, the immature and unequal *Eleanore*:—

> As thunder-clouds, that hung on high,
>   Roof'd the world with doubt and fear,
>   Floating thro' an evening atmosphere,
> Grow golden all about the sky.

And for imaginative intensity, such as the great Greek poets would have delighted in, and indeed wholly in their manner, it is hard to excel the phrase in which Tithonus describes the glory of the dawn:—

> And the wild team
> Which love thee, yearning for thy yoke, arise
> And shake the darkness from their loosened manes,
> And beat the twilight into flakes of fire.

Or the farewell of Ulysses, when he cries:—

> Come, my friends,
> 'Tis not too late to seek a newer world,
> Push off, and, sitting well in order, smite
> The sounding furrows ; for my purpose holds
> To sail beyond the sunset, and the baths
> Of all the western stars until I die.

These are but random samples of the perfection to which Tennyson has wrought his art in the faithful and accurate depiction of Nature. Every word tells : it tells because it is true, because it expresses the very spirit of the scene that he would paint, not less than its external show. The labour and culture which lie behind such perfect phrases as these are immense. Not infrequently

the source of some fine image is to be found in some remote page of the older poets, and part of the charm of
the Tennysonian phrase is that it is often reminiscent—a
subtle echo, as it were, of a more ancient music, which
does not offend but fascinate. Thus the image of the
" ploughed sea " is one of the very oldest since the dawn
of language, and the picture of the dawn in *Tithonus*
has its counterpart in Marston's noble lines —

> But see, the dapple-gray coursers of the morn
> Beat up the light with their bright silver hoofs,
> And chase it through the sky.[1]

But the more enduring element of beauty in such lines
is their delightful truthfulness. " The sounding furrows"
is an exact representation to ear and eye of what happens when the heaving waters are suddenly smitten with
the level sweep of oars. The darkness trampled into
flakes of fire is the precise effect of the instantaneous
irruption of the splendour of the dawn, when the thin
clouds that lie across the east are broken up into floating
fragments, and hang quivering, like golden flames, in the
lucid air, and the world lies still and windless, waiting
for the day. " The fiery dawn," the great burst of
streaming yellow, not graduated into crimson or purple,
but all vast and lurid, like an angry conflagration in the
east, is a spectacle which the seaman knows too well,
when the night has been " wild with wind," and the
storm pauses at the dawn, only to gather strength for the
riotous havoc of the day. It is the exact truth of Nature
which is fixed in phrases like these. It is the truth
Turner painted, the vision of the miracle of Nature
which he strove with infinite toil and true inspiration to

[1] *Vide* Lamb's *Specimens of Elizabethan Poetry.*

retain in his immortal canvases. And because it is true art, therefore it is fine art. Much that might be said of Nature, Tennyson has not said; to much that others have said he is indifferent. But this at least he has done: he has approached Nature, not with the hot and hasty zeal of the impressionist, but with the cool eye of the consummate artist; and every sketch of Nature which he has given us, whether of the commonplace or the extraordinary, is finished with admirable skill, and has the crowning merit of absolute fidelity, accuracy, and truth.

XX

TENNYSON: LOVE AND WOMAN

JUST as one of the most crucial points about a poet is his treatment of Nature, so again, his view of Womanhood affords a key to the character of his mind and the quality of his genius. The love-poetry of the world is one of its most fascinating inheritances, and ranges through many keys. Love has always furnished the impulse to poetry, and has often been its staple. It would be difficult to find any poet who has nothing to say of love; it would be easy to find many poets who have never written exquisitely till they became lovers. The new divine warmth of the heart has liberated the faculties of the intellect, and has given inspiration and insight to the soul. Even when the warmth has been sensuous rather than divine, it has not the less had some effect in the liberation of the mind. Burns displays his highest genius in his love-lyrics. Some of the Elizabethan poets are famous only by a single stanza, or a single poem, which expresses the passion of the human heart with such felicity, such delicate skill, such fire and tenderness, that the world cannot forget their phrases. Rossetti lives in the vision of womanhood, with every sense perpetually tingling to the keen delight of passion. Even Wordsworth kindles at the vision of love: he sees the ideal woman glowing before him, not with any heat of passion indeed, but with a calm and spiritual radiance, which is to him a sacred flame, searching the spirit and purifying the heart. Perhaps the poet of our day least affected by the enchantment of love is Matthew Arnold. He is too reticent for passion, is too sadly philosophical to sing the rapture of the lover. But even Arnold has written love-verses—not inspired lyrics like Burns', but, nevertheless, verses which have sprung from a lover's yearning. Tennyson is so far from an exception that love forms the great motive in all his larger poems. Everywhere he testifies to the pre-eminence and influence of woman. He has been an ardent student of womanhood, and has struck out with admirable skill and genuine artistic feeling many typical portraits of womanhood. He has mastered the difficult secret of how to write voluptuously, and yet retain the bloom of a delicate and almost virginal purity. He knows how to be passionate, but his passion never passes into that sensuous extravagance which is the sign of weakness. There is always a gravity and earnestness about it which preserves him from an excess which becomes ridiculous. In this he stands nearer to Wordsworth than to either Keats or Burns. But whereas in Wordsworth woman has no commanding position, and is almost forgotten and obliterated in the presence of Nature, in Tennyson woman is always preëminent, and the fascination of woman is at least as strong as the charm of Nature.

As with Byron, so with Tennyson, we cannot help tracing the treatment of woman in his poetry to the early influences which surrounded his boyhood. He was never cast upon the world, to sink or swim as he could, in the great seething whirlpools of sensual temptation. He carried with him no evil heritage of passionate blood, as did Byron; he was not brought face to face with any dar-

ing theories of free-love, as was Shelley ; he was not de-
pendent on the coarse orgies of village society for recreation, as was Burns.   He breathed an atmosphere of
refinement from the very first.   He was trained by every
sight and influence of early life into that fastidious purity
which characterizes him.   He grew into vigour in what
might be called the cloistral calm of clerical life in a remote English village.   The baser side of human life was
not seen ; the carnal meanings of love never so much as
named ; the coarser aspects of passion were smothered in
flowers and fragrances.   Behind all the love-lyrics of
Tennyson one sees the picture of a calmly-ordered home,
where domestic love moves like a shining presence, with
hands busy in silent ministrations, and heart full of the
tenderness of a pure devotion.   The portrait of Tennyson's mother is the key to his reverence for womanhood.
It is a beautiful and tender face, delicately moulded,
lighted with a spiritual radiance of sympathy and hope,
and yet, too, bearing pathetic traces of resigned sadness
and sorrowful experience.   We can understand how
Tennyson was preserved from the fatality of recklessness,
how it is he wore the white flower of a blameless life, and
ruled himself with chivalrous regard for womanhood,
when we study his mother's face.   What such a woman
must have been in the home, and what sort of home it
must have been where she moved like a ministering
spirit, we can readily imagine.   And how divinely pure
and penetrating may be the influence of such a woman
Tennyson has told us in a passage of the *Princess*, which
might without much risk of misinterpretation be taken as
a personal reminiscence.

> I loved her ; one
> **Not learned, save in gracious household ways**

> Not perfect, nay, but full of tender wants,
> No angel, but a dearer being, all dipt
> In angel instincts, breathing Paradise,
> Who looked all native to her place, and yet
> On tiptoe seemed to touch upon a sphere
> Too gross to tread, and all male minds perforce
> Swayed to her from their orbits as they moved,
> And girdled her with music.   Happy he
> With such a mother ! faith in womankind
> Beats in his blood, and trust in all things high
> Comes easy to him, and tho' he trip and fall
> He shall not blind his soul with clay.

The first point to be noted, therefore, in Tennyson's treatment of love is its conspicuous purity.   It is the love of the chivalrous knight, not of the Bohemian profligate, which he paints.   His whole conception of love is reverential.   It is a spiritual passion, not an earthly.   He perceives it in its spiritual working, and not in its fleshly. With rare exceptions he shuns altogether the fleshly aspects of love.   One exception is found among the early poems in the striking ballad called *The Sisters*, but this is an obvious imitation of the ancient ballad poetry, in which passion is indeed a prime motive, but is always treated with a healthy frankness.   But the poem partially fails as a perfect imitation of the anciet ballad, simply because Tennyson cannot allude to unchaste passion without a burst of terrible denunciation.

> She died : she went to burning flame,
> She mixed her ancient blood with shame,
> The wind is howling in turret and tree.

He leaps upon the desecrator of human love with a bitter wrath, and with words like the sword-flash of an avenging angel.   The other great example of Tennyson's

treatment of the baser side of love is the unlawful love of
Guinevere. But even here again, he manifests the same
sternness of avenging purity. Not by one touch, one
veiled hint or implication, does he seek to move the
springs of evil concupiscence in his reader. What he sees
again is not the fleshly side of unlawful passion, but the
spiritual. From the sin of Guinevere springs the ruin of
an empire. Her outrage upon purity is avenged in the
downfall of that great kingdom of chivalry which Arthur
had built up with infinite toil. The great purpose of that
kingdom was that it should be God's kingdom on earth.
The work of its great knights was

> To ride abroad redressing human wrongs.

Their rule of conduct was

> To speak no slander, no, nor listen to it,
> To lead sweet lives in purest chastity,
> To love one maiden only, cleave to her,
> And worship her by years of noble deeds
> Until they won her.

And now what happened? Arthur tells her she has
spoiled the purpose of his life —

> Well is it that no child is born of thee.
> The children born of thee are sword and fire,
> Red ruin, and the breaking up of laws.

The carnal sin of one guilty woman has shattered into
utter ruin the noblest kingdom ever built upon the earth.
That is the one awful fact which Tennyson sees, and that
is the key-note to the whole poem. Where other poets
might have seen a subject on which they could lavish all
the wealth of sensuous imagery, he sees not the manner

of the sinning, and is not careful to paint it, but the infinite consequences of the sin streaming on, like a loosened
flood of flame, working havoc and infinite wreck upon
every side. Just as it is the spiritual cleansing of love
which he paints when he tells us —

Love took up the harp of Life, and struck on all the chords with
    might,
    Smote the chord of self, that, trembling, passed in music out
    of sight,

so it is the spiritual and moral effect of the base selfishness of unchaste passion which he describes, when he
paints the breaking up of the Round Table, and Arthur
turning sadly away to lead his disheartened hosts

Far down to that great battle in the west.

It is this perfect and pellucid purity of Tennyson's
mind which has enabled him to do many things impossible to others. Take, for instance, such a poem as *Godiva*.
A subject more difficult of handling it would be hard to
find. The slightest prurience of thought would have been
ruinous. So difficult and delicate is the theme, that the
merest featherweight of over-description, a word too
much, a shade of colour too warm, a hint only of human
heat, would upset the balance, and turn a poem which
sparkles with a crystal purity into a poem brilliant only
with the iridescence of corrupt conception. Such a
theme could not have been entrusted to Rossetti;
scarcely, indeed, to Keats; absolutely not to Swinburne.
To make it acceptable not merely the most delicate lightness of touch was needed, but the most pellucid freshness
of thought. Both Keats and Rossetti would have over-
coloured the picture, and left upon the taste the taint of

an unwholesome voluptuousness. What Swinburne
would have made of it needs no sort of explanation.
But Tennyson is able to treat it nobly, with simplicity
and severity of touch, and he does so in sheer virtue of
his own purity of heart.   There is about him something
of that divine quality which Guinevere discovers in King
Arthur —

> The pure severity of perfect light.

He has no cunning eye to discern anything in the subject which can minister to the baser man.   What he sees
is a noble woman performing an heroic deed.   He describes her in imagery which clothes her as with a garment of light : —

> She lingered, looking like a summer moon
> Half-dipt in cloud : anon she shook her head,
> And showered the rippled ringlets to her knee ;
> Unclad herself in haste ; adown the stair
> Stole on ; and, like a creeping sunbeam, slid
> From pillar unto pillar.
> Then she rode forth clothed on with chastity.

It is the moral significance of the scene which fascinates Tennyson,—the spectacle of a woman sacrificing
herself for the people's good, and so building for herself
an everlasting name.   *Godiva* is a short poem, but it is
invaluable as an index to the purity of Tennyson's
genius, for no poet, who was not penetrated by the utmost reverence for womanhood could have treated such
a subject with such daring, or such conspicuous success.

This reverence of Tennyson for womanhood is marked
in all his poems, and is an influence more or less apparent
throughout his work.   The early poems no less than the
later abound in evidence of its sincerity.   The very fact

that so many of his poems describe women, and bear the names of women, is in itself significant. He bears constant testimony to the " finer female sense," and is careful that he shall not offend it by his " random string." Woman, as he conceives her, is the divinely purifying element in human life. Chivalry to woman is no mere romantic echo of the past : it is the sign-manual of every noble soul. The apprehensions of woman are more delicate than man's ; her instincts are surer, her intuition more certain, her spirit more gracious, more tender, and more divine. He who despises the intuitions of pure womanhood quenches a light which God has set in the world for his guidance and illumination. Of course this is no new doctrine, either in poetry or morals. But it came upon the world almost as a new doctrine in 1830. The women of poetry fifty years ago—the women of Byron, to wit—had no sign of any divine intuition about them. They were warm, weak, and foolish. They never exercised the slightest control over men, except the sensuous control of passion. They were neither reverenced nor obeyed. They were the toys of desire, the beautiful and fragile playthings of an hour. The reverential chastity of Tennyson's treatment of womanhood was nowhere found in the poetry of sixty years ago. The revolution and emancipation of woman had not yet come. It was easy, therefore, for writers like Bulwer Lytton, throughout whose works there are very few examples of reverence for woman, and in which the prevalent conception of woman is debasingly gross and offensive, to mock Tennyson as " school-miss Alfred." It was easy to use the femininity of tone in the earlier poems as a weapon of insult against him. Bulwer Lytton had yet to discover that reverence for woman did not imply any lack

of virility in manhood.   No more stinging retort was
ever made than the verse which " Miss Alfred" fixed
upon the dandy author of *Pelham :* —

> What profits it to understand
> The merits of a spotless shirt,
> A dapper foot, a little hand,
> If half the little soul be dirt !

For it was not weakness of fibre which bred in Tennyson a reverence for woman, but nobility of spirit.   And
it was something more than this.   It was the outcome
of pure training under the gracious eyes of good women.
The home was to Tennyson the highest and noblest expression of human life.   His sympathy with romance
and chivalry gave us exquisite sketches of mediæval
thought, like the *Lady of Shalott*, and finally worked out
that noblest series of poems, *The Idylls of the King*.
The same romantic sympathy is apparent in such a poem
of fairy fancy as the *Day Dream*.   But the strongest
movement of Tennyson's mind in the direction of woman-
worship is towards domestic life.   It is in married love
that the noblest fruit of love is found.   It is there the
divinest dreams of love are realized.   Happy he to whom
such joy is given, but the joy is not for all.

> Of love that never found his earthly close
> What sequel?   Streaming eyes, and breaking hearts?
> Or all the same as if he had not been?

Not so.   When Love and Duty strive together, the victory is with Duty.   Any love snatched in defiance of
Duty is not true love : because it forgets reverence to
womanhood, therefore it is base, and can only lead to
moral disintegration and corruption.   Better far

> Such tears as flow but once a life,
> In that last kiss, which never was the last!

For to Tennyson so supreme is the passion of reverence for womanhood, so infinitely high and dear is womanly purity, that it becomes the key to everything really noble in human life, and any outrage upon that is the vilest of all sin—such sin as shakes the pillars of society, and over-throws the majesty and might of empire. Reverence for woman and reverence for self go hand in hand.

> Self-reverence, self-knowledge, self-control,
> These three alone lead life to sov'reign power,
> Yet not for power (power of herself
> Would come uncalled for), but to live by law,
> Acting the law we live by without fear:
> And, because right is right, to follow right
> Were wisdom in the scorn of consequence.

But high as Tennyson sets woman, yet he retains a clear conception of the just and proper place of woman in society. She may inspire and lead man, but she is not equal with man. She may, indeed, govern men, but it is not by the right of superior intellectual endowment, but by the force of her nobility of soul. Her passions matched with man's

> Are as moonlight unto sunlight, and as water unto wine.

That is a rough and dramatic way of expressing the truth, which Tennyson has worked out at large, with great subtlety and skill, in the remarkable poem of the *Princess*.

The central point of the whole argument in the *Princess* is that woman was never meant to wrestle with man in the arena of intellectual preëminence or the active business of the world. He will reverence her to the utmost, but he will not abdicate in her favour. In fact, his very reverence is founded on her possession of certain qualities which man has in only a less degree, and those qualities are the highest, because they lead to the noblest results

in the actual administration of human life. Man rules
through the brain : woman through the heart. If man
is to be ruled by woman it can only be a spiritual rule,
not an intellectual. In nothing is the reasonableness of
Tennyson's mind better seen than in this poem. It would
have been easy for him to become an impassioned advocate of women's rights. On the contrary, his very
reverence for womanhood leads him to put certain limitations upon woman's empire, which do not hinder its influence, but rather intensify it. The power of woman is not
to be wasted in vulgar strife with men for social preëminence : it is too rare, too subtle, too ethereal. That power
finds its highest exercise in moulding men to morality,
and penetrating nations with the spirit of purity. The
woman who is " slight-natured, miserable," prevents by
her peevishness the growth of man. There is no strife
between man and woman —

> The woman's cause is man's : they rise or sink
> Together, dwarfed or godlike, bond or free.

They are " distinct in individualities," and the only bond
of common life and toil is —

> Self-reverent each, and reverencing each.

And the noble conclusion of the whole argument once
more leads to that vision of the perfect home which
never fades from the poet's heart —

> For woman is not undevelopt man
> But diverse : could we make her as the man
> Sweet Love were slain : his dearest bond is this,
> Not like to like, but like in difference.
> Yet in the long years liker must they grow ;
> The man be more of woman, she of man ;
> He gain in sweetness and in moral height,
> Nor lose the wrestling thews that throw the world ;

> She mental breadth, nor fail in childward care,
> Nor lose the childlike in the larger mind :
> Till at the last she set herself to man
> Like perfect music unto noble words ;
> And so these twain, upon the skirts of Time,
> Sit side by side, full-summed in all their powers,
> Dispensing harvest, sowing the To-be.

Finally, we may say of Tennyson's view of womanhood, that it is not easy to exaggerate the immense service he has rendered to society by his constant insistence on the nobility of purity, the Divine grace of chastity. He has never glorified the wanton, or clothed evil with a golden mist of glowing words. He has kept his moral sense acute and sensitive, and has never confused the limits of right and wrong. With a clear and steady eye he has gazed upon the acts of unchaste passion, but not with sympathy, not with delirious yearning, not with any voluptuous quickening of the pulse : but always with loathing, with hatred, with the strenuous abhorrence of a noble heart, strong in its virgin purity. He has known where the secret of strength lay : —

> His strength was as the strength of ten,
> Because his heart was pure.

For him vice has had no seduction : a jealous virtue has sat enthroned in the heart of his genius, and preserved his mind unsullied. When we consider the bulk of his work, the multitude of his readers, the greatness of his influence, and when we contrast with him the influence and work of such a poet as Byron, we begin to understand how vast a service Tennyson has rendered to the cause of righteousness by the reverent ideal of womanhood he has maintained, and the great example of purity which he has set.

XXI

TENNYSON'S VIEW OF SOCIETY
AND POLITICS

I T is hardly to be expected of a poet that he should
be required to define his views on sociology, or that
he should begin his work in imaginative literature
with any cut-and-dried social creed, which it is his mission to propagate. No great poet has ever set out with
any such propaganda. Wordsworth and the Lake poets
did profess a definite creed, and drew up a statement of
their principles, but they were purely literary principles.
There was nothing in these principles to lead the Lake
poets towards any common view of human life, or human
society. Each took his own course apart from the
literary principles they professed in common, and it was
inevitable that he should. Training, idiosyncrasy, environment, the social status of the poet, the methods of
his education, the opportunities he may have of knowing
the world, or the reverse — all these, and a thousand
other causes, contribute to the shaping of his thought,
and the consequent attitude of his mind towards human
life. But though a poet may have no definite intention
of drawing up any philosophic interpretation of life, he
usually succeeds in doing so. He cannot help himself.
He is bound to furnish himself with some answer to the
great social problems that press upon him hungrily, with
a dreadful insistence, demanding solution or recon-
ciliation. Some ideal of human society he must have,

and he cannot help comparing things as they are with things as he would make them. When at last the finished work of a poet lies before us, then we perceive, and perhaps he also perceives for the first time, that there is a unity and sharpness of outline in his thought, which is clear and distinctive. A hint there, a phrase here, a verse yonder—and silently the underlying thought of the poet emerges. Bone comes to its bone till at last, with every reticulation complete, the skeleton rises clothed in flesh, and the ideal of human life which was jealously hidden in the poet's heart stands before us complete and undisguised.

Now, perhaps, the first thing that occurs to the reader who approaches Tennyson from this point of view is his sense of order. The tendency of his mind is distinctly conservative. He hears, indeed, " the roll of the ages," and he is not unconscious of the revolutionary elements which seethe in society; but he hears, if not with unsympathetic stoicism, at least with an equanimity too settled for disturbance. He is full of reverence for antiquity, he is filled with an all-sufficing sense of the perfection and indestructible stability of all English institutions. His mind is too calm and steady to be sympathetic towards the passionate revolts and despairing heroisms of those who seek an immediate reform of society; he is, indeed, too cool in temper to catch the glow of such movements as these. The place in which he habitually walks and meditates is like that pathway which he has described in the *Gardener's Daughter*:—

> A well-worn pathway courted us
> To one green wicket in a privet-hedge ;
> This, yielding, gave into a grassy walk
> Thro' crowded lilac-ambush trimly pruned ;

And over many a range
Of waving limes the gray cathedral towers,
Across a hazy glimmer of the west,
Revealed their shining windows.

Now what are the details of this picture? What is the
effect it produces on the imagination? The chief idea it
conveys is a sense of perfect order. The pathway is
well-worn with the feet of generations; the green
wicket is framed in a perfectly neat and symmetrical
privet-hedge; the lilac-bush, in its utmost joy of bur-
geoning and blossom, must be allowed no license—it is
" trimly pruned "; and finally, as if to complete the sense
of well-established use, of absolute propriety, of faultless
order and reverent conservatism, the gray cathedral walls
bound the view, and the shining windows seems to reflect
the glory of the past.   In this passage we have a not in-
apt illustration of the strongest tendency of Tennyson's
mind.   It is from such a neat and quiet bower of peace
he looks out upon the world.   He is a recluse, shut up
with his own thoughts, and weaving the bright thread of
his fancy far from the loud commotions of the world.
He loves to surround himself with influences which minister to this studious calm.   In the garden where he walks
no leaf is out of place, no grass-blade grows awry.   If
the world he looks upon hardly matches the spotless
propriety of his retreat, yet, at least, the world shows itself upon the whole a very proper and well-governed
world.   Accidents will happen in the best-regulated societies, but in England at all events they are blessedly rare.
Our roots run deep, and we stand above the shocks of
time.   We have gray cathedrals, excellent clergy, gracious noblemen, stately homes surrounded by the greenest
of lawns, which might almost justify the eloquent eulogy

of the Cambridge gardener, who remarked that such turf could only be got " by mowing 'em and rolling 'em, rolling 'em and mowing 'em, for thousands of years ! " The axiom that " Order is heaven's first law " has been fully accepted by Tennyson, and has received additional development : to him order is also earth's best excellence.

One has only to glance through Tennyson's poems of modern life to see that this criticism is neither spiteful nor unjust. He is usually found in the company of lords and ladies, princesses, scholars, and generally refined people, whose place in society is fully assured. There are exceptions to this statement, of course, which will occur to every reader. He has studied the northern farmer to good effect, and in the *May Queen* and *Dora* we have admirable pictures of homely life. But this does not affect the general truth of the statement. Claribel, Lilian, Isabel, Mariana, are not daughters of the people. Lady Clara Vere de Vere certainly receives condign chastisement, but still she is Lady Clara Vere de Vere. Maud lives in the stately hall, and the village where her lover meets her is the sort of perfect village, " with blossomed gable-ends" which we only see upon a great estate. When he bitterly assails a lord, it is a new-made lord, with a gewgaw title new as his castle, " master of half a servile shire," and clothed with the rank insolence of recent wealth. When he alludes to trade it is with the usual aristocratic contempt, and the ear of the merchant

> Is crammed with his cotton, and rings,
> Even in dreams, to the chink of his pence.

It is true that he can cry,

> Ah, God, for a man with a heart, head, hand,
> Like some of the simple great ones gone

Forever and ever by :
One still strong man in a blatant land,
Whatever they call him, what care I —
Aristocrat, democrat, autocrat, one
Who can rule and dare not lie !

But this is, after all, merely the wail of an angry pessimism. It is the sort of jeremiad in which timid minds usually indulge when the ancient order of things seems threatened. Of true democratic feeling Tennyson is singularly destitute. His leaning is all the other way. It is the sustained splendour and delicate refinement of aristocratic life which fascinate him. His heart is with the ancient order of things, and all his modern poems breathe the spirit of this sentiment.

It follows, therefore, that Tennyson never has been, and never can be, in the true sense, a people's poet. That he has written poems which the very poorest value, and which might rejoice the heart of the peasant, we gladly admit. Probably the *May Queen* is the most popular poem he ever wrote, and it is so because it touches the hearts of homely people. But in the main there is little for the common people in Tennyson's poetry. It knocks at the door of the lady's bower, but not at the poor man's cottage. Its troops of knights and ladies, and exquisitely-dressed and admirably-nurtured people, seem out of place amid the coarse realities of grimed and toiling life. To those who stand among the shadows of life, those who suffer or fight in the hard battles of humanity, and feel the cruel irony and mockery of circumstance, it may well seem that Tennyson's laudation of order is in itself an irony, that the puppets on his stage know little of the great throbbing heart of the common people, and that their fine talk is, after all,

a little too finical to pierce into the most secret chambers
of the human memory.

A further evidence of this limitation of sympathy in
Tennyson is found in his treatment of social questions.
He does not ignore them; he sees them indeed, and some
of his lines, such as the following from the opening of
Maud, quiver with a passionate indignation : —

> And the vitriol madness flushes up in the ruffian's head
> Till the filthy by-lane rings to the yell of the trampled wife,
> And chalk and alum and plaster are sold the poor for bread,
> And the spirit of murder works in the very means of life.

But it is not in mere denunciation of existing evils that
the true poet should spend himself.   The true poet seeks
to probe the heart of the world's sorrow, and we turn to
him to know what verdict he can give, and whether there
is any hope.   Tennyson has no distinctive reply to such
questions as these, or if any reply, it is a hopeless one.
He perceives the glorious growth of science, he fore-
shadows the vast discoveries of a larger age, he is sure
that on the whole the world means progress ; but when
he brings himself face to face with the actual details of
life lived in poverty, squalor, and crime he is sullenly unhopeful.   He looks upon the whole question from the
point of view of the comfortable burgess, not of the poor
man himself who stands amid the grime of the actual
sacrifice.   He gazes down from his sunny vantage-ground
of æsthetic refinement, where " no wind blows roughly,"
and ponders, speculates, sympathizes, but his philosophic
calm is undisturbed.   He never steps down into the thick
of the struggle, and makes those who unjustly suffer feel
that in him they have a comrade and a champion.   When
the sudden light of some glowing, some delusive hope is
flung across their wasted faces, he is quick to tell them

that the hope *is* delusive, and to rebuke them for their excess of fond credulity.   One of his characters is described as running

> A Malayan muck against the times ;

but when we wait to be told exactly in what his offending lies, we find that it simply amounts to this, that he

> Had golden hopes for France and all mankind.

This is typical of Tennyson's point of view of social questions.   There is no living heat of enthusiasm in him: he is wrapped in a chilly mantle of reserve, and he chills the ardent as he talks with them.   When he proposes a great concession to the poor, what is it?

> Why should not these great sirs
> Give up their parks some dozen times a year
> To let the people breathe ?

That is all: a mere act of justice, an imperfect recognition of the truth that property has duties as well as privileges; but it is announced as though it were a revolution, and as if the poet himself were astonished at his own daring. Perhaps, however, the sense of daring is not surprising when we find that the proposal was made to a stalwart baronet,

> A patron of some thirty charities,
> A pamphleteer on guano and on grain,
> A quarter-sessions chairman, abler none,
> Fair-haired, and redder than a windy morn.

And, practically, this is as far as Tennyson ever goes in his treatment of social questions.   He does not really grasp them.   He does not understand the intensity of peril, or the grave considerations of justice which underlie them.   He stands aloof, in the company of baronets and princesses, courtly and cultured people, whose life is perfumed with pleasure and cut off from all intrusion of tragic misery ; those who fare sumptuously every day, to whom poetry is an exquisite luxury of the mind as fine colour is to the eye, or delicate flavour to the appetite : and it is to these Tennyson sings, and it is their view of life which finds the fullest reflection in his poetry.

It is characteristic of the scientific spirit that it rigidly attends to facts, and classifies them, finally deducing from them great laws which appear to underlie and control all things.   Thus, in his treatment of Nature, Tennyson's love of science has worked in the direction of accuracy of statement and fidelity of delineation.   But in his view of life it has checked generous enthusiasm, and produced coldness of temper.   The survival of the fittest is not in truth a doctrine likely to produce a sympathetic temper towards the crippled and the unfortunate.   It does indeed kindle a great light in the future.   It pictures the final evolution of man into some unimagined state of strength and joy, when he shall have attained his majority, and entered into the scientific paradise which Truth is preparing for him.

So many million of ages have gone to the making of man,

that we may well consider him not as having reached his true height, but as toiling on to something higher even than he dreams.   But however bright may be the vision of the future, the survival of the fittest is poor comfort in the vast interval.   It has nothing to say to the halt and maimed, except that they deserve to be halt and maimed. It can rejoice in the vast movements of society which, like immense waves, carry it onward to its infinite goal, but it has no compassion for the lives sacrificed every day in this predetermined progress.   And as one turns over the pages of Tennyson, he sometimes finds himself wondering whether Tennyson has ever suffered deeply Personal suffering, the agony of severed love which comes to all, he has known ; but there is another form of sorrow, the sorrow of early disappointment and rebuff, which does far more to educate men into breadth and charity of view; and by the buffeting angels of vicissitude he has been unvisited. Life may be too fortunate, things may go too well with men in this world. The liquor of life may corrupt with excess of sweetness ; and for lack of that wholesome bitter of disappointment, which is God's frequent medicine to the greatest, a man's heart may stagnate in an undiscerning content.   Is this absence of vicissitude part of the reason for the comparative limitation of sympathy which we find in Tennyson's view of life ? He has been attended by worldly fortune and success never before vouchsafed to any English poet. How different the life that closed in sorrowful isolation at Dumfries, or the life cut off by the violence of tempest at Spezzia, from the close of this life in fortune, fame, and a peerage ! How different the plain life and simple house from which came to us the *Ode on Intimations of Immortality* from the cultured life of artistic ease in which the *Idylls of the King* were slowly fashioned and made perfect in fastidious patience !   Doubt it as we may, resent it as we do, nevertheless the truth remains that those whose words live longest in the hearts of men have " learned in suffering what they taught in song."   In them the heart has most maintained a childlike simplicity and sympathy : and to them it has been given to survey life with the largest charity of hope. Is it this lack of vicissitude in the life of the poet himself which has dulled the larger sympathies of his nature, and narrowed the range and

spirit of his poetry? Has he too long, like his own
Maud,

> Fed on the roses and lain in the lilies of life?

It is hard to judge: but no one can be unconscious of the
fact of this limitation. Its causes lie partly in the order
of the poet's life, but mainly in the character of his own
mind, which is dispassionate rather than ardent, philosophic rather than sympathetic, and better fitted to touch
with subtle delicacy the fringe of a great problem than to
penetrate its gloom with true imaginative insight.

The same deficiencies are notable in Tennyson's treatment of politics. He has a deep and genuine love of
country, a pride in the achievements of the past, a confidence in the greatness of the future. And, as we have
already seen, this sense of patriotism almost reaches insularity of view. He looks out upon the larger world
with a gentle commiseration, and surveys its un-English
habits and constitution with sympathetic contempt. The
patriotism of Tennyson is sober rather than glowing:
it is meditative rather than enthusiastic. Occasionally,
indeed, his words catch fire, and the verse leaps onward
with a sound of triumph, as in such a poem as the
Charge of the Light Brigade, or in such a glorious ballad
as the story of the *Revenge*. Neither of these poems is
likely to perish until the glory of the nation perishes, and
her deeds of a splendid and chivalrous past sink into an
oblivion which only shameful cowardice can bring upon
her. But as a rule Tennyson's patriotism is not a
contagious and inspiring patriotism. It is meditative,
philosophic, self-complacent. It rejoices in the infallibility
of the English judgment, the eternal security of English
institutions, the perfection of English forms of government. This is his description of England:

It is the land that freemen till,
    That sober-suited Freedom chose —
    The land where, girt with friends or foes,
A man may speak the thing he will ;

A land of settled government,
    A land of just and old renown,
    Where Freedom slowly broadens down
From precedent to precedent ;

Where faction seldom gathers head,
    But by degrees to fullness wrought,
    The strength of some diffusive thought
Hath time and space to work and spread.

In these verses we have the gist of Tennyson's
general view of English political life. Freedom is not
to him a radiant spirit, flooding the world with Divine
splendour ; nor a revolutionary spirit, moving through
the thunders of war, whose habitation is cloud, and
smoke, and the thick darkness ; nor a Godlike spirit,
putting the trumpet to his mouth, and sounding the
Divine battle-call, which vibrates through the heart of
the sleeping nations, and wakens them to victorious
endeavour ; it is " sober-suited Freedom," a " diffusive
thought," a scientific growth evolving itself through long
ages of patient struggle, a heritage only won by patience,
and only kept by sobriety of judgment and mutual
compromise. Freedom indeed makes " bright our days
and light our dreams," but she also stands disdainfully
aloof from over-much contact with tumultuous passions,

Turning to scorn with lips divine
The falsehood of extremes.

Of the falsehood of extremes Tennyson is keenly conscious. His philosophic insight perceives the peril, and
holds him back from any unregulated enthusiasm.

There is no abandonment about his patriotism. It is the cool and scholastic patriotism of the moralist, not the ardent patriotism of the man standing in the full stream of action and moving with it. And for this reason it lacks vigour, and it does not inspire men with any real warmth. There is little in Tennyson's patriotism that could feed the flame of spiritual ardour in a time when men actually had to fight and die for liberty. It is retrospective ; it gilds the past with a refined glory, but it does not mould the present. It immortalizes the work of the fathers —

> The single note
> From that deep chord which Hampden smote
> Will vibrate to the doom ;

but if the work of Hampden had to be done over again we should scarcely look to Tennyson for encouragement ; and when the new Roundheads " hummed a surly hymn " and went out to battle, we are pretty sure Tennyson would be found with the king's armies, and would be the accepted laureate of the ancient order.

There is no doubt room for this species of patriotism, and it is certainly a not unpopular species. It is the patriotism of the well-bred and cultured classes, of the merchant who has made his fortune, the aristocrat who lives in feudal security, the student or specialist whose money is safely invested in the funds, and brings in its uneventful dividends. Nothing is more common than the praise of English institutions by men who have an imperfect sympathy with the processes by which they have been created. It is the cant of after-dinner speeches, the infallible note which always wakens thunders of applause for the utterances of otherwise indifferent speakers. Nor can we be surprised at the popularity of this kind

of patriotism.   It produces a gentle stimulating warmth
of self-complacency which is very pleasant to the average
Englishman.   It tells him what he most loves to hear,
that upon the whole he possesses the monopoly of
political wisdom, and holds the patent for the only perfect form of political government.   But we usually find
in this species of patriotism a very deficient sense of
present needs as compared with past glories.   And this
is preëminently true of Tennyson.   When he is brought
face to face with the actual conditions of modern political
life he recoils in angry dismay.   It is one thing to praise
the British constitution in theory, it is quite another to
approve it in fact.   The spirit of Freedom which moves in
the thick turmoil of present affairs is anything but " sober-
suited."   The phrase " sober-suited Freedom " may admirably describe a Freedom which has been tamed and
domesticated, but it does not describe the spirit of Liberty
which actually worked in the fiery clangour of the
English civil wars, or the French Revolution, or that
moves in the hot parliamentary encounters of to-day.
Both there and here, then and now, Freedom is the
radiant and constraining spirit, inspiring stormy impulses
and emotions, trampling on ancient wrongs, ever busy
and never resting, carrying on the continual war for the
rights and heritages of man.   When that actual reality of
what Freedom means is grasped, the mere connoisseurs
of a tame and domesticated Freedom, adapted to house-
hold uses, always fall back alarmed, and repudiate
Freedom in something like dismay.   Tennyson does not
do this altogether, but the recoil is nevertheless evident.
He fears " the many-headed beast " the people.   He distrusts their instincts and impulses.   Their idea of liberty
is not

That sober freedom, out of which there springs
Our loyal passion for our temperate kings.

The pulse of the democracy throbs too fast for him,
and liberty moves with an undignified breadth of stride
in these modern days. His contempt for trade breaks
out at every pore, and he thanks God " we are not cotton-
spinners all." And so it happens that while no poet has
had a keener patriotic sense of the greatness of the past
of England, yet Tennyson usually fails to sympathize with
the modern spirit, or to recognize the revolutionary stress
of the modern England. We instinctively feel that he
distrusts the age, and is afraid of the growth of popular
liberty. There was a great England once, but that was
long ago: over the England of to-day, too frequently
in Tennyson's vision, the darkness of decadence gathers,
and the work of slow disruption and decay is threatening,
even if it be not already commenced.

One result of this philosophic and tempered patriotism
of Tennyson is that he naturally has little sympathy with
forlorn hopes and unpopular causes. The men who fail,
the great, eager, hasty spirits of humanity who fling
themselves with a noble impulsiveness on the spears of
custom, and gather the cruel sheaf into their hearts, do
not fascinate him. He does not see the noble side of
failure, the quickening vitality of a true impulse, even
though it be misguided, and fail wholly of attainment.
The steady growth of constitutional liberty, " broadening
slowly down from precedent to precedent," always respecting precedent, never failing in a proper loyalty to
the reigning classes, is a drama on which he can brood
with sober pleasure ; but the angry uprising of the multitude to whom the bitter yoke can no longer be made
tolerable does not thrill or inspire him.

For illlustration of this mood and temper, take, for instance, his attitude to France. The French Revolution was unquestionably the turning-point in European liberty, and it has been the sad irony of history that every nation has had a larger share of the spoil of freedom than France herself.   It has been her unhappy fate to undergo the martyrdom, and Europe has reaped the victory. Two great poets, Byron and Shelley, had a large enough conception of liberty to be true to France in the hour of her agony, and in spite of the excess of horror which made the last stages of the Revolution a hideous nightmare of unbridled cruelty.   Two other poets, Wordsworth and Coleridge, forsook her and fled.   It is not difficult to understand why.   We can comprehend how the revulsion of horror fell on both, and how in that hour of darkness the face of Liberty seemed forever obscured. But it *is* difficult to understand how a great poet who professes a love of freedom can to-day fling jeer and jest against the great people whose sufferings in the cause of liberty have been for the healing of the nations.   Yet this is Tennyson's description of the French : —

> But yonder, whiff!   There comes a sudden heat,
> The gravest citizen seems to lose his head,
> The King is scared, the soldier will not fight,
> The little boys begin to shoot and stab,
> A kingdom topples over with a shriek
> Like an old woman, and down rolls the world
> In mock-heroics stranger than our own :
> Revolts, republics, revolutions, most
> No graver than a schoolboy's barring out,
> Too comic for the solemn things they are,
> Too solemn for the comic touches in them.

There is nothing in this forlorn yet noble quest of liberty which touches the higher note of sympathy in Tennyson.

His sole reflection is that such are not we, and a pious pharisaic congratulation —

> God bless the narrow sea which keeps her off,
> And keeps our Britain whole within herself,
> A nation yet, the rulers and the ruled ;
>   God bless the narrow seas !
> I wish they were a whole Atlantic broad !

How different is this to the spirit in which Browning regards the same spectacle !   To him there is a perennial nobleness in any true impulse whose aim is lofty, and its failure of attainment simply invests it with a pathetic grandeur, a tragic dignity, a new claim upon our honour and admiration.   Failure in a great cause is to Browning better than victory in a mean ambition, and to perish in the right, even when the right is dimly comprehended, is better than to succeed with a merely conventional success.   It is not through any deficiency of analytical penetration that Browning does not pass as shrewd criticisms as Tennyson on the national defects of others, but he is better employed : it is his mission to mark the good that lurks in evil, and the high ideals which often penetrate and underlie even the most defective human action. When he goes to the French Revolution for a subject, it is not to find a text for British self-complacency, but to catch the dying whisper of the patriot's soul as it passes out of this wild earthly confusion, and to report it thus : —

> I go in the rain, and, more than needs,
> A rope cuts both my wrists behind ;
> And I think, by the feel, my forehead bleeds,
> For they fling, whoever has a mind,
> Stones at me for my year's misdeeds.
>
> Thus I entered, and thus I go !
> In triumphs people have dropped down dead.

> " Paid by the world, what dost thou owe
> Me?'' God might question ; now instead,
> 'Tis God shall repay : I am safer so.

The difference between the two poets is precisely the difference between an insular and cosmopolitan view of politics. Tennyson sounds no keen clarion of hope, he is in no sense the leader of men. Men will never go to him for inspiration in the dark and difficult hour of national peril. But, on the other hand, it cannot be said that the general note he strikes is pessimistic. He says that his faith is large in time : he anticipates the hour when

> The war-drums throb no longer, and the battle-flags are furled,
> In the Parliament of man, the Federation of the world.

Human progress is a Divine certainty : —

> This fine old world of ours is but a child
> Yet in the go-cart—Patience ! Give it time
> To learn its limbs : there is a Hand that guides.

The work of political evolution, like the work of natural evolution, is slow, and asks for its development the breadth of the ages. There will be widening thoughts with the process of the suns ; there will be steady increase of strength and wisdom, and growing " harmonies of law." Tennyson's reverence for law is complete and absorbing : it is a temper of mind nurtured by his knowledge of and reverence for science. Even in his treatment of so light and delicate a fancy as the *Day-dream* he remembers the majesty of law, and pictures how the world may

> Sleep through terms of mighty wars
> And wake on science grown to more —
> On secrets of the brain, the stars,
> As wild as aught of fairy lore.

All the defeats and renunciations of to-day are but the
Divine discipline shaping us for a great to-morrow, and
far away, in the unmeasured and immeasurable spaces of
the future, lies a fair and renovated world.   He is as one
who watcheth for the morning.   His vision is not always
clear, his hope is not always strong; and often in the
dark night his faith seems to suffer sorrowful eclipse.   In
such hours, when we ask him, " Watcher, what of the
night?" his voice is mournful and his speech is bitter.

> At last I heard a voice upon the slope
> Cry to the summit, Is there any hope?
> To which an answer peal'd from that high land,
> But in a tongue no man could understand.

But it is at least a high land on which the poet stands,
and, confused as his reply may often be, yet he never
fails to see far off the promise of the future, how

> On the glimmering limit, far withdrawn,
> God makes Himself an awful rose of dawn.

And for this noble hope we thank the poet.   He does
not fight in the ranks with us, but he foresees the hour
of victory.   He does not stand amid the heat and dust
of battle; but he that is not against us is for us.   He is
one of those of whom Arnold speaks, one

> Who hath watched, not shared the strife ;

but at least he " knows how the day has gone," and he
waits in patient hope for the breaking of a larger dawn.

XXII

IDYLLS AND THE IDYLLS OF THE KING

W E have now come to the point in our study of Tennyson where his two greatest poems, the *Idylls of the King* and *In Memoriam*, come into review. There are, however, certain groups of poems which can scarcely be passed unmentioned, and before turning to the two greatest works of Tennyson it may be well to glance at these. Everywhere throughout Tennyson's books there are to be found exquisite clusters of lyrical poems, and it may be said with confidence that in this domain of poetry his power is unrivalled and his excellence supreme. It is this excellence which redeems *Maud*, in all other respects the weakest and least artistic of his long poems. The *Princess*, again, wearisome and dull as it becomes in parts, contains three or four of the most musical lyrics Tennyson has ever written, and snatches of melody which will bear comparison with the finest lyrics in the language. The art in which Tennyson's rarest excellence lies, the art of musical expression, the subtle cadence of rhythm which produces a recurring and never-forgotten sweetness in the memory, is seen at its very best in these short and lovely lyrics. The lines in the *Princess* commencing,

> The splendour falls on castle walls,

may be mentioned in this category as the nearest approach to the effect of fine music which language is able

229

to produce, and in glamour and sweetness they are un-approached by any modern poet.   Of poems like these nothing can be said but praise.   They have gone far to constitute the charm of Tennyson.   They have found their way into the general memory without effort, by virtue of an enchantment all their own.   They will probably be remembered when much of his more ambitious work is forgotten.   Indeed, it may be said that already this process has been accomplished in part, and the chief thing which preserves *Maud* from oblivion is the famous garden-song, " Come into the garden, Maud," one of the most finished and impassioned lyrics that is to be found in the whole range of modern English.   In lyrical power and sweetness, in the power of uttering that "lyrical cry," as it has been called, that species of poem which is, in truth, not so much a poem as a cry, a voice, a gust of thrilling music—in this art Tennyson has few rivals and no peer.

To another class of poems in which Tennyson has at-tained high excellence he has himself given an appropri-ate title when he calls them English Idylls.   The more famous is *Enoch Arden*, the most exquisite is *Dora*.   When *Enoch Arden* was published great exception was taken to its method and structure, and its obvious want of simplicity in diction was held to disqualify its title to be called an English idyll.   In subject it is purely idyllic, in diction it is elaborately ornate.   One of the acutest and most brilliant of English critics, Mr. Walter Bagehot, has pointed out the fact that in no single instance throughout the poem is Tennyson content to speak in the language of simplicity.   The phrases are often happy, often expressive, but always stiff with an elaborate word-chiselling.   To express the very homely circumstance that Enoch Arden was a fisherman and sold fish, we are told that he vended " ocean-spoil in ocean-smelling osier." The description of the gateway of the Hall is almost pretentious in its combination of complex phrases : " portal-warding lion-whelp, and the peacock yew-tree." This is no doubt an excellent description of tropic scenery :—

> The sunrise broken into scarlet shafts,
> Among the palms and ferns and precipices ;
> The blaze upon the waters to the east,
> The blaze upon his island over head,
> Then the great stars that globed themselves in Heaven,
> The hollower-bellowing ocean, and again
> The scarlet shafts of sunrise—but no sail.

But this is not a shipwrecked sailor's description of what he would see, nor is there a single phrase such as a homely seaman would be likely to use in all this elaborate passage. " The hollower-bellowing ocean " is a combination such as an ornate poet, anxious to combine his impressions in a complex phrase, might use; but it would not by any possibility be the phrase of Enoch Arden. As an English idyll, therefore, *Enoch Arden* fails. But in *Dora* we have the simplest story of country life told in the simplest words, and with an almost Wordsworthian austerity of phrase. There is nothing to disturb the charm of perfect verisimilitude. It is, however, a poem almost by itself. Nowhere else does Tennyson work so high an effect by such simple means. In the main he is an ornate poet, and errs in over-elaboration of phrase. In the *Idylls of the King* the same strength and weakness are always associated, and the excellence and defect run side by side. As his narrative rises in passion the phraseology becomes terser, clearer, less involved; when his invention slackens, and his poetic impulse ebbs, he always falls back upon elaborate phrase-coining to cover his defect. The result is a curious combination such as exists in no other poet. In a score of pages we pass a dozen times from the noble severity of Wordsworth to the fanciful conceit of Keats. It is never difficult to know how the tide of poetic impulse runs in Tennyson : when the impulse is strong the style clarifies into nervous simplicity; when weak, it abounds in ornate decoration and scholastic word-mongering.

The *Idylls of the King* are the work of Tennyson's mature manhood, and give us the ripest result of his art. The history of their inception and completion is curious ; it covers fifty years, beginning with a lyric; " then with an epical fragment and three more lyrics ; then with a poem, *Enid and Nimue*, which is suppressed as soon as it is written ; then with four romantic idylls, followed ten years later by four others, and two years later by two others, and thirteen years later by yet another idyll, which is to be placed not before or after the rest, but in the very centre of the cycle." Thus the world of Arthurian romance is first touched in the *Lady of Shalott*, published in 1832; and last, in *Balin and Balan*, published in 1885.

In the life of every great poet there comes a time when a desire seizes him to accomplish some great design, a poem on a scale of magnitude which shall give scope to all his qualities. As a rule such ambitions have resulted in failure. Wordsworth is not known after all by his *Excursion*, but by his lyrics, and his *Ode on Immortality*. Mrs. Browning's *Drama of Exile* cannot contest the awards of fame with the *Lines on Cowper's Grave*. The only long poem by an English author which has held an uncontested place in memory is Milton's *Paradise Lost*, and it has been pointed out that this is largely owing to the fact that it is written in sections, and each section can be read at a sitting. No doubt Tennyson was fully conscious of the peril of his task, and the warning of these great examples, when he began to work upon the *Idylls*. He began at the end of his theme, with the *Morte d'Arthur*, as though to judge of his chances of success by an experiment on the public taste. He was fortunate also in the choice of a subject. In the noble myths which had gathered round King Arthur there was a vast field of poetry which was wholly unworked. Over and above their moral and poetic elements they possessed a national value. For Tennyson they had always had a peculiar charm; and we are told that in his solitary boyhood at Somersby, a favourite recreation was to enact scenes from the Round Table with his brothers. These myths provided him with precisely what he was least able to provide himself, a splendid story, or series of stories, ready to his hand. No critical reader can help noticing that in the power of pure invention Tennyson is singularly weak. It is the weakness of his invention which led to the vicious elaboration of style which we have remarked in *Enoch Arden*. But in the old chronicle of Sir Thomas Malory of the fabulous deeds of the Knights of the Round Table, there is a series of stories complete in every incident and detail. The chronicle is full of graphic force and poetic merit. It is indeed so full of the genuine elements of poetry that many persons, who have carefully read Sir Thomas Malory, refuse to think that Tennyson has improved upon him. In many senses he has not. He has often failed where Malory is strongest, necessarily perhaps, because to make Malory acceptable to modern

ears it was needful to smooth over a good many awkward details. But what Tennyson has done is to imbue
the old chronicle with new life and spirit, to interpret it
by a Christian insight, and to apply its ancient lessons to
the complex conditions of modern life and thought.

Probably one reason why Tennyson chose Sir Thomas
Malory's famous chronicle for his greatest experiment in
verse was that it exactly coincided with his own natural
bent towards romantic allegory. We have to remember
the force of the pre-Raphaelite movement, as it was
called, if we are to understand the reasons of Tennyson's
choice. From the simple nature-worship of Wordsworth,
and the more ethereal and ecstatic nature-worship of
Shelley, there had come a revulsion towards the glowing
spectacle of mediæval life and the chivalrous bent of
mediæval thought. Just as the publication of the *Reliques of English Ballad Poetry*, by Bishop Percy, in the
end of the eighteenth century, worked a revival of
mediæval sentiment, whose best fruit is found in the
great romances of Sir Walter Scott, so the experiments
of Rossetti and Morris worked a similar revival in our
own. Among the weird half-lights of mediæval history
there lay a land of old romance, full of material for the
poet. Tennyson's *Lady of Shalott, Sir Galahad*, and
St. Agnes were early experiments in this field of poetry,
and indicate how deeply he had felt its fascination. It
was only natural that he should pursue the clue which he
had thus discovered. In the mediæval England of
knight and lady, tournament and battle, spell and incan-
tation, adventure and romance, Tennyson found an atmosphere entirely suited to his genius. It was the land
of glamour and enchantment. There the imagination
and fancy could move untrammelled. Every knight was

brave and every lady fair. Magnificent spectacles continually passed before the imagination, and afforded a decorative artist like Tennyson the finest possible opportunity for the exercise of that species of art in which he most excelled. And over and above all this, there ran throughout the record of the history a strong moral sentiment, a deep religious bias. The fall of King Arthur's Round Table was the fall of a kingdom, and the causes of its fall were moral causes. In this respect it was more than a mere mediæval record : it was an eternal parable of human life. It touched the moral sense in Tennyson, which had always been quick and sensitive. What theme was there more likely to stimulate his genius than this, and more suitable for a great epic ? The greatest of all themes Milton had taken, but even if he had not, it was too late to write a religious epic. The *Paradise Lost* could only have been written in a theological age—an age like the Puritan, deeply saturated with the theological spirit. To hit the taste of the nineteenth century an epic might be a morality, but it needed also human sentiment and passion in all their fullness. With that perfect artistic insight which has rarely failed him, Tennyson saw the value of his theme, and the result is that he has produced the only long poem which has been read by multitudes since *Paradise Lost*, and a poem which, in parts at least, may fairly challenge comparison with the noblest work of Milton.

The *Idylls of the King*, as Tennyson handles them, are a very different thing from the simple chronicle of Malory. It is extremely interesting to compare passages and see how far Tennyson has followed and where he has left Malory. As regards the story itself, he has inserted many poetic fancies, but he has invented little or nothing.

The incidents run parallel. In many points, as we have said, there is a graphic force in Malory which we miss in Tennyson, and the short, simple words of the mediæval chronicler produce a deeper effect upon the mind than the rich and subtle diction of the modern poet. It is the difference between the rude but thrilling ballad-tune and the skillful variations made upon it by a great musical composer. In Malory we think of the theme ; in Tennyson more frequently of the artist. But if any one desires to see how finely a poetic fancy can breathe life into a bald history, he has only to mark how faithfully Tennyson has seized upon the salient points of Malory, and what a wealth of artistic skill he has lavished on them. For the chief fact to be observed in Tennyson's use of Malory is that to the plain facts of the chronicler he always gives an allegorical significance. He never loses sight of the moral lesson. King Arthur stands out as a mystic incarnation, a Christ-man—pure, noble, unerring : coming mysteriously into the world, and vanishing mysteriously, according to the prophecy of Merlin :

> From the great deep to the great deep he goes.

He is the perfect flower of purity and chivalry, and the kingdom he seeks to found is the very kingdom of Christ upon the earth. Lancelot, in many respects the more subtle and powerful study, is of the earth earthy, and by turns base and noble, and rightly describes himself in the hour of his remorse : —

> In me there dwells
> No greatness, save it be some far-off touch
> Of greatness to know well I am not great :
> There is the man.

It is round these two men and Guinevere that the great

interest of the poem culminates. The very over-noble-
ness of Arthur works disaster, and Guinevere cries : —

> He is all fault who has no fault at all,
> For who loves me must have a touch of earth ;
> The low sun makes the colour.

The pathos of the whole poem is that in Arthur we have
the incarnation of a high ideal which men vainly strive
after, and its tragedy is that men do strive vainly, and that
all the noble work of Arthur is undone by the weakness
and folly of his followers. In the lesser characters of the
epic the allegorical bent is more fully developed. Sir
Galahad is the type of glorified asceticism, visionary aims,
spirit triumphant over flesh, but after all following wandering fires in a vain quest, and " leaving human wrongs
to right themselves." *Gareth and Lynette* is but a variation of the story of Arthur and Guinevere, and it points
to the severity of struggle which awaits him who overcomes the flesh. In this poem the allegory is more distinct and beautiful than in either of the others, and Tennyson has given us no nobler conception of victory over
death than this :—

> The huge pavilion slowly yielded up
> Thro' those black foldings that which housed within ;
> High on a night-black horse, in night-black arms,
> In the half-light, thro' the dim dawn, advanced
> The monster, and then paused, and spake no word.

It is the King of Terrors, the spectral form of the last
enemy. But when Gareth rides forth to the combat, and
strikes the helm of his grisly foe —

> Out from this
> Issued the bright face of a blooming boy,
> Fresh as a flower new born.

And this is immortality, the life which springs out of death.

Of the tenderness of *Lancelot and Elaine*, with its immortal picture of the dead Elaine sailing to her last home, oared by the dumb servitor; the grandeur of the *Last Tournament*, with its ever-present sense of desolation; the genuine pathos of *Guinevere*, increasing stanza by stanza in passionate depth and tragic force, till we reach the parting with Arthur in the misty darkness, amid the faint blowing of the unhappy trumpets; and of the solemnity of the *Passing of Arthur*, with its dramatic fullness, its farewell counsels of neglected wisdom, its tragic mixture of human despair and mystic heavenly hope,—of these poems it is needless to speak. If we had to choose the greatest poem of Tennyson, we should choose *Guinevere ;* if the most solemnly impressive, the *Passing of Arthur.* Nothing which he has written rivals these two, or approaches them in the highest qualities of poetry. They are the mature work of a great poet. They express his deepest convictions, and sum up his best wisdom. Such passages as —

> More things are wrought by prayer
> Than this world dreams of.   Wherefore let thy voice
> Rise like a fountain for me night and day ;
> For what are men better than sheep or goats
> That nourish a blind life within the brain,
> If, knowing God, they lift not hands of prayer
> Both for themselves and those who call them friend ?
> For so the whole round earth is every way
> Bound by gold chains about the feet of God,

or —

> The old order changeth, yielding place to new,
> And God fulfills Himself in many ways,
> Lest one good custom should corrupt the world,

have already passed into the permanent currency of literature. They contain noble truths nobly expressed. And among the artistic lessons of the *Idylls of the King* none is better worth marking than the perfection of Tennyson's blank verse. Blank verse is the one distinctively English measure, and the most difficult of all. Apparently it is easy of attainment; in reality there is nothing harder. There is no form of verse which so severely tests the ear and musical faculty of a great poet. Keats attempted it in *Hyperion* with magnificent success, but he gave it up after that one supreme effort. Wordsworth's success is only partial, and there are many passages in the *Excursion* which are little better than prose cut up into metrical lengths. Byron never touched it without complete failure. Milton only has chosen it as his supreme method of utterance for epic poetry, and he has used it as only a giant could use it. Next to Milton stands Tennyson. He sinks far below Milton in grandeur, but he often excels him in musical modulation. He does not fill the air with the wave-like majesty of sound and movement which characterize Milton, but he soothes it with an unfailing melody of phrase. It is so distinctive that the merest tyro could not fail to recognize the peculiar charm of Tennyson's blank verse, and distinguish it at once in any company. Often it is mannered, and mannerism is always a vice. But in the finest qualities of assonance and resonance Tennyson rarely fails. His verse moves with perfect ease, with perfect music, with perfect strength ; and apart from the charm of thought and subject, the *Idylls of the King* show his metrical talent in its finest operation. But the theme also is great and solemn, and in the *Idylls of the King*, we have his noblest work, and work such as the very greatest poets might have been proud to produce and covetous to claim.

XXIII

TENNYSON AS A RELIGIOUS POET

WHILE Tennyson has touched, with more or less success, almost every stop in the great organ of poetry, yet perhaps the strongest impression which he leaves upon the mind is that he is essentially a religious poet, and it is in the realm of religious poetry that his noblest work is to be found. It may be said, indeed, that the religious spirit pervades all that he has written. He might almost be called an ecclesiastical poet, for his writings abound in references to the familiar sanctities of the Church,—the font, the altar, the church clock measuring out the lives of men, the graveyard with its yews whose roots grasp the bones of the dead, the Eucharist, in which

> The kneeling hamlet drains
> The chalice of the grapes of God.

How deep a reverence he has had for the Bible may be inferred from the fact that no fewer than three hundred Scripture quotations have been discovered in his poetry. He has played with agnosticism, and expressed its doubts and ponderings, but he has never become an agnostic. " Poetry is faith " was the saying of a great critic, and assuredly without living faith the highest poetry is impossible. One may fairly suppose that the religious tendency in Tennyson was hereditary, and every influence of his life conserved that tendency and strengthened it. There is a remarkable passage in a letter of

Tennyson's, which throws considerable light upon this side of his character, and which it is interesting to compare with Wordsworth's similar confession of his early inability to realize the potency of death. The letter is dated Farringford, Isle of Wight, May 7, 1874, and is written in reply to a gentleman who had communicated to him certain strange experiences he had undergone under the effects of anæsthetics. Tennyson says: " I have never had any revelations through anæsthetics, but a kind of waking trance (this for lack of a better name) I have frequently had, quite up from boyhood, when I have been all alone. This has often come upon me through repeating my own name to myself silently till, all at once as it were, out of the intensity of the consciousness of individuality, the individuality itself seemed to dissolve and fade away into boundless being ; and this not a confused state, but the clearest of the clearest, the surest of the surest, utterly beyond words, where death was an almost laughable impossibility, the loss of personality (if so it were) seeming no extinction, but the only true life. I am ashamed of my feeble description. Have I not said the state is utterly beyond words ? "

This is a perfect description of the philosophic and religious dreamer, and narrates an experience commoner in the East than in the West. The deduction which Tennyson himself makes from his experience is that it verifies the truth of the separate existence of the human spirit, and that that spirit " will last for æons and æons." Something of the same state and experience is described in *In Memoriam*, and especially in the *Ancient Sage*,

> And more, my son ! for more than once when I
> Sat all alone, revolving in myself
> The word that is the symbol of myself,

The mortal limit of the Self was loosed
And passed into the Nameless, as a cloud
Melts into Heaven. I touched my limbs—the limbs
Were strange, not mine—and yet no shade of doubt,
But utter clearness, and through loss of Self
The gain of such large life as matched with ours
Were Sun to spark—unshadowable in words,
Themselves but shadows of a shadow world.

A poet so sensitively constituted, and liable to such moments of spiritual trance as this, could hardly fail to be a religious poet. To him the unseen world would be an ever-present reality, and he would live as seeing that which is invisible. Gazing into what Arthur Hallam has called " the abysmal deeps of personality," he would be always conscious of the greatness of the soul, and the thought of final annihilation would be to him impossible. For him death would be already abolished, and his vision would be of life for evermore.

'Tis life whereof our nerves are scant,
More life and fuller, that we want,

is his own utterance of his own desire. And from this calm and steadfast belief in immortality, this infallible assurance of the eternity of personal life, all that is noblest and serenest in the poetry of Tennyson has risen.

But from personal belief in immortality to the embodiment of religious beliefs in religious forms, it is a long step, and Tennyson has shown considerable antagonism to religious forms. If we glance over his writings, leaving out the *In Memoriam*, which is the greatest achievement in religious poetry which our age has produced, we see that he has carefully studied religious problems, and has reached certain memorable conclusions. First of all, we find in the three poems of *St. Simeon Stylites, Sir*

Galahad, and *St. Agnes' Eve,* Tennyson's statement of, and judgment upon, religious mysticism. *St. Simeon Stylites* is something more than a historical portrait: it is a satire upon the monastic spirit and ideal of life. The figure of *St. Simeon* on his pillar, alternately coveting and cursing the world, sighing for the shade of comfortable roofs, warm clothes, and wholesome food, and then dilating with pride at his own heroic renunciation, as he cries:

> I wake ; the chill stars sparkle, I am wet
> With drenching dews, or stiff with crackling frost,

is a monument of all that is harshest, grossest, and most repellent in the monastic ideal of life. The very humility of the man is loathsome ; it is the pride which apes humility. He may be all he says he is,

> The basest of mankind,
> From scalp to sole one slough and crust of sin,
> Unfit for earth, unfit for heaven, scarce meet
> For troops of devils, mad with blasphemy ;

but his depth of self-humiliation is farcical when it becomes a plea for sainthood, and when the secret hope of his life is that

> A time may come, yea, even now,
> When you may worship me without reproach,
> And burn a fragrant lamp before my bones,
> When I am gathered to the glorious saints.

The most virulent poison of monasticism is in the man's blood, and one knows not which is more loathsome, the humiliation or the ambition of *St. Simeon.* Yet in the main it is a just and true portraiture, and appearing, as it did, at a time when the public mind was being roused into frenzy over the revival of mediæval-

ism in the Church of England, it was a tremendous rebuke. Tennyson marks in *St. Simeon* his utter abhorrence of the monastic ideal of life. Self-renunciation he
can preach, but renunciation which despises and forsakes
the glad activities of daily life, as in themselves foul and
unclean, he will not regard as other than a form of ecclesiastical madness.

Nor is his sense of the imperfection of religious mysticism less strong in such poems as *St. Agnes' Eve* and *Sir
Galahad.* Just as *St. Simeon* expresses all that is most
degrading in monasticism, these two beautiful poems express all that is loveliest and most tender in its forms of
life. In *St. Simeon* the mediæval religious spirit is intense
self-consciousness, sinking into uttermost degradation; in
St. Agnes it is renunciation of self, rising into rapture
and beatific vision. It is the pure and yearning spirit of
a true woman-saint which sighs for the heavenly Bride-
groom, and cries, as the trance of ecstasy deepens into
the vision of death,

> He lifts me to the golden doors;
> The flashes come and go;
> All heaven bursts her starry floors,
> And strows her light below,
> And deepens on and up! The gates
> Roll back, and far within
> For me the Heavenly Bridegroom waits
> To make me pure from sin.
> The Sabbaths of Eternity,
> One Sabbath deep and wide —
> A light upon the shining sea —
> The Bridegroom with His bride.

Not merely is the expression of the sentiment in these
verses beautiful, but the sentiment itself is beautiful. It
is the essence of all that is most devout in conventual

piety.   It is the sentiment we can fancy floating forth in
silence from the half-opened lips of *St. Helena,* as she
sleeps on that memorable summer afternoon, in that attitude of pathetic weariness which a great artist has so
exquisitely interpreted, when she sees in dreams the de-
scending cross, and her soul smiles to greet the solemn
presage of approaching martyrdom.

The picture of *Sir Galahad,* going forth in his pure
and noble youth upon his lifelong quest of the Holy
Grail, is not less touching in its aspect of saintly conse-
cration.   He, too, moves in his vision of holy things :

> A gentle sound, an awful light ;
>   Three angels bear the Holy Grail ;
> With folded feet in stoles of white,
>   On sleeping wings they sail.
>
> The clouds are broken in the sky,
>   And through the mountain-walls
> A rolling organ-harmony
>   Swells up, and shakes and falls.
>
> Then move the trees, the copses nod,
>   Wings flutter, voices hover clear :
> " O just and faithful Knight of God,
>   Ride on ! the prize is near ! "

This is a noble picture of the religious knight, the ideal
knight of chivalry, but not the less his religious mysticism
is his weakness.   This does not appear in this poem,
because here Tennyson only attempts to reproduce in accurate form and outline what the spirit of religious mysticism in the days of chivalry had to say of itself, and in
so far the poem is a dramatic personation ; but when, in
later life, Tennyson touches the same theme, it is with a
difference of handling, or rather a fuller handling.   It is
mysticism not less than wrong-doing which helps to break

up the knightly Order of the Round Table.   And this is
the reproach of King Arthur when he says :

> Was I too dark a prophet when I said,
> To those who went upon the Holy Quest,
> That most of them would follow wandering fires,
> Lost in the quagmire ?
> And out of those to whom the vision came,
> My greatest hardly will believe he saw ;
> Another hath beheld it afar off,
> And leaving human wrongs to right themselves
> Cares but to pass into the silent life ;
> And one hath had the vision face to face,
> And now his chair desires him here in vain,
> However they may crown him otherwhere.

That is the reply of Tennyson to religious mysticism.
For some it is a wandering fire, dying down at last in
darkness and confusion ; for some a pious cheat, a beautiful delusion which in saner moments they themselves cannot accept ; for the purest spirits of all, capable of the
highest and devoutest religious ecstasy, it is after all only
something seen afar off—a fitful and capricious radiance,
as though one dreamed he dreamed, and hoped he hoped,
but held no certainty or assurance of either faith or vision.
Its effect is to produce in men that fatal " other-world-
liness," which cares but to pass into the silent life, and
passes through the evil gloom of this world with blinded
eyes, leaving human wrongs to right themselves.   It is
not the solitary rapture of the idealist which helps the
world, and if human piety has no help in it for the world,
wherein lies its virtue, and what title has it to our reverence ?   It is, after all, a sort of sublimated selfishness,
and on that ground Tennyson condemns it, and dismisses
it as wholly ineffectual to meet the real needs of the
human soul.   And it is almost with a touch of mournful

scorn he adds that the mystic may be crowned in other worlds, but it is clear that he has neither won nor merited a coronation here.

Two other poems of Tennyson deserve mention here, as still further illustrating his religious attitude.   In the *Vision of Sin* he describes the perversion of nature which follows the pursuit of carnal lusts, and its bitter end in despairing infidelity and cynicism.   That which a man sows he also reaps, and the wages of sin is death. The man he paints is already a dead man, though he moves still with some ghastly semblance of life.   He is " gray and gap-toothed," a cold wind of death comes with him, a ruined inn receives him ; a mocking merriment, which jeers at all things sacred and Divine, is the one temper which survives in him.   His memory is stored only with sensual recollections, leprous delights, unclean and hateful pictures.   He has no faith left in anything.

> Friendship ! to be two in one,
>   Let the canting liar pack ;
> Well I know, when I am gone,
>   How she mouths behind my back.
>
> Virtue ! to be good and just —
>   Every heart, when sifted well,
> Is a clot of warmer dust
>   Mixed with cunning sparks of hell.

He has sown the wind, and reaps the whirlwind.   He has gone to the farthest opposite of religious mysticism, and has sunk in gross and unredeemed animalism.   The sated voluptuary usually develops into the aged cynic, and, having outraged purity and virtue through a long life, finally brings himself to believe that neither has any real existence.   And it is thus, with true insight, Tennyson moralizes on the portrait he paints :

> Then some one spake : " Behold, it was a crime
> Of sense avenged by sense that wore with time,"

for the senses carry in themselves their own secure retribution.

> Another said, " The crime of sense became
> The crime of malice, and is equal blame ; "
> And one, " He had not wholly quenched his power,
> A little grain of conscience made him sour."

In the last suggestion only is there any hope, but Tennyson confesses it is at best but a shadowy and inarticulate hope. So far as we can see the man has slain himself, and there is no escape from the retribution he has merited. The failure of mysticism is great, but infinitely greater is the failure of materialism ; for while one errs by overstrained yearning after Divine things, falling into credulous fantasy and rapture, the other errs by love of carnal things, and falls at last into such a depth of moral debasement that it can hardly be said the spirit lives at all. The one may be crowned other-where ; it is at least certain that the other is avenged even here.

The other poem, which completes Tennyson's view of the religious needs of life, is the *Palace of Art.* There is a sort of midway house which men seek, a halting-place between the material and the mystical. They turn from the mystical in incredulity, and revolt from the carnal in disgust. They retain spiritual purity and intellectual integrity, and are quick to respond to the promptings of the æsthetic temper, which continually begets in them vague dissatisfactions. Why not then find rest in Art ? Why not gratify the religious instinct in the worship of Beauty ? Is not the worship of beauty the only real religion ? As for the world, full as it is of unredeemed animalism, let that be forsaken and forgotten, as an impure vision which is best ignored and put out of sight. There is splendour in the sunrise, glory in the flower, grace in the statue, delicate suggestion and subtle pleasure in the tapestry and the picture, infinite delight and solace in the revelations of art; let it be ours to seek these, and find in these our peace. So the soul builds herself a lordly pleasure-house wherein at ease for aye to dwell.

It realizes the utmost dreams of beauty. Before it streams the rainbow's "orient bow"; the light aerial gallery, golden-railed, "burns like a fringe of fire"; the air is sweetened with perpetual incense, and made musical with the chiming of silver bells; slender shaft, rich mosaic, wreaths of light and colour, "rivers of melodies," singing of nightingales, and fragrance of "pure quintessences of precious oils" are everywhere, and it is a veritable palace of delight, which poets only build, and human eyes have never seen. The world lies far beneath the huge crag-platforms, and the men labouring in it are as

> Darkening droves of swine,
> That range o'er yonder plain.

Creeds have ceased to perplex the mind —

> I take possession of man's mind and deed,
> I care not what the sects may brawl.
> I sit as God, holding no form of creed,
> But contemplating all.

And in what does it all end? It ends in the bitter cry of *Vanitas vanitatum*, as all such experiments must always end. Dull stagnation closes on the soul, and the pursuit of selfish ease ends in agonizing despair. Beauty becomes loathsome, and its daily vision is as a fire which frets the flesh, until at last the soul exclaims :

> I am on fire within ;
> What is it that will take away my sin,
> And save me lest I die ?

And the only answer is —

> Make me a cottage in the vale, she said,
> Where I may mourn and pray.

It is a great and memorable lesson memorably taught. Human responsibility cannot be ignored, whether in the monastery, the tavern, or the palace of art. The first duty of man is to his brothers, and that is the soul of all religion. Society annexes obligations to its privileges, and the one must be shared with the other. These poems represent the religious attitude of Tennyson, and it is an attitude eminently sane and noble. They breathe the spirit of a rational and serviceable human piety. They rebuke at once asceticism and sensuality. They pierce to the essential hollowness of all mere art-worship as a substitute for the worship of God, and they contain teachings which were never more needed than in the generation which Tennyson has addressed.

XXIV

TENNYSON'S IN MEMORIAM

WE now come to the most distinctive, and, in many essential characteristics, the greatest of Tennyson's poems, *In Memoriam*. Published in 1850, it is the work of his prime, and contains the most perfect representation of his genius. The personal history on which it is founded is well known. It commemorates one of the noblest of human friendships, and one of the noblest of men. Arthur Hallam, the son of Henry Hallam, the celebrated historian, was born in Bedford Place, London, on the 1st of February, 1811. The family afterwards removed to Wimpole Street, which is thus described in *In Memoriam* —

> Dark house, by which once more I stand,
>   Here in the long, unlovely street,
>   Doors, where my heart was wont to beat
> So quickly, waiting for a hand.

In October, 1828, Arthur Hallam went into residence at Cambridge, and it was there he met Tennyson. The affection which sprang up between them must have been immediate, for in 1830 we find them discussing a plan for publishing conjointly a volume of poems. One of Tennyson's most striking phrases in the *Palace of Art*, " the abysmal deeps of personality," is directly borrowed from a phrase of Hallam's : " God—with whom alone rest the abysmal secrets of personality." It was one of those rare and beautiful friendships which sometimes visit the morning hours of life, in which intellectual sympathy, not less than love, plays a foremost part. On the 15th of September, 1833, Arthur Hallam lay dead. On the 3d of January, 1834, his body was brought over from Vienna, where he died, and was interred in manor aisle, Clevedon Church,[1] Somersetshire —

> The Danube to the Severn gave
>   The darkened heart that beat no more ;
> They laid him by the pleasant shore,
>   And in the hearing of the wave.
>
> There twice a day the Severn fills ;
>   The salt sea-water passes by,
> And hushes half the babbling Wye,
>   And makes a silence in the hills.

When and where *In Memoriam* was conceived or commenced it is impossible for us to know, but it will thus be seen that seventeen years elapsed between the death of Arthur Hallam and the publication of Tennyson's exquisite elegy. It is tolerably certain that the poem was actually in process of construction during the whole of this long period, for it bears in itself marks of slow growth, of gradual accretion and elaboration. Probably the work was begun with one or two of the earlier sections, which simply bewail in poignant verse Tennyson's sense of unspeakable loss, and which possess the solemnity and self-containedness of separate funeral hymns, rather than the consecutiveness of an elaborate poem. The history and character of the poem sustain this view. In seventeen years the anguish of the deepest sorrow must needs show signs of healing. Grief grows less clamant, and more meditative. It passes somewhat out

---

[1] In the first edition of *In Memoriam* Tennyson says in " the chancel." This was not strictly correct, and is altered in subsequent editions to " dark Church."

of the region of personal bitterness into the realms of philosophic reflection and religious resignation. Time does not destroy the sense of loss, but it lifts the soul to a place of broader outlook and calmer vision. As we read *In Memoriam* this process is clearly detailed, and there is much in the structure of the poem to suggest that from a few mournful verses, cast off in the bitterest hour of bereavement as a solace to the wounded spirit, Tennyson gradually enlarged his plan, till he had woven into it all the philosophic doubts, the religious hopes, the pious aspirations, which the theme of human loss could suggest to a thoughtful mind and noble spirit.

Concerning the general structure and character of the poem, one or two things are worth remark. It differs essentially from any other elegy in the English language, both as to metrical arrangement and artistic colour. English literature is not rich in elegy, but it possesses in Milton's *Lycidas*, in Gray's famous poem, in Shelley's *Adonais*, and in Arnold's noble lamentation for his father and his *Thyrsis*, isolated specimens of elegiac poetry as fine as any literature can boast. Of these great elegies, Shelley's *Adonais* is the longest and the noblest; Milton's *Lycidas* the most classic in gravity and sweetness; Gray's *Elegy in a Country Churchyard* the most perfectly polished; Arnold's *Lines in Rugby Chapel* the most effective in moral view and spirit. But of the last two it will be at once perceived that neither aims at the constructive breadth of a prolonged poem, nor would the metrical form sustain the burden of great length. The constant evil which menaces elegy is monotony, and it is the most difficult to be avoided by the very nature of the theme. Gray avoids it by aiming at aphoristic brevity, and by polishing every phrase with the most consummate artistic skill and patience.   Arnold adopts for his purpose a peculiar unrhymed metre, which stimulates the ear without wearying it, but which could not be sustained except within the limits of brevity which he has set for himself.   Milton is similarly brief, and *Lycidas* reads more like a noble fragment of the antique than an English poem written for English readers.   No ·doubt Milton's genius would have served him perfectly if he had attempted a *Lycidas* of thrice the length, for he has attempted no form of poetry without absolute success ; but, however that may be, he was taught by his artistic instincts in writing elegy to compress within the narrowest limits of space his lament for the noble dead.   Shelley does indeed write at length, but there are two things to sustain him in his daring effort; first, he uses a metre singularly pliable and resonant; and, secondly, he leaves his theme at will, and weaves into his poem a hundred exquisite suggestions of natural beauty and imaginative vision, so that while his theme is mournful his poem is often ecstatic, and monotony is avoided by richness of fancy and variety of theme. In what respects does *In Memoriam* differ from these great masterpieces ?   Wherein does its distinctive charm and greatness lie ?

   In the first place it differs entirely in metrical form and arrangement.   Properly speaking, it is hymnal in form. Some of its stanzas are admirably suited for Christian worship, and no doubt will appear, with slight alterations, in the hymnal collections of the future.   In this respect it is distinctively English, and appeals strongly to English tastes.   But what is there that could be conceived as more monotonous than a hymn of a thousand stanzas ? The hymnal form may be excellently suited for elegy, but how is it possible to combine a form in itself monotonous with a theme whose chief peril is monotony without producing a poem which would be insufferably dull and tedious? That was the problem Tennyson had to solve, and he solved it in two ways. Instead of the ordinary hymnal ·quatrain, he adopted a form, not unknown indeed in English literature, but virtually new to modern readers, in which the first and last and the two middle lines of the verses rhyme. Any one who will take the trouble to compare these forms will at once see how greatly Tennyson's variation gains in modulation and flexibility. He had already attempted it in one of his earlier poems, " Love thou thy land with love far brought," and had no doubt been struck with its power of musical expression. If, as we surmise, *In Memoriam* grew slowly from certain fragmentary stanzas, thrown off in the first agony of grief, no doubt that was the metrical form in which they were written. A form more perfect for elegiac poetry could not be conceived; but how could it be applied to an elaborate poem of many hundreds of lines? This Tennyson answered by dividing his poem into short sections, each one complete in itself, and expressing some particular thought or sentiment. It is to this division of the poem, in part at least, that much of its popularity must be attributed. I have already quoted the saying of an acute critic that the reason why people read *Paradise Lost* is that it is arranged in sections, and can therefore be put down and resumed at will. This is eminently true of *In Memoriam*. It is a brilliant constellation of short poems, held together in rhythmic order by one great sustaining sentiment. We can open it where we will, read as much as we wish, and put it down again, without any perplexing sense of having missed the poet's meaning, or destroyed his clue of

thought. Of course this is not the student's method
of reading *In Memoriam*, but it is a method often forced
upon busy men by the necessities of their position ; and
the fact that *In Memoriam* is as truly a cluster of small
poems as a great poem in itself, has no doubt helped its
popularity, and has fully justified the artistic instinct
which suggested its division into sections.

Another point worthy of special remark is that not
merely in form, but in all its colouring, *In Memoriam* is
a distinctively English poem.   Milton's noble elegy we
have already spoken of as a fragment of the antique,
and its whole conception and spirit is severely classic.
Shelley goes to the same source to find inspiration for
his elegy on Keats.   Save the passages which directly
touch on the unhappy fate of Keats, there is nothing in
the poem which is distinctively English.   Its allusions
are classic ; its sky is the sky of Italy ; its scenery has
a gorgeousness of colour and a pomp unknown in the
gray latitudes of the north.   Over the dead body of
Keats, Shelley builds a glorious and fantastic tomb—a
sepulchre of foreign splendours, and the earth that holds
him in her bosom is a warmer and more glorious earth
than that land of sombre skies and gray seas where his
genius was suffered to blossom and decay unheeded.
Gray, indeed, is English ; Arnold is English, but with the
trace of Greek culture always perceptible ; but Milton and
Shelley both go boldly to the classics for their inspiration,
and have written elegies which are English in name indeed, but classical in spirit and design.   It is the charm of
In Memoriam that it is steeped in English thought and
spirit.   Its sights and sounds are the familiar sights and
sounds of rural life in England.   It is England, and no
other land, that is described in lines like these : —

Now fades the last long streak of snow,
    Now burgeons every maze of quick
    About the flowery squares, and thick
By ashen roots the violets grow.

Now rings the woodland loud and long,
    The distance takes a lovelier hue,
    And, drowned in yonder living blue,
The lark becomes a sightless song.

Now dance the lights on lawn and lea,
    The flocks are whiter down the vale,
    And milkier every milky sail,
On winding stream or distant sea :

Where now the sea-mew pipes, or dives
    In yonder gleaming green, and fly
    The happy birds, that change their sky
To build and brood.

All the colour of the pictures drawn from life and nature
is English, and can be mistaken for no other.   It is the
Christmas Eve we all have known which he thus describes
for us :

The time draws near the birth of Christ ;
    The moon is hid, the night is still :
    A single church below the hill
Is pealing, folded in the mist.

It is the English summer, whose mellow eventides we all
have rejoiced in, when " returning from afar " :

And brushing ankle-deep in flowers,
    We heard behind the woodbine veil
    The milk that bubbled in the pail,
And buzzings of the honeyed hours.

Nowhere in Tennyson's works will there be found
more perfect pictures of English scenery and seasons
executed with more artistic delicacy and skill than in
In Memoriam.   They are all exquisitely finished, with

something of the laboured patience of pictures on ivory or porcelain, and each is perfect in its way. The effects are often gained in single phrases, so happy, so luminous, so exact, that we feel it is impossible to surpass them. This, at least, is one of the qualities which have made *In Memoriam* famous. It is not merely a noble threnody upon a dead Englishman, but it is one of the most distinctively English poems in the language, expressing universal sentiments indeed, but with a perpetual reference to national scenery, customs, and life.

One other point should not be overlooked in estimating such a poem as *In Memoriam*. To its many other great qualities, it adds one of the rarest of all—it is the most perfect expression we have of the spirit of the age. It is a poem of the century; indeed, we may say, *the* poem of the century. It sums up as no other work of our time has done the characteristic intellectual and religious movements of the Victorian epoch. Nowhere has Tennyson borrowed so largely from modern science as here. The well-known lines,

> Break thou deep vase of chilling tears
> That grief hath shaken into frost,

afford an excellent specimen of these obligations; the metaphor is very beautiful, but it cannot be understood without a knowledge of elementary chemistry. At first this was esteemed a startling innovation, and was used against him as a reproach, but if the great poet is he who concentrates in his poetry the spirit of his time, Tennyson was bound to take account of the scientific tendency, which is one of the most marked features of the century. But he has done more than this. He has stated not merely scientific arguments and facts, but also the religious doubts, the perplexities, the philosophic difficulties of the day, with equal skill and force. He has perceived the intellectual and religious drift of his age with unerring accuracy. He himself has passed through its various stages of doubtful illumination, of dark misgiving, of agonizing search for light, and lastly of clear and even triumphant faith. Like another poet of our time, Arthur Hugh Clough, Tennyson has known what it is

> To finger idly some old Gordian knot,
> Unskilled to sunder and too weak to cleave,
> And with much toil attain to half-believe.

But he has done what Clough could not do, he has cut the Gordian knot, and found " a surer faith his own." · The process by which he has attained this victory we shall see in the analysis of *In Memoriam*. In the meantime, it is sufficient to observe that the hold which this poem has taken on the minds of men must be attributed not only to its literary genius, but to its prophetic qualities. Not only is it original in metrical design, and thoroughly English in colour, but it is also an interpretation of the deepest religious yearnings and philosophic problems of our time, and as such has become the indispensable companion of all who share, and seek to understand, or to direct, the intellectual life of the century.

A great poem should interpret itself, and, in the larger sense, *In Memoriam* needs no comment or elucidation. But there is another sense in which elucidation is needed, and cannot but be useful. Because the *In Memoriam*, is, as we have seen, not merely a great poem in itself, but really a series of short poems held together by a common sentiment, it is not always easy to perceive the thread of thought that binds each to each. The transitions of thought and theme are always subtle, and often sudden. The various suggestions of loss crowd thickly on the mind of the poet, and it is sometimes difficult to perceive the link which connects them into an organic whole. It may be well, therefore, to attempt, not an elaborate analysis, for that has been ably done by others, but a sort of indicatory comment whereby we may perceive the course and current of the poem.

The opening poem of the series is an after-thought, and sums up much that is said hereafter in detail. It is a final confession of religious faith, " Believing where we cannot prove," in which Tennyson craves forgiveness for " the wild and wandering cries " of the poem, which he terms " confusions of a wasted youth." The poem proper then begins. From i. to v. we have a statement of those common states of mind which attend all great bereavements. There is a sacredness in loss (v.) which almost makes it a sacrilege to embalm the sorrow of the heart in words, and yet there is a use in measured language, for at least the labour of literary production numbs the pain. Then follows (vi.) a beautiful and pathetic vision of what loss means to others beside himself. Such a sorrow as his is not peculiar : at the moment while the father pledges his gallant son, he is shot upon the battle-field, and while the mother prays for her sailor-lad, his

> Heavy-shotted hammock-shroud
> Drops in his vast and wandering grave.

Memory wakens (vii.-viii.), and then Fancy (ix.-x.) ; the one recalling ended joys of fellowship, the other picturing the ship that bears homeward the dead body of his friend ; and fancy suggests that it at least is something to be spared an ocean burial, and to sleep in English earth, that

> From his ashes may be made
> The violet of his native land.   (xviii.)

Nature is calm (xi.), but if the poet has any calm it is a calm despair. Yet while he pictures the processes of death, he marks it as curious that it is almost impossible to believe his friend is dead. If again they struck hand in hand, he would not feel it strange (xiv.), for death seems unimaginable. Then again the light fades, and he pictures the final obsequies and place of rest (xix.). Pain may be meant to produce in him the firmer mind (xviii.). Perhaps some will say that this brooding over grief is unmanly, the pastime of the egotist, the vain torture of a morbid mind; to which he can only reply they know neither him nor his friend.

> I do but sing because I must,
> And pipe but as the linnets sing.   (xxi.)

Again he recalls lost days, and how on the "fifth autumnal slope" of those brief ended years, Death met and parted them (xxii.). Let those mock who will. He has no envy of those more callous of heart than he, who have never known the joy of a perfect love, and, therefore, cannot understand what its loss may mean. A man's capacity of agony is his capacity of rapture:

> I hold it true, whate'er befall,
> I feel it, when I sorrow most;
> 'Tis better to have loved and lost
> Than never to have loved at all.   (xxvii.)

The time of happy family gatherings draws near, and

> Christmas bells from hill to hill
> Answer each other in the mist.

To him it is a sad time of forced mirth and empty joy.
But there is something in the very season that suggests
nobler thoughts :

> Our voices took a higher range ;
>   Once more we sang : " They do not die
>   Nor lose their mortal sympathy,
>   Nor change to us, although they change."   (xxx.)

That, at least, is the promise of faith, and with a cry to
the Divine Father, who lit " the light that shone when
Hope was born," the first great halting-place in the poem
is reached.

In the next section of the poem (xxxi.) a new line of
thought begins with the touching picture of Lazarus redeemed from the grave's dishonours, and seated once
more among the familiar faces of Bethany.   During
those four days of sojourn in the realm of death, did
Lazarus yearn for human love, or miss it?   Did he retain
a conscious identity, and know where and what he was?
If he had willed, surely he could have solved all the
deep mystery of death for us.   But if such questions
were proposed to him " there lives no record of reply,"
or, if he answered them, " something sealed the lips of
that evangelist," and the world will never know the secrets of the prison-house.   At this point Tennyson
begins to state and combat the doubts that perplex him.
Yet he half hesitates to do so.   Simple faith is so beautiful and rare, that he may well ask himself what right he
has to disturb its serenity with his uneasy questionings.
Let any who, after toil and storm, think that they have
reached a higher freedom of truth, be careful how they
disturb the faith of simple souls, who have nothing but
their faith to sustain them, and whose " hands are quicker

unto good" than ours (xxxii.).   Yet we cannot help asking : " Is man immortal ? "   If he is not, then

> Earth is darkness at the core,
> And dust and ashes all that is.

The thought of God is lost, and the best fate were to
drop

> Head-foremost in the jaws
> Of vacant darkness and to cease.   (xxxiv.)

In the hour of such awful questionings the heart instinctively turns to Christ, who wrought

> With human hands the creed of creeds,
> In loveliness of perfect deeds
> More strong than all poetic thought.   (xxxvi.)

Doubt and hope now alternate like shadow and light in
the poet's mind.   When he sees the sun sink on the wide
moor, a spectral doubt makes him cold with the suggestion that so his friend's life has sunk out of sight, and he
will see his " mate no more " (xli.).   Perhaps his friend
is as the maiden who has entered on the new toils of
wedded days, and is content to forsake the home of
childhood : yet even she returns sometimes to

> Bring her babe, and make her boast,
> Till even those who missed her most
> Shall count new things as dear as old.   (xl.)

" How fares it with the happy dead ? " (xliv.)   May
not death be in itself a new birth, the entrance upon
fuller life ? (xlv.)   Only it were hard to accept the suggestion literally, for that would mean forgetfulness of
that which preceded the entrance on eternal life.   " In
that deep dawn behind the tomb " will not " the eternal
landscape of the past " be clear " from marge to marge " ?
(xlvi.)   With those who speak of death as re-absorption

into the universal soul he has no sympathy. It is " faith as vague as all unsweet " ; it means destruction of identity, and his hope about his dead friend is that he

> Shall know him when we meet,
> And we shall sit in endless feast,
> Enjoying each the other's good.   (xlvii.)

With the glow of that thought burning in him he calls upon the dead ever to be near him—when the light is low, when the heart is sick, when the pangs of pain conquer trust, when the folly and emptiness of human life appal him, and, finally, when he fades away on that low dark verge of life which is

> The twilight of eternal day.   (l.)

Yet even this wish he is keen to question a moment later ; do we really desire our dead to be near us in spirit, and is there no baseness we would hide from their purged and piercing vision ? (li.)   In fact, his soul has become so sick with sorrow, that he now only suggests hopes to himself that he may fight against them.   He philosophizes on his own errors of conduct, but rebukes his conclusions with the fear that he may push Philosophy beyond her mark, and make her " Procuress to the Lords of Hell! (liv.)   Yet in the moment of the uttermost darkness, full of distemper and despair, he breaks forth into one of the noblest confessions of faith,

> That nothing walks with aimless feet,
> That not one life shall be destroyed,
> Or cast as rubbish to the void,
> When God hath made the pile complete.   (liv.)

It is true that Nature teaches no such doctrine ; she is careless of the single type, and cries,

> A thousand types are gone ;
> I care for nothing, all shall go.   (lv.-vi.)

Yet will he stretch lame hands of faith, and " faintly trust
the larger hope." Nay, it seems a sin against the dead
to doubt that it is forever and forever well with them
(lvii.). The lost Arthur is in a " second state sublime " ;
and he has carried human love with him there. Will he
still love his friend on earth ? (lxi.) Will he not still love
the earth and earthly ways? It is a question Emily
Brontë answered in her daring picture of a spirit in
heaven sighing unceasingly for the purple moors she
loved below, until the angels in anger cast her out, and
she wakes, sobbing for joy, on the wild heather, with a
skylark singing over her. Tennyson pictures the great
statesman who still yearns for the village-green of childhood, and consoles himself that Love cannot be lost :

> Since we deserved the name of friends
> And thine effect so lives in me,
> A part of mine may live in thee,
> And move thee on to nobler deeds.   (lxiv.-v.)

He dreamed there would be Spring no more, but now he
perceives that his life begins to quicken again (lxix.).

> So many worlds, so much to do,
> So little done, such things to be,   (lxxiii.)

is his reflection on the premature ending of his friend's
life, but it also marks an awakening of purpose in his
own. Here again, upon the verge of another Christmas,
the poem seems to pause with the personal reflections of
the seventy-seventh section, on the possibility that what
he has written of his friend may never find readers, nor
touch any heart but his own. There is a virility and
spirit in this section which marks the movement of a

healthier mind. That he can begin to think about the publication of his own verses is significant of the rekindling of human ambition in him, and is the token that the lethargy of grief is broken. He has not recovered his strength yet; but the crisis of the disease is over.

From this point the poem moves in a clear and less grief-laden atmosphere; the assurance of faith becomes stronger, and a note of triumph breathes in the music, gradually heightening and deepening to its majestic close. He can bear now to pass in review the lost possibilities of earthly felicity which were in his friend (lxxxiv.), because he has learned to believe that a diviner felicity is his. He holds sacred " commune with the dead," and asks

> How is it? Canst thou feel for me
> Some painless sympathy with pain ? (lxxxv.)

He gives us a portrait of his friend; he pictures him eager in debate, a master-bowman cleaving the centre of the profoundest thought, quick and impassioned in oratory,

> And over those ethereal eyes
> The bar of Michael Angelo ; (lxxxvii.)

that is, the deep furrow between the eyebrows,[1] which was indicative of individuality in the great Italian artist. He recollects how he left " the dusty purlieus of the law," and joined in simple rural sports with boyish glee (lxxxix.); and how they talked together, and in prolonged and eager converse

---

[1] This is a disputed point. According to Dr. Gatty the reference is the straightness and prominence of Hallam's forehead, in which it resembled Michael Angelo's.

> Discussed the books to love or hate,
>   Or touched the changes of the state,
>   Or threaded some Socratic dream.

This portraiture of Arthur Hallam is completed later on, in the striking stanza of the hundred and eleventh section, when Tennyson exclaims,

> And thus he bore without abuse
>   The grand old name of gentleman,
>   Defamed by every charlatan,
>   And soiled with all ignoble use.

Again he implores his presence, and he will have no fear; for whereas he once thought of him as lost forever, now he feels his presence, "Spirit to Spirit, Ghost to Ghost," and actually believes that in dream or vision his friend does visit him —

> So word by word, and line by line,
>   The dead man touched me from the past,
>   And all at once it seemed at last
> The living soul was flashed on mine.   (xci.-v.)

It is mind breathing on mind from the past; he feels that whatever is lost, *that* survives, and is with him alway. It is true that his friend has doubted, but it was honest doubt, which he defends in the famous lines,

> There lives more faith in honest doubt,
>   Believe me, than in half the creeds.   (xcvi.)

He draws a lovely picture of a wife who lives with a husband whose intellectual life is beyond her apprehension, but who can say at least, as he has learned to say, " I cannot understand; I love" (xcvii.). It is the only outcome from bewilderment; he will follow not the reason but the heart; a truth stated with yet greater force and fullness in section cxxiv.:

> If e'er when faith had fallen asleep,
> I heard a voice, " Believe no more,"
> A warmth within the breast would melt
> The freezing reason's colder part,
> And like a man in wrath the heart
> Stood up, and answered, " I have felt."

He recalls how he and his friend travelled together in unforgotten summer days, and that leads to a series of those beautiful cabinet pictures of scenery which lend so great a charm to the poem (xcviii.-ci.). He relates how he has dreamed, and saw in dreams the glory of his friend ; how " thrice as large as man he bent to greet us "—a symbol of the larger manhood which he has inherited; and how he stood upon the deck of some great ship with shining sides, that sailed o'er floods of " grander space " than any earthly—a pathetic reference to the ship that bore his dead body home to England, and again a symbol of that voyage of life on which his spirit now passes through an ever-broadening glory (ciii.). Then again the Christmas comes : charged still with too great memories of sorrow to allow the dance and wassail-song, but yet bringing a genial change in him, for he has abandoned wayward grief, and " broke the bond of dying use " (cv.). This Christmas is spent in " the stranger's land," away from home, and the bells are not the bells he knows. The Christmas bells peal " folded in the mist " as before : but when the New Year is near its dawning there is a new music in the bells, a hope and triumph in their chime, which sets his heart vibrating with a new and wholesome vigour, and he breaks out into that memorable apostrophe :

> Ring out, wild bells, to the wild sky,
>   The flying cloud, the frosty light,
>   The year is dying in the night.
> Ring out, wild bells, and let him die.   (cvi.)

The happy clangour of the New Year bells celebrates his final emancipation from the perplexities of doubt, his final recovery of healthful life, the sanctification of his sorrow, the triumph of his faith. It is the anniversary of Arthur Hallam's birth, the bitter February weather, which " admits not flowers or leaves to deck the banquet," yet the day shall be kept with festal cheer —

> With books and music ; surely we
> Will drink to him, whate'er he be,
> And sing the songs he loved to hear.   (cvii.)

He has soared into the mystic heights of perplexed speculation, only to find his " own phantom singing hymns " ; henceforth, he says,

> I will not shut me from my kind ;
>   And lest I stiffen into stone,
>   I will not eat my heart alone,
> Nor feed with sighs a passing wind.   (cviii.)

Science, which teaches him how the world and human life have grown out of the fierce shocks of age-long discipline, the cleansing fire and cyclic storm, may also teach him that sorrow is to man a sacred discipline, and that fear, and weeping, and the shocks of doom, do but batter him to shape and use (cxviii.). Natural science can tell us much, but not all; we are not " magnetic mockeries," nor " cunning casts in clay." There is a spiritual science also which the wise man seeks to learn, and which unfolds a truer map of the mysterious nature of man (cxx.). It is the reality of spiritual existence that his sorrow has revealed to him. Love is immortality, and through his love he has already entered on eternal life.   The knowledge that his lost friend is really alive for evermore; that death for him has been simply emancipation and enfranchisement; that all which he loved in him, not merely survives, but is perfected in excellence, freed from all human blemish or limitation,— this fills him with an almost ecstatic joy.   In the early morning, when the city is asleep, he again stands before those dark doors in Wimpole Street, but it is no longer with agonized upbraidings of fate.   The calmness and hope of morning are with him, as they were with that forlorn woman who long since sought her Master, when it was yet early, in an Eastern garden, and found not a corpse within the tomb, but a shining Figure walking in the dewy freshness of the day, and he says:

> And in my thoughts with scarce a sigh
> I take the pressure of thy hand.   (cxix.)

It is more than resignation, it is more than hope.   It is the voice of living certainty, of an entire and undivided triumph, which lifts itself above the dark confusions of the past, and sings,

> Far off thou art, but ever nigh,
>   I have thee still and I rejoice ;
>   I prosper, circled with thy voice,
> I shall not lose thee tho' I die.   (cxxx.)

The long anguish has done its work in the purification of the soul and the strengthening of the faith ; all the bitter sounds of wailing and distress die away, and it is with a perfect Hallelujah Chorus of glory in the highest, and peace upon earth, that the poem ends.

There is, however, annexed to it one other section, and not the least lovely ; the epithalamion on his sister's marriage. We learn that this marriage took place " some thrice three years " after Arthur Hallam's death, but whether the bride was the sister Hallam hoped to marry we have no means of knowing. This epithalamion is one of those happy after-touches in which Tennyson displays so perfectly his artistic skill. It is suggestive of how life goes on, and must go on, in spite of the gaps made in our ranks by death; and " the clash and clang " of the wedding bells, carried on the warm breeze, is a noble contrast to that mournful pealing of bells through the mist which is heard so often in the earlier stages of the poem. The winter is over and gone, the time of the singing of birds is come, and the voice of the turtle is heard in the land. And now, whether life bring joy or sorrow, funeral chimes or marriage bells, the poet has an all-sustaining and purifying faith in God —

> That God, which ever lives and loves,
>   One God, one law, one element,
>   And one far-off divine event,
> To which the whole creation moves.

That " one far-off divine event " can be no other than the perfecting of love in human life, the complete recognition by every living soul of the love of God, and the final vindication of that perfect Divine love in all its varied dealings with men, in things past, in things present, and in things that are to come. This is the vaguely sketched, yet noble vision, which crowns with spiritual glory the completion of his thought and labour. He has led us through the darkest valleys of Apollyon, but we reach with him the Beulah land at last. We hear the trumpets pealing on the other side, and behold it is morning! Fair and sweet the light shines, and heavenly voices tell us we shall walk in night no more. It is morning; the morning of a deep and clear-eyed faith; and doubt and sorrow, fear and pain, are past forever. They are not forgotten indeed; but we see them now only as distant clouds touched with glories of celestial colour, lying far and faint behind us on the radiant horizon, transfigured and transformed by the alchemy of God. The phantoms of the night are slain, the anguish of the night is ended; the true light shineth with healing in its wings, and the soul rejoices. It may well rejoice with joy unspeakable, for

> Out of the shadow of night
> The world rolls into light,
> It is daybreak everywhere.

We may here conclude our study of Tennyson. Fortunate beyond almost any poet in his life, he was equally fortunate in his death. The finest elements of his power remained with him to the last; his intellectual force was not abated, nor his magic wand broken. His eightieth birthday brought him the homage of the entire intellectual world, and found him writing the noblest, and what is probably destined to be the most famous, of all his hymns of faith.

> Sunset and evening star,
>   And one clear call for me,
> And may there be no moaning of the bar
>   When I put out to sea.
>
> But such a tide, as moving seems asleep,
>   Too full for sound or foam,
> When that which drew from out the boundless deep
>   Turns again home.

*　　*　　*　　*　　*　　*　　*

For tho' from out our bourne of Time and Place
  The flood may bear me far,
I hope to see my Pilot face to face
  When I have crost the bar.

And then came that night of wondrous moonlight, when he lay majestic in the final weakness; with his Shakespeare open at the noble dirge of Cymbeline beside him, confronting the unknown with complete tranquillity and faith, and like his own Arthur, encouraged with the vision of a land of larger life beyond the sea. Never was a poet's exit from life contrived with a finer dignity, and the picture of that majestic death-bed will remain forever as one of the immortal memories of literature.

What Tennyson's final position in the hierarchy of the great poets may be it is premature and indeed impossible to decide. We are yet too fully under his immediate influence for our discernment to be just, or our judgment to be wise. That he is among the few great creative poets of humanity, no one will assert; that he is nevertheless a poet of great and varied excellence, none will deny. He has been compared with Milton, and has been set so high above Wordsworth, that one of his critics[1] has ventured to say that in the future, when men call the roll of poets, " they will begin with Shakespeare and Milton—and who shall have the third place if it be not Tennyson?" But Emerson, whose judgment is worthy of general deference, has said that Wordsworth is *the* poet of modern England, and that "other writers have to affect what to him is natural." And that pregnant saying illumines at once the whole question, laying bare at one stroke the secret of Wordsworth's supremacy and of Tennyson's deficiency. We cannot but feel that he lacks the massive ease of

[1] Henry Vandyke.

Wordsworth and the deep interior strength of Milton. If we still hesitate to grant him equality with the foremost poets of the older centuries, or of his own, it is for the sound reason that while in Tennyson artistic culture has never been surpassed, yet the original poetic impulse is weaker in him than in either Keats or Shelley, Dante, Wordsworth, or Milton.   But happily it is not necessary for us to determine the rank, before we can discern the genius, of our masters; it is enough for us to receive with thankfulness and admiration the writings of a great poet, who for sixty years fed the mind of England with visions of truth and beauty, and who, through all that length of various years, has never ceased to be a source of inspiration and delight to that diffused and dominant race who

Speak the tongue that Shakespeare spake.

XXV

ROBERT BROWNING

Born at Camberwell, London, May 7, 1812. Pauline published, 1832. Marries Elizabeth Barrett, September 12, 1846. The Ring and the Book published 1868. Asolando, his last volume, 1889. Died in Venice, December 12, 1889. Buried in Westminster Abbey, December 31, 1889.

THE two greatest figures in the world of modern poetry are Tennyson and Browning. To each was accorded old age : both have been keenly alive to the intellectual and social movements of their time, and have endeavoured to reflect them. Each also has been an observant student of life, as all true poets must be, and each has constructed a huge gallery of human portraits, representing many types, and arranged with artistic instinct and consummate skill. But while Tennyson has proved himself the greater artist, Browning has proved himself the greater mind. He has brought to the work of the poet a keen and subtle intellect, a penetrating insight, the experience of a citizen of the world, and in all things the original force of a powerful individuality. The result of his artistic deficiency is that he has relatively failed to obtain popularity. He has not known how to deliver his message to the popular ear, and it may be doubted if he has ever cared to try. With a touch of justifiable scorn he has declared that he never intended his poetry to be a substitute for a cigar or a game of dominoes to an idle man. The grace and music of Tennyson's verse have compelled delight, but in Browning there is no attempt at verbal music. It is with him an unstudied, perhaps an uncoveted, art. When the Hebrew Psalmist sought to express the consummate union of the opposite qualities which constitute perfection he said, " Strength and beauty are in His sanctuary." In Browning we have the strength, in Tennyson the beauty. And the result of this artistic deficiency, this inability to clothe his thoughts in forms of grace, is, that Browning has failed in any large degree to charm the ear of that wide public who care less for the thought that is uttered than for the manner of its utterance.

It is, however, necessary to remember another fact about Browning's poetry, viz., that to the first minds of the age, the men who lead and govern the world of thought, Browning has been and is a potent and inspiring force. He has disseminated ideas, he has pervaded the literature of his time with his influence. He has found an audience, few but fitting, and to them has addressed himself, knowing that through them he could most effectually reach the world at large. The test of popularity is at all times an imperfect test, and in Browning's case is wholly inadequate and unsatisfactory as an index of his true position in the literature of his day. The influence of a poet is often out of all proportion to his popularity, and is by no means to be measured by the number of his readers, or the poverty or copiousness of public praise. If mere popularity were to become the solitary test of influence, we should have to rank Longfellow above Dante, and Martin Tupper above Tennyson. But while popularity is in itself a testimony to the possession of certain serviceable qualities, or a certain happy combination of qualities it fails wholly as a just measurement of the real formative force which a writer may be able to exercise upon his time, and still more hopelessly as an indication of the position such a writer may take up in the unknown judgments of posterity. A man may catch the ear of the public, and win its empty plaudits, without touching in more than an infinitesimal degree the public conscience or the public thought.

The deeper and diviner waves of intellectual life indeed have more often than not owed their origin to men who have quarrelled with their age, and received from their contemporaries little but the thorn-crown of derision and the sponge of gall and vinegar—men wandering in the bitterness of exile like Dante, or starving in the scholar's garret like Spinoza. Most truly great writers, to whom has been committed the creative genius which opens new wells of thought and new methods of utterance, have had need to steel themselves against the indifference of their time, and to learn how to say: "None of these things move me." They have appealed from the contemptuous ignorance of their contemporaries to the certain praises of posterity, and not in vain. Where such men find readers they make disciples, and each heart upon which the fire of their genius falls becomes consecrated to their service. Theirs it is to found a secular apostolate, a school of prophets united by a common faith, and pledged by the sacredness of an intense conviction to urge on the teaching of the new doctrine and the new name, till the world acknowledges the claim and gives adhesion to the master whom they love and reverence.

Let us grant, then, that we have in Robert Browning undoubtedly a great poet, but also a relatively unpopular poet. With the exception of the *Ride from Aix to Ghent*, the *Pied Piper of Hamelin*, and the tender and pathetic *Evelyn Hope*, few or none of his poems have won the ear of the common people. Yet he has produced no fewer than twenty-four volumes, characterized by enormous erudition, intense passion and insight, and the most astonishing ingenuity of metrical device. No writer of our time has manifested greater fecundity of genius, versatility of style, or capacity of industry. Few writers have ever had a firmer faith in themselves, or have trusted more fully to the secure awards of time. Now that the poetry of Browning has become a cult, his less known works have probably found readers; but at the time of their publication few but the reviewers had the courage to read them. There is a story told of a great critic, who had *Sordello* sent him for review at a time when he was in weak health and low spirits. After an hour's fruitless effort, he flung the book aside, crying: " My brain is failing! I must be mad! I have not understood a word." His wife then took the book up, and it was agreed that upon the test of her ability to understand it the question of her husband's sanity must turn. She at length flung it down, saying: " My dear, don't be alarmed. You're not mad; but the man who wrote it is!" Many persons have closed *Sordello* with the same angry comment, and there are isolated passages in Browning more difficult than anything in *Sordello*. How is it, then, that the man whose mastery of humour is so finely displayed in the *Pied Piper*, whose pathos and power of narrative have such splendid attestations as *Evelyn Hope* and the *Ride from Aix*, who can write with such terseness, simplicity, and vigour as these poems display, is, nevertheless, to the bulk of English readers a stone of stumbling and a rock of offence ?

The answer to this question is not difficult. Let it at once be granted that Robert Browning can write as clearly as any English poet when he likes, for he has done it. Open Browning at random, and it will be hard if, in half-an-hour, you do not come upon a score of noble thoughts, admirably expressed in clear ringing English, with delicate attention to phrase and perfect adherence to the laws of construction. Yet it must be owned that in the same half-hour it is quite possible to alight on passages where the nominative has lost its verb beyond hope of recovery, and phrases seem to have been jerked out haphazard, in a sort of volcanic eruption of thought and temper. What is the underlying cause of these defects of style ?

There are two main causes. The first springs from Browning's theory of poetry. Browning's theory of poetry is a serious one. Like all truly great artists, he has uniformly recognized the dignity and responsibility of art. With him poetry is not the manufacture of a melodious jingle, nor the elaboration of pretty conceit ; it is as serious as life, and is to be approached with reverent and righteous purpose. It is, moreover, the noblest of all intellectual labours and should therefore minister to the intellect not less than to the emotion. Into his poetry Browning has put his subtlest and deepest thought, and he uniformly puts a higher value on the thought than the method or manner of its expression. In *Pauline*, his earliest poem, published in 1832, he says, with a true forecast of his own powers and limitations,

> So will I sing on, fast as fancies come ;
> Rudely, the verse being as the mood it paints.

With him the sense is more than the sound, the substance is more than the form, the moral significance is more than the rhetorical adornment. He has something to say, something of infinite moment and solemn import, and he is comparatively careless of *how* he says it. He is the Carlyle of poetry : the message is everything, the verbal vesture nothing. It is in this respect that Browning's divergence from all other modern poets is greatest. He is not indifferent to the art and music of words, but he habitually treats them as of secondary importance. Naturally, the growth of this temper has led Browning into extravagances of style, as it did Carlyle; many a fine thought is hopelessly embedded in insufficient and faulty phrases; and therefore, to the mass of readers, who do not approach poetry with the patient spirit of scientific research, is hopelessly lost.

The second cause of the occasional obscurity of Browning's poetry is found in the condensation of his style. When *Paracelsus* was published it was declared unintelligible, and John Sterling, one of the acutest critics of his day, accused it of "verbosity." This saying of Sterling's was reported to Browning by Miss Caroline Fox, who went on to ask : " Doth he know that Wordsworth will devote a fortnight or more to the discovery of a single word that is the one fit for his sonnet ? "

This criticism filled Browning with a dread of diffuseness, and henceforth he set himself never to use two words where one would do. The result of this resolve is that often he does not use words enough to express his meaning. He uses one word, and expects his reader to supply two. It is this which makes *Sordello* the puzzle it is. It is a vast web of words, in which the filaments are dropped, confused, tangled, like the crumpled gossamer of a spider s web hastily detached and more than half-ruined by the touch of carelessness.

There are beautiful thoughts and passages in *Sordello*, but they savour so much of bookishness, and demand so much antiquarian knowledge in the reader, that few are likely to disinter and appreciate them. For instance, take this passage from Book the Third: " Factitious humours " fall from Sordello, and turn him pure

> As some forgotten vest
> Woven of painted byssus, silkiest,
> Tufting the Tyrrhene whelk's pearl-sheeted lip,
> Left welter where a trireme let it slip
> I' the sea and vexed a satrap : so the stain
> O' the world forsakes Sordello : how the tinct
> Loosening escapes, cloud after cloud.

Now what is the picture painted here ?   Analyze it, and this is the result: An eastern satrap, sailing upon a galley or trireme, wears a vest of byssus, dyed with Tyrian purple.   He lets it fall overboard, and as he looks down through the clear sea sees the purple dye escaping and clouding the water.   So Sordello is cleansed from the stain of the world.   It is a very beautiful illustration ; but its beauty is not perceived till we recollect that purple is taken from the tuft of the " whelk's pearl-sheeted lip," and that a garment so dyed, if cast into the sea, throws off its colour in tremulous clouds.   Does any one see the meaning at first sight ?   And how many might read it and never see any meaning in it at all ?   This is an example of Browning in his worst mood ; and we cannot wonder, when we consider it, that simple-minded poets like Charles Mackay called him the " High Priest of the Unintelligible " ; or that Browning societies have had to be invented to reduce his recondite fancies to lucidity.

These, then, are the two main sources of all that is obscure in Browning's writings. The very fact that for many years he was a solitary worker, writing almost for his own pleasure, naturally confirmed the defects of his style. The obscurity is never of the thought; that, indeed, is so clear and luminous to him that he seems incapable of conceiving it as confused in the vision of his reader. The thought is clear as the sun; but the atmosphere of words through which we perceive it is murky, and the body of the thought looms through it dim and strange. And so Swinburne has spoken with equal felicity and truth of Browning's faculty of " decisive and incisive thought," and has said, " He is something too much the reverse of obscure; he is too brilliant and subtle for the ready readers of a ready writer." The case cannot be better put than in the words of one of his most earnest and intelligent students : " He has never ignored beauty, but he has neglected it in the desire for significance. He has never meant to be rugged, but he has become so in the striving after strength. He never intended to be obscure, but he has become so from the condensation of style which was the excess of significance and strength." This should constantly be remembered, if we are to approach Browning's poetry with the intelligence which interprets, and the sympathy which appreciates.

Were Browning not a great poet it would be difficult to forgive him such defects as these. We should be inclined to dismiss him with the brief aphorism of the Swedish poet, Tegner, who said, " The obscurely uttered is the obscurely thought." But Browning is one of the greatest of poets, and has so profoundly affected the thought of his time, that however the ordinary reader may be repelled by the grotesqueness of his style, it is

eminently worth the while even of that distinguished individual to endeavour to understand him. We freely
grant that poets should not need interpreters ; but where
there is something of infinite moment to be interpreted
it is well to set aside fixed rules and habitual maxims.
Genius is so rare a gift that we must take it on its own
terms, and we cannot afford to quarrel with the conditions
it may impose on us. It speaks its own language, and is
indifferent alike to the reproach or desire of those whom it
addresses. The only question for us is, whether it is
worth our while to endeavour to penetrate the meaning
and ascertain the teaching of any writer who, through
natural limitations or willful indifference, renders the study
of his works difficult and perplexing ? In the case of
Browning I reply that no more remunerative study can
be found than in the careful reading of his works. He
embodies some of the most curious and pervasive tendencies of nineteenth-century literature, and in subsequent
chapters I shall endeavour to show what Browning's
teaching is, and to estimate his influence in literature.

XXVI

BROWNING'S PHILOSOPHY OF LIFE

ONE of the most interesting facts about Robert Browning is that he has no touch of the recluse about him; he is the child of cities, not of solitudes. In the writings of Wordsworth and Tennyson, dissimilar as they are in many respects, there is this bond of likeness—they breathe the air and silence of seclusion. With the one it is the silence of the mountains, with the other the ordered calm of English rural life. All that Wordsworth has written is steeped in the very spirit of solitude, and the mighty silence of the hills has lent a majesty to his conceptions—an atmosphere, as it were, of dignified simplicity. In Tennyson, also, one is always conscious of the presence of Nature. The wind that blows across his page is full of the dewy freshness of green lawns and rustling trees. The city, with its moil and grime, its passionate intensity of life and action, is far away. He sees its distant lights flaring like a dusky dawn: but he has little care to penetrate its mysteries. And in most modern poets the same remoteness from the passionate stress of life is felt. What is true of Wordsworth and Tennyson is equally true of Keats and Morris. The fundamental idea in each seems to be that the life of the recluse is alone favourable to poetry, and that the life of action in the great centres of civilization is fatal to works of imagination.

To this temper Browning furnishes a splendid exception. Born a Londoner, and proud to own himself a citizen of the greatest city upon earth, it is with London, Florence, and Venice that his name is imperishably interwoven: not the Lake district of Wordsworth, nor the Geneva of Byron, nor the Spezzia of Shelley. In continental travel he is evidently more familiar with the bookstalls of Florence than the snow-solitudes of the high Alps. He was a familiar figure in society for many years. He does not shun the crowd : he seeks and loves it. The sense of numbers quickens his imagination. The great drama of human life absorbs him. The glimpses of pure nature he gives us are curiously few. He can describe a lunar rainbow : but he saw it not among the Alps, but from the dull greensward of a London common. Practically, he has little to say about Nature as such. When he does describe any bit of scenery he does it with scientific accuracy. His pictures of Italy are full of the very spirit of Italian scenery, and have an almost photographic exactitude. But they are the mere by-play of his mind. It is Italian life which fascinates him, not Italian scenery. It is life everywhere that moves him to utterance, and in the crowd of men, and in the tangled motives of men, and the constant dramas and tragedies bred by the passions and instincts of the human heart, Browning has found the food upon which his genius has thriven. In this respect Browning occupies an entirely unique position among modern poets. He concerns himself so little with the message of nature, and so much with the soul of man, that his whole poetry may be called the Poetry of the Soul : its

> Shifting fancies and celestial lights,
> With all its grand orchestral silences
> To keep the pauses of the rhythmic sounds.

If Wordsworth's was the priestly temperament, and

Tennyson's the artistic, it may be said that Browning's was something broader than both: the nobly human temperament, which cleaves to man, and seeks to understand his hopes and fears, and judges him by the standard of a catholic charity. In this respect it is no exaggeration to say that Browning more nearly resembles Shakespeare than any poet of the last three hundred years; for we can imagine Shakespeare as having moved among men with the same genial and understanding sympathy, and as interpreting the men of his day with an insight similar to, if broader and more profound than, Browning's.

The immediate result of this temper in Browning is that no poet has exhibited such variety, and this variety springs from the multiplicity of subjects in which he is interested. His poems cover dissertations on art and music, stories of adventure, strangely vivid and exact reproductions of mediæval life and thought, glimpses of the authentic life of the ancient world not less than of the modern, yet all touched with that precision which marks the student and the scholar. In the company of Robert Browning you see from the prosaic eminence of a London common the overthrow of Sodom, and the dread vision of the Last Judgment, as in the wonderful poem called *Easter Day ;* you sail in Venetian gondolas witnessing the drama of passion and crime ; you hide with conspirators in the ruined aqueducts of modern Italy; the scene changes from the Ghetto to the Morgue; from the byways of London to the deserts of Arabia ; from the tent of Saul to the plains of " glorious guilty Babylon " ; from the Shambles' Gate, where the patriot rides out to death upon his hurdle, to the splendid chambers of the connoisseur, crowded with the spoils of Renaissance art, where

the Bishop orders his tomb in St. Praxed's. Nothing in
the drama of human life seems to escape Browning ; its
minutest by-play rivets his attention not less than its
master passions.   He writes, in fact, like a citizen of the
world, with a shrewd, hard, piercing intelligence, which
goes straight to the heart of things, touching them with
gentle cynicism, or laying them bare with the lightning
flash of inspired insight.   He is essentially dramatic—
that is to say, he habitually loses himself in the individuality of the person he represents, his main question
being, " Now, what did this man think, that he acted
thus?"   He frequently labours with minute care to build
up his picture of the man's condition, till we begin to be
impatient of his patience ; then suddenly, with some short,
sharp flash of thought, the whole soul of the man is revealed as by lightning, and the poem ends.   What, then,
is Browning's view of life?   His view of religion we may
conveniently leave for a separate chapter.   Let us ask
now, What is his view of life?

The first and chief point in Browning's view of life is
his intense sense of the reality of God and the human
soul.

> He glows above
> With scarce an intervention, presses close
> And palpitatingly, His soul o'er ours.

These are the twin Pharos-lights of earthly life ; the wild
surge of circumstance breaks and darkens on all sides,
but these abide.   It matters not what is lost if God be
found, or how much is swept down into the roaring wells
of the hungry sea of oblivion if the soul be saved.

> In man's self arise
> August anticipations, symbols, types
> Of a dim splendour ever on before,
> In that eternal circle run by life.

In all moments of supreme passion and impulse we feel how thin is that veil which shuts us from eternity. The lover in the *Last Ride* utters this thought when he cries,

> Who knows but the world may end to-night?

These moments of exaltation are the true index to the greatness of the soul of man, and therefore are to be sought and cherished above all other gain. What are progress, science, knowledge, love, art, in the light of these higher thoughts? They are simply so many golden roads which lead to God, so many shining stairs on which the half-visible shapes of spiritual presences go up and down. There is a world of spirit as of sense, and the gleams of spiritual knowledge which visit us

> Were meant
> To sting with hunger for full light.

Art is not to be praised for what it achieves, but for what it aspires to. It is the yearning of the spirit, not the skill of the hand, which gives it its real value.

> Progress, man's distinctive mark alone,
> Not God's, and not the beasts' ; God is, they are,
> Man partly is, and wholly hopes to be.

No English poet has written so fully upon art and music, or has shown more conclusively an exact knowledge and delicate taste in both ; but no poet is less of a *dilettante*. Art is simply an aspiration ; when the artist is satisfied with his work, then he has renounced all that made his art true and worthy. The mere visible results of art are worthless in themselves, and the passion of accumulating them an ignoble passion, if it has no higher purposes. Contempt can go no farther than to picture such a connoisseur, who —

> Above all epitaphs
> Aspires to have his tomb describe
> Himself as sole among the tribe
> Of snuff-box fanciers who possessed
> A Grignon with the Regent's crest.

On the other hand, it is in the pursuit of true art that
Abt Vogler gets his vision of truth itself, and cries : —

> All we have willed and hoped or dreamed of good shall exist,
>   Not in semblance, but in itself ; no beauty, nor good, nor power
> Whose voice has gone forth, but each survives for the melodist,
>   When eternity affirms the conception of an hour.
> The high that proved too high, the heroic for earth too hard,
>   The passion that left the ground to lose itself in the sky,
> Are music sent up to God by the lover and the bard.
>   Enough that He heard it once ; we shall hear it by and by.

Upon the general text of this view of life Browning
perpetually engrafts other lessons.   For instance, he is
fond of showing that it is better and grander to fail in
great things than to succeed in little ones.   What though
the patriot goes out at the Shambles' Gate, remembering,
as he rides, the flags flung wide for him a year before ?

> Thus I entered, and thus I go !
>   In triumphs people have dropped down dead.
> " Paid by the World—what dost thou owe
>   Me ? " God might question ; now instead
> 'Tis God shall repay !   I am safer so.

So, again, in the *Grammarian's Funeral*, Browning
puts into four terse and epigrammatic lines the same
truth : —

> This low man seeks a little thing to do,
>   Sees it and does it ;
> This high man, with a great thing to pursue,
>   Dies ere he knows it.

A truth which Browning is never weary of illustrating is that to all men there come moments of half-inspired

insight, the keen and, perhaps, momentary thrill of great impulses, and that a man's whole eternity hangs upon the use of such visitations. The revelation may be made in human love; it may be a vision of knowledge, or of duty; but it is imperative that when such transfiguring moments come we should be ready to seize them. In such Divine moments we see the narrow way that leads to life eternal.

> There are flashes struck from midnights,
>   There are fire-flames noondays kindle,
> Whereby piled-up honours perish,
>   Whereby swoln ambitions dwindle ;
> While just this or that poor impulse,
>   Which for once had play unstifled,
> Seems the whole work of a lifetime,
>   That away the rest has trifled.

What if it be said such moments are transient, that ecstasy is rare, that such high visions fade as soon as born ? The vision may perish, but the lesson it reveals remains. Life which is not vivified by faith and emotion is scarcely life at all. The worst of all woes is worldliness; to sink down in tranquil acquiescence before the customs of a low-pitched life, and never to break through into that eternal world which invests the visible world like an invisible atmosphere,—this is spiritual death, and there is no death to be feared but that. Why, the very grasshopper

> Spends itself in leaps all day
> To reach the sun, you want the eyes
> To see, as they the wings to rise
> And match the noble hearts of them.

Would the grasshopper, with his " passionate life " change estate with the mole that gropes in his " veritable muck "? Thus the vision of life which shapes itself to Browning is the vision of a great world in which the spiritual is ever in peril of being throttled by the sordid.

The general issue of Browning's philosophy of life is, then, that life is probation and education. Nothing is of value in itself, but for that to which it leads, for the help that it may yield the spirit in its long battle to gain enfranchisement from the flesh, and inheritance with God. Just as the utmost spoil of knowledge only serves to sting us with hunger for fuller light, so the utmost wealth of love only reveals to us the infinite possibilities of the love of God. There is "no pause in the leading and the light ":

> There's heaven above, and night by night
> I look right through its gorgeous roof ;
> For I intend to get to God.

Life has manifold sweet and pleasant uses ; let the odour of the April, and the freshness of the sea, the miracle of science, the ineffable yearning of perfect music, or the spell of perfect art, find their just and proper place in the category of life ; and be accepted with no ascetic scruple, but genial gratitude. But they are nothing more than broken hints, by which men learn the alphabet of better life. And it is because to rest in these things is death that Browning so eagerly applauds any life that flings itself away in endeavours after the distant and unattainable, and is at all times so merciful towards earthly failure. He loves to show us that beneath the rough husk of lives which seem wasted, there lies hidden the true seed of a life which will one day bloom consummate in beauty. He loves equally to take up some apparently successful life, and pierce it with his caustic humour, and point out its essential emptiness with an irony so keen and stern that it would be bitter were it not softened by the pathos of a human-hearted pity. Above all, there is no touch of pessimism in him; he looks undismayed above present evils to the brightening of a diviner day.

> Therefore, to whom turn I, but to Thee, the ineffable Name?
>   Builder and Maker, Thou, of houses not made with hands!
> What, have fear of change from Thee, who art ever the same?
>   Doubt that Thy power can fill the heart that Thy power expands?
>   There shall never be one lost good!   What was, shall live as before.
> The evil is null, is nought, is silence implying sound ;
> On the earth, the broken arcs ; in the heaven, a perfect round.

XXVII

THE SPIRIT OF BROWNING'S RELIGION

HAVING said so much as I have about Browning's intense interest in life, it naturally follows that something should be said about his attitude to religion, and the spirit of his religious teaching. The great poet is necessarily a great believer. The faculty which pierces to the unseen, and works in constant delicate contact with the invisible, is a faculty absolutely necessary to the equipment of a true poet. The poetry of faithlessness is an abnormal growth. It has little range or vitality. It never attains to really high and memorable results. When the spring of faith is broken, every faculty of the mind seems to share in the vast disaster. And especially do the faculties of imagination, spiritual insight, and tender fancy, which are the master-architects of poetry, suffer. The loss of faith strikes a chill to the central core of being, and robs the artist of more than half the material from which the highest poetry is woven.

On the other hand, the power of spiritual apprehension is one of the surest signs whereby we know a great poet. It is the function of the great poet to be a seer and interpreter. He sees farther, deeper, and higher than ordinary men, and interprets for the common man what he dimly feels but does not fully apprehend. It is quite possible that the message of the poet, the result of his spiritual insight, may not shape with our preconceived notions and theories; but where the spiritual insight is sure and real, the true poet never fails to quicken insight in his reader.

Perhaps no man has done more in our generation to quicken and sharpen the spiritual insight of men than Browning.   Preëminently he is a religious poet.   Religion enters into all his work, like a fragrance or a colour which clings to some delicate and lovely fabric, and, while occasionally subdued or modified, is never lost.   Browning's vast knowledge of the world never degenerates into worldliness.   He seeks to know the world in all its aspects, all its strange and vague contradictions, and seeks rather than shuns its sad and seamy side.   If he is an optimist it is not because he is an idealist, and the most striking thing about his optimism is that it thrives in the full knowledge of the baseness and evil of the world.   But the curiosity which impels Browning to investigate the darker side of life is never altogether an artistic curiosity: it is a religious curiosity.   What then is the net result?   What are the great facts on which he builds his faith?   What are the sources of that religious buoyancy which is so remarkable in so thorough a citizen of the world, and especially in an age when so many of the foremost writers and thinkers have given themselves over to agnosticism or despair?

Now, the actual religion of a man can usually be reduced to a few simple truths which are grasped with entire belief, and thus become the working principles of his life. Few men believe with equal conviction all the various dogmas of religious truth; but while many may remain obscure, there are others which are revealed with a vividness of light and force which constitute them henceforth the pillars of a man's real life.   Thus, for instance, St. James has defined what pure religion and undefiled meant to him in one simple and sufficing formula—charity and unworldliness, visiting the fatherless, and keeping the soul unspotted from the world. So Browning has grasped, with all his force, certain religious truths which appear to him the soul and marrow of Christianity, and these constitute the spirit of his religion.

The best illustration of the working of Browning's genius in the realm of religious truth may be found in such a poem as *Easter Day*. This poem is a wonderful poem in more respects than one: it is wonderful in its imagery, its intensity of insight, its daring, its vividness, the closeness of its reasoning, the sustained splendour of its diction, the prophetic force of its conclusions. It begins with the discussion of two speakers, who agree " How very hard it is to be a Christian." But each speaker utters the phrase in a different sense: the one finds Christianity hard as a matter of faith, unproved to the intellect; the other as a matter of practice, unrealized in the life. It would not be difficult to be a martyr, and find a Hand plunged through the flame to pluck the soul up to God, if, indeed, one could be certain of any such result; it *is* hard to believe on less than scientific evidence. To renounce the world on such evidence as we have would be folly. Suppose, after such renunciation, a man found he had given up the only world there was for him? Then ensues the poem itself, which consists of the description of a vision of the final judgment which the man of faith received, and which shook him out of the very web of negation in which his friend struggles. Suddenly, as he crossed a common at midnight, occupied with these very thoughts, all the midnight became " one fire." There shot across the dome of heaven, " like horror and astonishment,"

> A fierce vindictive scribble of red,
>   And straight I was aware
> That the whole rib-work round, minute

> Cloud touching cloud beyond compute
> Was tinted, each with its own spot
> Of burning at the core, till clot
> Jammed against clot, and spilt its fire
> Over all heaven.

This awful vision burned away all darkness from his spirit, and he knew that he had chosen not God, but the World.   Instantly he resolved to defend and applaud his choice.   God had created him to appreciate the beauties of life, and he had not put aside the boon unused—that was all.   But at that instant there came a final belch of fire, and he saw God —

> **Like the smoke**
> Pillared o'er Sodom when day broke —
> I saw Him.

Then God spoke.   He had chosen the World; let him glut his sense upon the World, but remember he was shut out from the heaven of spirit.   But what was the World, with all its brave show of beauty?   Merely one rose of God's making, flung

> Out of a summer's opulence,
> Over the Eden barrier, whence
> Thou art excluded.

Well, then, he would choose Art, to which the voice of God replies yet more sternly that Art is less than Nature; and its highest trophies the shame and despair of artists, who sought therein to express the invisible whole of which they perceived but a part.   Then he will choose Mind, the joys of Intellect; but what again, replies the Judge, is Mind but a gleam which to the devout thinker

> Makes bright the earth an age—
> Now, the whole sun's his heritage !

Lastly, he perceives there is nothing left but Love, and that shall be his choice.

> God is : thou art—the rest is hurled
> To nothingness.

He has doubted the story of Christ because he could not conceive so great love in God —

> Upon the ground
> That in the story had been found
> Too much love !   How could God love so ?
> He, who in all His works below,
> Adapted to the needs of man,
> Made love the basis of His plan,
> Did love, as was demonstrated.

In that moment he saw that God's love was the solution of all intellectual difficulties, and then, as he lay prone and overwhelmed,

> The whole God within his eyes
> Embraced me.

So the poem ends—a vision of Divine unalterable love as the solution of the mystery of the universe.

The infinite issue of human choice is, again, one of those strong beliefs which with Browning form the spirit of his religion.   He reiterates persistently and in many forms that any choice which falls short of God is ruinous in its sequence.   For instance, the speaker in *Easter Day* is taught the folly of choosing Mind by perceiving that the highest genius of man is but a gleam from the unexhausted sun which pours light through an eternal world.   But Browning, in one of his greatest poems, *Paracelsus*, has gone much farther than this.   In that poem he has shown that Intellect without Love, without Morality, without Character, is of all forces the most perilous.   Paracelsus has sought to *Know*.   What has his desire brought him but bitterness and disappointment ?   So poignant is his sense of failure that he even cries :

> Mind is nothing but disease,
> And natural health is ignorance.

And in the final pathetic scene he derides the folly of such intellectual passions as those which have consumed him, and sees clearly that to Love is better than to Know

> No, no ;
> Love, hope, fear, faith—these make humanity,
> These are its sign and note and character,
> And these I have lost.

Throughout his writings Browning shows himself inexorably opposed to the modern theistic philosophy which makes the individual the centre of the universe, and steadily teaches the more ancient doctrine of Him who, being rich, for our sakes became poor, that we, by His poverty, might become rich —

> Renounce joy for my fellow's sake ?   That's joy
> Beyond joy.

But this all-present sense of God's love implies also such truths as communion, prayer, providence ; and these also are incorporated in Browning's religion.   The noblest example of Browning's expression of these doctrines is found in the short but splendid poem, *Instans Tyrannus*. It is the Tyrant who speaks.   Out of the million or two of men he possesses there is one man not at all to his mind. He struck him, of course, but though pinned to the earth with the persistence of so great a hate he neither moaned nor cursed. He is nothing but a toad or a rat, but nevertheless the Tyrant cannot eat in peace while he lives to anger him with his abominable meekness. So he soberly lays his last plan to extinguish the man —

> When sudden . . . how think ye? the end
> Did I say "without friend"?
> Say, rather, from marge to blue marge,
> The whole sky grew his targe,
> With the sun's self for visible boss,
> While an arm ran across!
> Do you see? Just my vengeance complete,
> The man sprang to his feet,
> Stood erect, caught at God's skirts, and prayed!
> — So *I* was afraid?

The poem is a sort of magnificent version of the familiar hymn-lines : —

> Strong to deliver, and good to redeem
> The weakest believer who hangs upon Him.

The centre of Browning's whole world of religious thought lies in his abiding sense and conviction that God is Love. It reconciles him to the mysteries of faith, it casts a bright bridge of gleaming hope across the profound gulfs of human error, and like the lunar rainbow he describes, a second and mightier bow springs from the first, and stands vast and steady above the mysterious portals of human destiny, on whose straining topmost arc he sees emerge the foot of God Himself. "God is good, God is wise, God is love," is the perpetual whisper of spiritual voices, floating over him, and piercing with

their divine sweetness the evil darkness of the tortuous
way he threads in tracking out the strange secrets of
human impulse and achievement. All knowledge is but
the shadow of God's light; all purity and constancy of
human passion but the hint of His love; all beauty but
the fitful gleam of His raiment as He passes us—that
King in His beauty whose face itself we shall at last behold in the land that is very far off. If Browning stands
amid the ruins of that mighty city, which in a single year
sent its million fighters forth, and

> Marks the basement whence a tower in ancient time
> Sprang sublime,
> And a burning ring, all round, the chariots traced
> As they raced,

it is to turn at last from the vision of that domed and
daring palace, the splendid spectacle of power and pomp,
to cry:

> Shut them in,
> With their triumphs, and their glories, and the rest;
> Love is best!

If he considers the failing of human power in the presence of death, it is only to exclaim, with a sense of triumphant gladness:

> Grow old along with me!
> The best is yet to be,
> The last of life for which the first was made;
> Our times are in His hand,
> Who saith : " A whole I planned,
> Youth shows but half ; trust God ; see all, nor be afraid ! "

He has infinite faith in God, that His love will, in
ways unknown to us, work out ultimate blessedness for
His children, and that the world will not pass out in darkness, but in the end of the ages it will be daybreak every-

where. Not only is there no despair: there is no touch
of disheartenment even in Browning —

> Languor is not in his heart,
> Weakness is not in his word,
> Weariness not on his brow.

He awaits the revelation of eternity; then all will be
made clear. The lost leader, who has forsaken the great
cause of progress—"just for a handful of silver he left
us"—may never be received back save in doubt, hesitation, and pain by his old comrades; but the estrangement
of earth will not outlast earth —

> Let him receive the new knowledge and wait us
> Pardoned in heaven, the first by the throne !

Caponsacchi, the great and noble priest, the " soldier-
saint" of *The Ring and the Book*, must needs henceforth
pass through life with the shadow of Pompilia's sweet
presence laid across his heart, and all the purest aspiration of his life covered in her grave. Well, is there not a
further world, where they neither marry nor are given in
marriage ?

> Oh, how right it is ! how like Jesus Christ
> To say that!
> So let him wait God's instant, men call years ;
> Meanwhile hold hard by truth and his great soul,
> Do out the duty !

The dying Pompilia sees how the love of souls like his
interprets the meaning of the love of God, and cries :—

> Through such souls alone
> God, stooping, shows sufficient of His light
> For us i' the dark to rise by. And I rise.

Even when Browning stands in such a place as the
Morgue, amid the ghastliness of tragic failure and de-

spair, touched though he be with mournfulness, yet this strong and living hope does not leave him, and he still can write:

> It's wiser being good than bad,
>   It's safer being meek than fierce,
> It's fitter being sane than mad.
>   My own hope is, a sun will pierce
> The thickest cloud earth ever stretched ;
>   That, after Last, returns the First,
> Though a wide compass first be fetchèd ;
>   That what began best can't end worst,
>   Nor what God blest once prove accurst.

In other words, whatever dreary intervals there may be of folly, darkness, misery, the world God blessed in the beginning will roll round into the light at last; and when His purpose is complete, there will be a new heaven and a new earth wherein dwelleth righteousness.

XXVIII

BROWNING'S ATTITUDE TO CHRISTIANITY

IN the last chapter we noticed that one of the abnormal growths of modern poetry is a poetry of negation. We may add that this, in its last development, has become a poetry of despair. And the source of that despair is inability to receive the truths of Christianity. Since the advent of Goethe a movement very similar to the Renaissance in Italy has passed over the whole of Europe. There has been a return to Paganism, concurrently with a wide-spread revival in art and culture. The dogmas of the Church have been vehemently assailed, and the ethical teachings of Christianity disputed. The movement initiated by Goethe has spread throughout the world. It has received impulse from strange quarters, and given impulse in strange directions. Its legitimate outcome in Germany is found in the long line of great scholars who have devoted indefatigable genius and patience to the work of destructive Biblical criticism. There may appear to be a wide enough gulf between the calm paganism of Goethe and the vehement controversial temper of German theological scholarship, but nevertheless the one is a true child of the other.

Added to this, there must be reckoned the extraordinary growth of natural science during the present century. The minds of the greatest thinkers have been riveted on the problem of the origin of things. The results of their investigation have been published with the hardihood and confidence of complete conviction. In their researches as to the working of natural law they have completely ignored all that is supernatural. Their temper towards the supernatural has been one of contemptuous indifference or embittered hostility. Thus, then, two forces of immense strength have been steadily at work upon the structure of received opinion; the one force, fearless rationalism, the other, fearless paganism. Culture has been preached as the true substitute for Christianity, Art and Beauty as the all-sufficient gospels for human life. We have only to turn to the literature of the last half-century to see how far these influences have permeated. The essayist and poet have alike conspired to preach the new doctrine. The stream of tendency thus created has sufficient examples in the beautiful paganism of Keats and the garrulous mediævalism of Morris.

But there is another class of writers who have not been able so easily to dismiss the great beliefs by which centuries of men and women have lived and striven. They have been allured, fascinated, and repelled alternately; they have hoped and doubted; in their voices is the sound of weeping, in their words the vibration of long suffering; for whatever attitude they may have taken towards Christianity they have never relapsed into reckless indifference. This eager scrutiny of religious dogmas by the best and keenest minds of the age is, at least, a proof that such men have been alive, and even agonizingly alive, to the tremendous importance of those dogmas. Poetry in the nineteenth century has sought to be the minister of theological truth not less than of artistic beauty, and as a consequence the theological problems of the century, and in less degree the scientific problems also, have been inextricably interwoven with its fine warp and woof of exquisite creation. So that let what will be said about the faithlessness of the nineteenth century, nevertheless the presence of Jesus Christ in nineteenth century literature is one of its most remarkable and indisputable characteristics.

But the solitary issue of this intermingling of theology with poetry is not perplexity or sadness. There is found a very different culmination in one poet at least, and that poet is Browning. Browning has attacked theology with the zeal and fervour of a born disputant. He is not merely a great religious poet, but is distinctively a theological poet. He has deliberately chosen for the exercise of his art the most subtle problems of theology, and has made his verse the vehicle for the statement of theological difficulties and personal beliefs. The historical evidences and arguments of Christianity have exercised upon him a deep and enduring fascination. In *Pauline*, his earliest poem, the vision of Christ has visited Browning, and he cries —

> O Thou pale form, so dimly seen, deep-eyed,
> I have denied Thee calmly—do I not
> Pant when I read of Thy consummate deeds,
> And burn to see Thy calm pure truths out-flash
> The brightest gleams of earth's philosophy ?
> Do I not shake to hear ought question Thee ?
> If I am erring, save me, madden me,
> Take from me powers and pleasures, let me die
> Ages, so I see Thee !

That vision of Christ has been not only an ever-present, but an ever-growing, vision with Browning.

This spirit of passionate reverence for Christ, which Browning thus expresses in his first considerable poem, is the spirit which dominates his entire writings. The deepest mystery of Christianity is Christ Himself; that, indeed, is its one mystery. Browning has been quick to realize this, and habitually perceives and teaches, with unerring keenness, that in Christ all mysteries have solution, or without Him are left forever dark and impenetrable. The method of argument he pursues is peculiarly his own. He ranks himself for the moment with the Rationalist, and having detailed his conclusions, goes on to probe them. For this purpose dialectic skill, irony, humour, and the subtlest analysis are his weapons. He refuses to be content with negation; it is not enough to say what you do not believe, you must realize what you do believe. He pushes back the burden of proof upon the doubter, and says men have an equal right to demand the demonstration of a doubt as of a creed. When every shred of evidence has been weighed and tested, then comes the moment to ask what is left, and the final verdict depends not on the letter of the evidence, but the spirit; not on any body of oral attestation, but on the soul which witnesses within a man. This, with many variations and differences, is, upon the whole, a fair statement of Browning's method of argument, and the result is never left in doubt. In *A Death in the Desert*, where St. John is supposed to utter his last words of belief, the verdict, not indeed of the man Cerinthus, who hears the great confession, but of the man who adds the final note, is: —

> If Christ, as thou affirmest, be of men,
> Mere man, the first and best, but nothing **more,**
> Account Him, for reward of what He **was,**
> Now and forever, wretchedest of all.
>   Can a mere man do this?
> Yet Christ saith this He lived and **died to do.**
> Call Christ then the illimitable God,
> Or lost!

and he significantly adds —

But 'twas Cerinthus that is lost.

In the *Epistle of Karshish*, in which the strange story
of Lazarus is debated from the physician's point of view,
the writer finally rises into a very ecstasy of faith, and the
poem closes with this passionate exclamation:

> The very God! think, Abib; dost thou think?
> So, the All-Great were the All-Loving too —
> So, through the thunder comes a human voice,
> Saying, " O heart I made, a heart beats here !
> Face, My hands fashioned, see it in Myself!
> Thou hast no power, nor may conceive of Mine.
> But love I gave thee, with Myself to love,
> And thou must love Me who have died for thee."

It cannot be said that there is the faintest touch of in-
tolerance or scorn for honest doubt in Browning's poetry.
Yet no man of our days has pierced it with so many telling shafts of irony and reason. He acknowledges the
difficulties of belief, and it is plain to every reader that
Browning has wrestled sorely with the angel in the night,
with that impalpable and dreadful shape which has all but
overwhelmed him. But the morning has broken and
brought its benediction. If the difficulties of belief are
great, the difficulties of unbelief are greater. He assumes
that there must be many unexplored remainders in the
world of thought. Well, what then? Because some
things are hidden, are there none revealed?

> What, my soul? See so far and no farther? When doors
>   great and small,
> Nine-and-ninety flew ope at our touch, should the hundredth
>   appal?
> In the least things have faith, yet distrust in the greatest of all?

That were the last unreasonableness of ignorance, the

final folly of imbecility. No; the wiser act is to trust where actual knowledge fails. Faith is a very fine word, but

> You must mix some uncertainty
> With faith if you would have faith be.

If a scientific faith is absurd, and " frustrates the very end 'twas meant to serve," he will rest content with a mere probability —

> So long as there be just enough
> To pin my faith to, though it hap
> Only at points ; from gap to gap,
> One hangs up a huge curtain so,
> Grandly, nor seeks to have it go
> Foldless and flat along the wall.
> What care I if some interval
> Of life less *plainly* may depend
> On God? I'd hang there to the end.

Moreover, it is part of God's good discipline to educate us by illusion ; the point of victory, the prize of the high calling, perpetually recedes to the man who presses towards the mark.

> We do not see it, where it is
> At the beginning of the race ;
> As we proceed, it shifts its place,
> And where we looked for crowns to fall,
> We find the tug's to come—that's all.

Thus the uncertainties of knowledge are in themselves a beneficent training for the spirit of man ; they sting him with this Divine hunger for full light, they soften him to childlike blessedness of mere trust, and tend to the more real and vivid hold upon the creed itself, by shaking from it " the torpor of assurance."

No poet of our time has so consistently attacked the

darker and more tangled problems of human conduct. He confesses that " serene deadness " puts him out of temper. His sympathies, on the other hand, go out irresistibly towards any sort of life, however strangely mistaken or at variance with custom, which has real, throbbing, energetic vitality in it. To him there is an overwhelming fascination in misunderstood men, and the more tangled and intricate is the problem of character and action the more eagerly does he approach it. Not unnaturally this tendency of Browning's genius has led him through many of the darker labyrinths of human motive, and occasionally, as in *Mr. Sludge, the Medium*, the riddle has not been worth the prolonged application he has devoted to it. But in no class of poems is Browning's intense religious conviction more remarkably displayed. The same retreat upon mere faith which he makes in subtle questions of theology he observes also in dealing with the mysteries of human conduct. His method of treatment is twofold. The majority of his poems which deal with character and conduct deal with character and conduct more or less imperfect. In all such cases the blemish is laid bare with unerring accuracy. There are no glozing words to cover moral lapses, no spun purple of fine phrases to hide the hideousness of spiritual leprosy. But Browning describes such lives not to display their corruption, but to discover some seed of true life which may yet be hidden in them. Few lives are so evil but that some golden threads are woven in the coarse fabric ; some impulses are left which, if followed, may be the clue to life eternal.

> Oh, we're sunk enough, God knows !
> But not quite so sunk that moments,
> Sure, though seldom, are denied us

> When the spirit's true endowments
> Stand out plainly from its false ones,
> And apprise it, if pursuing
> On the right way or the wrong way,
> To its triumph or undoing.

The "poor impulse," the one obscure, true instinct, which vibrates under a smothered or sinful nature, may be the starting-point towards ideal goodness. But, if man be evil, God is good, and the soul of the universe is just. Browning is bound to admit that some natures seem hopelessly corrupt; at all events he fails to find the germ of renovation in them. They have chosen the evil part which cannot be taken away from them. They have had their choice —

> The earthly joys lay palpable —
> A taint, in each distinct as well ;
> The heavenly flitted, faint and rare,
> Above them, but as truly were
> Taintless, so, in their nature best.
> Thy choice was earth ; thou didst attest
> 'Twas fitter spirit should subserve
> The flesh.

When Browning confronts such natures, his second method comes into play; he falls back upon faith—faith in the wise order and infinite goodness of God. The most marked example of this method is in that splendid dramatic sketch, *Pippa Passes*. No more awful picture of guilt triumphing in its guiltiness, of corruption intoxicated with the abandonment and depraved joy of its own wickedness, has any poet given us than the Ottima of that poem. There stands the villa, with its closed shutters; within it the murdered man, and the guilty woman pouring out her confessions of passion to the man who slew him. Car. human action produce a more hideous combination? Yet the sun shines fair, and " God has not said a word." Has God's good government of things broken down, then ? No, indeed. Pippa passes—Pippa, the poor girl with her one day's holiday in the whole year, yet happy, cheerful, trustful; and as she pauses she sings rebuke to our doubts of God, and terror to the black heart of Ottima:

> The year's at the spring,
> And day's at the morn ;
> Morning's at seven ;
> The hillside's dew-pearled ;
> The lark's on the wing,
> God's in His heaven,
> All's right with the world.

It is thus Browning, like many a great spirit before him, falls back upon faith in God, saying in effect what Abraham said when confronted with the corruption of man and the judgment of God : " Shall not the Judge of all the earth do right ? "

XXIX

BROWNING'S SIGNIFICANCE IN LITER-
ATURE

BROWNING stands utterly alone in English poetry ; he has no prototype, and he can have no successor. He has created his style, as he has also created his readers. In almost every other poet of our day we can trace the course of influences, more or less defined, which have shaped the poetic form and moulded the poetic thought. Browning has had no model. If we except the faintest possible trace of Shelley's influence, which, like an ethereal fragrance, haunts the pages of *Pauline*, we may say that he shows no sign of the influence of any of the elder bards upon his style. He is unique in his rugged individuality, the subtlety of his analysis, the suggestiveness and intensity of his thought, the originality of his phrases, and, if one may use the term, the extraordinary agility of his intellect. His intuitions go by bounds and leaps, so that it taxes all our energy occasionally to keep pace with him. His pages are literally crammed full of thought. All the living poets of the English language taken together have produced nothing like the body of thought which he has produced. Moreover, of great latter day poets he is the most genuine humourist when it suits his purpose. " Humour," it has been said, " originally meant moisture, a signification it metaphorically retains, for it is the very juice of the mind, oozing from the brain, and enriching and fertilizing wherever it falls." Humour is, in fact, based on sympathy—a large, genuine, noble sympathy, which embraces all kinds and conditions of human life like a genial atmosphere. This gift Browning distinctly possesses, and it explains the variety of his poems. Nothing that pertains to man is foreign to him. But the humour of Browning does not manifest itself so much in individually ludicrous forms as in a general humorous attitude towards all sorts of forms. To quote a portion of the famous definition of humour given by Dr. Barrow, and which, according to Mackintosh, affords the greatest " proof of mastery over language ever given by an English writer," it may be said of Browning's humour, " Sometimes it lurketh under an odd similitude, sometimes it is lodged in a sly expression, in a smart answer, in a quirkish reason, in a shrewd intimation, in cunningly diverting or cleverly retorting an objection ; sometimes it is couched in a bold scheme of speech, in a tart irony, in a lusty hyperbole, in a startling metaphor, in a plausible reconciling of contradictions, or in acute non sense."

The worst form which Browning's humour has taken is in the purposed grotesqueness of his rhymes, and it is impossible to suppose that some of his verses could have been written without some sense on the part of their author of their extraordinary ludicrousness. What can one say to such verbal contortions as these : *Witanagemot* rhyming to *bag 'em hot, cub licks* to *Republics, vociference* to *stiffer hence, corrosive* to *O Sieve, spirito* to *weary toe ?* Or what mortal ingenuity is equal to the task of unravelling the meaning which may possibly be found in such a verse as this ? —

> One is incisive, corrosive ;
>   Two retorts, nettled, curt, crepitant ;
> Three makes rejoinder, expansive, explosive ;
>   Four overbears them all, strident and strepitant;
> Five . . . O Danaides, O Sieve !

Even Browning seems to have had some consciousness of the obscurity of his enigma, for he remarks in
the next verse, and his readers will heartily agree with
him —

> On we drift ; where looms the dim port ?
>   One, Two, Three, Four, Five contribute their quota ;
> Something is gained, if one caught but the import.

When Browning produces verses such as these, we can
hardly help suspecting him of perpetrating an elaborate
joke.   Nor can we discern any really welcome humour
in the " acute nonsense."   If there be humour it is after
the pattern of the celebrated German Baron, who wished
to be humorous, and accordingly took to dancing
on the dining-table.   It is grotesque, eccentric, curious,
even ridiculous, but not humorous.   It is Browning
amusing himself with conundrums, and slyly laughing at
the confusion of tongues they are likely to produce
among the critics, to say nothing of the depth of imbecility to which they will reduce his friends who are devoted enough to seek their " import."

It is necessary to consider Browning in these his most
willful moods if we are to estimate his significance as a
stylist in literature.   Poetry depends upon expression far
more than prose ; it is noble thought clothed in beautiful
language.   It is, therefore, impossible wholly to disregard
the defects of style, the maimed metres, the verbal somer-
saults, the unique grotesqueness of rhyme which Browning unquestionably displays.   It is only a great poet

who could have survived such literary escapades. But having survived them, in virtue of the immense genius of which they are but the excrescence, they nevertheless remain as part and parcel of his works, and have their influence. What is the significance of Browning, then, in a literary sense? Chiefly this—that he has introduced into English poetry a new, strong, fresh, and intensely masculine style. He is a transcendentalist in philosophy, but a realist in style. No word is too common for him, no phrase too hackneyed, or too idiomatic, or too scholastic, or too *bizarre* if it will carry his thought home. Wordsworth aimed at writing poetry in the language of prose, but Browning has ventured further, and has used vernacular prose. He makes his men and women speak as they would have spoken if alive. In this respect Browning is in line with the development of his age. We are becoming less idealistic and more realistic every day. The modern imagination is less concerned with the bright dreams of old chivalry than the present mysteries of sad humanity. It finds sufficient food for sorrow, wonder, faith, and passion in the things of the day. It fixes its piercing gaze on man rather than on Nature, knowing that he is of more value than many sparrows building in the summer eaves, or many lilies whitening happy hillsides in the spring. Browning is the interpreter of all that is highest, noblest, and most moral in this realism of to-day. His style is a protest against euphemism, as his poetry is a plea for realism. His significance as a man of letters is that he has enlarged the possibilities of English poetry by adding to it a bold, nervous, masculine vocabulary, and by using it as it was never used before, save by Shakespeare himself, for the analysis and portrayal of human character and motive.

But the moral significance of Browning in literature entirely eclipses the literary. Browning's literary method must have its effect upon the future of English poetry, and that effect will be in the direction of a less trammelled and ornate, a freer and more realistic, use of words. But where one reader catches some new inspiration from his method, a thousand will feel the overwhelming current of moral force which he has created. Here is a man who has tracked Nature home to her

> Inmost room,
> With lens and scalpel ;

who has been animated by vivid and potent interest in every form of human life, every mystery of human conduct ; who has sought knowledge of man, alike in the splendid chambers where kings live delicately and in the deserts where great spirits nerve themselves to strenuous heroism ; in the study of the artist, the organ-loft of the musician, the garret of the toiler, the warren of the outcast, the tents of great soldiers, and the cells of great mystics ; among the flower-like purities of little children, the shrewd schemings of characters half sordid and half lofty, the soiled grandeurs of great spirits overthrown, the shameful secrets of souls plunged deep in infamies— who has, in fact, acknowledged no height too high and no depth too low for the demand of his noble curiosity. And at what result has he arrived ? He himself has told us —

> I have gone the whole round of creation : I saw and I spoke :
> I, a work of God's hand for that purpose, received in my brain
> And pronounced on the rest of His handwork—returned Him again
> His creation's approval or censure ; I spoke as I saw,
> I report as a man may on God's work—all's love, yet all's law

He alone of our great latter-day poets has performed this great pilgrimage of inquiry, and has returned with absolute and happy assurances of hope. He has descended, like another Dante, through all the dreadful circles of flame and darkness, amid the woe and travail of mankind, but has never lost his vision of God's immortal love and tenderness. Where others have been overwhelmed, their voices reaching us from the thick blackness only in wild cries of anguish, rage, sorrow, and despair, he has stood firm, and has sung out of the deeps a song of limitless faith. He has passed out of the Purgatory and Inferno into the Paradise. Is there any other of our great poets of whom so much can be affirmed? Was not one of the latest bequests of the most melodious, famous, and successful poet of our time a bequest of bitterness and despair?[1] But where Tennyson found food for hopelessness, Browning found the seed, if not the fruit, of hope; where the one has been overwhelmed, the other has triumphed. Browning did not cast away faith because creeds are confused; nor expectation for his race because the haggard human army has been defeated oft and again in its onward march; nor patriotic hope because great movements and great reforms have failed, or seemed to fail to our bounded human vision. He teaches that each good deed done dies perhaps, but afterwards revives, and goes on to work endless blessing in the world. He believes that

> To only have conceived,
> Planned your great works, apart from progress
> Surpasses little works achieved.
> O, never star
> Was lost here but it rose afar!

[1] The second *Locksley Hall.*

And, believing thus, his voice rings out like a clarion blast of courage across the blank misgivings and confusions of our time, and it may be said of him as it was of Cromwell, " He was a strong man in the dark perils of war, and in the high places of the field hope shone in him like a pillar of fire, when it had gone out in others."

The significance of Browning in literature is, then, that he is a strong, resolute, believing teacher, who, amid the sick contentions of a doubting generation, has bated no jot of heart or hope. He has had the courage of his originality in creating his own style—a style which, for reasons already indicated, sometimes becomes obscure and not seldom is eccentric, but which is, nevertheless, wonderfully strong, nervous, and powerful, possessed of a vast vocabulary, idiomatic, free, resonant, and striking. He has had the courage of individuality also in resisting the Agnostic tendencies of his time, and amid the dismayed and doubtful has consistently delivered a testimony of hope. When the arrears of fame are paid, and the debts of praise are liquidated, as they will be in the just hands of Time, this and every succeeding generation will surely be acknowledged under heavy obligations to Robert Browning. The songs of mere loveliness charm us for a while, but it is the outpourings and upsoarings of the strong men of humanity which become the real marching songs of the race in the long run. What Browning has missed in melody he has gained in thought, and if he be deficient in form he possesses a far nobler efficiency—the inspiration and moral power of the noble thinker.

XXX

ROBERT BROWNING—CONCLUDING
SURVEY

THE prevalent impression which the work of Browning leaves upon the reader is twofold: he makes us feel the greatness of his mind, and the intensity and breadth of his sympathies. It is a vast world of thought to which Browning introduces his reader. He claims from him absolute attention, the entire absorption of the neophyte, whose whole moral earnestness is given to his task. Like all neophytes we have to submit to a process of initiation. In the world of Browning's thought there is much that is strange, much that is new, much that is grotesque. There is no problem of life that he does not attempt to solve, no mystery of life that he is not ready to explain or reconcile. He insists that we take him seriously, for he himself is profoundly serious and earnest. He is not a singer, but a seer. In every line that he has written there is the vigorous movement of a strong and eager intellect. If his reader is incapable of sustained thought, or too indolent to rise into something like intensity of attention, then Browning has nothing to say to him. He demands our faith in him as a master-teacher; he will work no miracle for him who has no belief. Sometimes this sense of the power of mind in Browning is almost oppressive. We long for a little rest in the arduous novitiate he imposes on us. We feel that the vehicle he uses for the exposition of his thought is unequal to the vast strain he imposes on it. The verse moves stiffly beneath the tremendous weight of thought. The forms of poetry seem to cramp and fetter him. We feel that an occasional lapse into the loose and liberated style of Whitman's rhapsodies would be of equal service to Browning and ourselves. No poet has ever so *tired* the minds of his readers. If Browning had possessed a less subtle and powerful intellect, if he had held a narrower view of life, he would have written with infinitely greater ease, and would have doubled and quadrupled his popularity.

But the compensating gain of this breadth of view is a corresponding breadth of sympathy. There is a perfectly unique catholicity in his affinities. Life in its shame as well as its splendour, life in its baseness, its distorted aims, its tragic failures, its limitless follies, is still life to him, and is worthy of his compassionate scrutiny. His unconventionality is startling to ordinary readers ; they never know where to find Browning, or can anticipate what he will say or teach. Thus, even for the Jew in the Roman Ghetto he has a good word. He interprets what may be the unspoken thought in the heart of many a Hebrew outcast. The Jew has slain Christ, and so has missed the one vast opportunity of Jewish history : but is there no excuse ? Is there no room for pity or apology ? This is what Browning makes the Jew in the Ghetto think and say—and no better example of the unconventional breadth of his sympathies could be found : —

> Thou ! if Thou wast He, who at mid-watch came
> By the starlight, naming a dubious Name !
> And if, too heavy with sleep, too rash
> With fear, O Thou, if that martyr gash
> Fell on Thee coming to take Thine own,
> And we gave the Cross, when we owed the Throne—

Thou art the Judge ! We are bruisèd thus,
But, the judgment over, join sides with us !
Thine too is the cause ! and not more Thine
Than ours, is the work of these dogs and swine,
Whose life laughs through, and spits at their creed,
Who maintain Thee in word, and defy Thee in deed !

The poet whose sympathies illumine the foul darkness of the Ghetto and the Morgue may well be a stone of stumbling and rock of offence to the careless and conventional reader.

Force, faith, and thought, the vigour of a strong intellect, the vitality of a victorious faith, the subtlety and logic of an acute insight, are, as we have seen, the dominating qualities in Browning's poetry. In so much all criticism must agree ; and M. Taine, the famous French critic, has acknowledged, not only that England is far ahead of France in the greatness of her poets, but that Browning stands first among modern English poets—the most excellent where excellence is greatness, the most gifted where genius is a common dower. When, however, we come to particularize certain poems as the greatest in the qualities of genius, probably opinions will differ. After all, there is no such thing as systematic or judicial criticism, and the efforts of such criticism to systematize itself have uniformly failed, and deservedly. Shakespeare defies the unities of the drama, and is great in spite of them, because he is the creator of a richer unity, which is based on the exposition of a richer and more complex life. Genius perpetually fashions new moulds for itself, and the history of criticism is in great part a list of defeats suffered by the critics at the hands of genius. Criticism ascertains qualities and describes them. The critic is an explorer who goes first with the lighted torch into the stalactite chamber roofed with gems, and in his most beneficent function only calls the public to admire that which he has illumined, but not created. His special preference for this or that particular form of beauty is, after all, his own affair, and is dictated by personal taste. An agreeable man, according to Lord Beaconsfield, was one who agreed with him ; the poem a critic calls the best is simply the one that agrees best with him. When, therefore, I state the work of Browning's which seems finest, noblest, weightiest in quality, I simply specify that which seems so to me, and can claim only the prerogative of a personal preference.

Lord Jeffrey, in almost the only well-known passage of his writings, has moralized on the perishable fame of poets, and has mournfully recounted how little of work famous in its day contrives ultimately to escape the devouring maw of oblivion. Lovelace lives by a single stanza, Wolfe by a single poem, and Jeffrey was probably too generous when he pictured posterity receiving with rapture the half of Campbell, the fourth of Byron, the sixth of Scott, the scattered tithes of Crabbe, and the three per cent. of Southey. The best way of sifting the perfect from the imperfect in Browning's work would be to ask what we should care least to lose, and what we would most willingly forget. If we had to submit to an ideal justice for the final jurisdiction of immortality the poems most likely to win him the award of age-long fame, which should we choose to support the claim ?

When we apply this test to Browning's poetry the result is soon reached. First of all stands the *Ring and the Book*. In force of conception, skill and delicacy of treatment, subtlety of thought, purity, power, and passion, the *Ring and the Book* is Browning's masterpiece. Wandering in Florence, Browning discovers on a bookstall an old manuscript volume containing the pleadings of a murder-trial at Rome in 1698. The whole case is one of those strange tangles of evidence which dull people usually discredit until the passions of human life flame forth, and the thing is a dramatic actuality, done before their very eyes. The murdered woman is Pompilia, who has fled from her husband with the priest Caponsacchi; the murderer is the husband. At first sight this appears merely a low drama of vicious passion and brutal revenge; but as Browning pores over the pleadings and unravels the tangled skein of evidence it reveals itself in a very different way. As he reads, the dark shadows of crime recede, revealing in transfiguring brightness the figure of Pompilia, " young, good, beautiful," clothed upon with the raiment which is from heaven, the beauty of holiness, the Divine dignity of goodness, the touching, inimitable freshness and purity of childlike innocence. A mere child in years, she is the spoil of her husband's avarice, then the victim of his malignity and disappointed cupidity, until at last she flies, to save her babe's life, with the young priest who has promised to defend her. Browning's method is to let each witness tell his own tale, making the written report his basis of fact, on which he casts his own quick, penetrating light of interpretation. This is accomplished in twelve books. The one-half of Rome gives its opinion, takes merely the outward appearance of the facts, and judges Guido justified in the murder. The other half of Rome accepts Pompilia's innocence, and perceives that from first to last she has been a victim. Then follow the chief actors in the drama. Guido makes his defence—the defence of a man thoroughiy shrewd, with more than a touch of fanaticism, alive to his position, and alert to use every waft of popular prejudice in his favour. After him Caponsacchi tells his tale; how he came to enter the Church, and was urged by great priests to put only an easy interpretation on the vows which seemed to him so strenuously solemn ; how he came to recognize in Pompilia a womanhood he had never before imagined—so sadly sweet, so grave, so pure, that he felt lifted into higher thoughts as by the vision of a saint ; how God and Pompilia kept company in his thoughts, so that when the hour came that he could serve her he seized it with a simple chivalry, and did it as God's plain duty, then and there made clear to him.   Then Pompilia herself, dying fast, in broken snatches tells the story of her life.   Finally, the old Pope sums up the case, giving verdict of death against Guido, and Guido himself pours out his last despairing utterances, which reach their tragic climax in the cry to his murdered wife to save him, thus unconsciously witnessing to the purity he had defamed and despised —

> Abate—Cardinal—Christ—Maria—God—
> Pompilia, will you let them murder me !

It is not too much to say that there is nothing like this in English poetry, and for certain parts of it we may claim that there is nothing since Shakespeare to surpass it.   The form is unique—one which Shakespeare would not have used—but, cumbrous as it is, it exactly suits Browning. The *Ring and the Book* is the work of a giant.   We could spare, perhaps, the pleadings of the advocates and the opinions of Rome, but the speeches of the great actors in the drama have the mintage of immortality upon them. Shakespeare himself has given us no more exquisite creation of womanhood made lovely by simplicity and purity than Pompilia.   She has grown like " an angel-

watered lily " born in polluted soil, but only the sweetness
and the light have been gathered up into her being, and
the sin of others has left no smirch on her.   The spoiled
and blackened life of Guido only serves the better to set
forth the grace and dignity of her purity.   Whenever any
of the speakers mention Pompilia, a hush of reverence
seems to fall upon their words, and even Guido, at the
last, turns to her in his extremity, as to a guardian saint,
for help.   It is impossible to read her own story of her
life without tears.   Her memories of early childhood,
ever shadowed with the mysterious sense of God ; her sad
married life, with its silent forgiveness of hateful wrongs ;
the most pathetic tenderness with which she describes the
rapture of her motherhood ; the joy she had in her babe
—how she seems now like that poor Virgin she often
pitied as a child,

> At our street-corner in a lonely niche,
> The babe that sat upon her knees broke off ;

her sad hope that people will teach her babe to think well
of her when she is dead ; her acknowledgment of that
sense within her which makes her know that she loves
Caponsacchi indeed, but with that spiritual love only
which Christ foreshadowed as the joy of that world where
they neither marry nor are given in marriage ; and always that deep abiding thankfulness to God that for a fortnight He has let her have her babe to love,

> In a life like mine
> A fortnight filled with bliss is long and much :
> I never realized God's birth before,
> How He grew likest God in being born, —

all this forms one of the loveliest and most pathetic
creations which English poetry has ever produced.   And

not less pathetic is Caponsacchi's account of his long ride
to Rome with Pompilia, and her simple wonder at a
kindness in him to which she was all unused: —

> She said—a long while later in the day,
> When I had let the silence be—abrupt —
> "Have you a mother?"—"She died, I was born."
> "A sister, then?"—"No sister."—"Who was it —
> What woman were you used to serve this way,
> Be kind to, till I called you and you came?"

And in the whole realm of English poetry it would be
hard to match for intensity and passion the concluding
passage of Caponsacchi's address to the judges, in which
he pictures Guido, not so much dying as "sliding out of
life," "parted by the general horror and common hate
from all honest forms of life," until upon creation's verge
he meets one other like himself,

> Judas, made monstrous by much solitude,

and there teaching and bearing malice and all detestabil-
ity, indissolubly bound, the two are linked in a frightful
fellowship of evil,

> In their one spot out of the ken of God,
> Or care of man forever and evermore.

The *Ring and the Book* is the most astonishing work
of genius of our time, and if the narrations of Guido,
Caponsacchi, and Pompilia do not escape oblivion, it is
hard to say what other poetry of our day is likely to endure and win the suffrages of posterity.

Another poem which it is impossible to omit in this
category of Browning's greatest works is, *Paracelsus*. It
may well take rank with the *Ring and the Book* in nobility of design and expression; but perhaps the most
wonderful thing about it is the vision of evolution which

is found in its concluding pages,—pages, let it be noted, which were written many years before Darwin had published his *Origin of Species*. Let him who would measure accurately the immense sweep and power of Browning's genius turn to the last fifty pages of *Paracelsus*. They contain passages which cannot be read, even after many readings, without astonishment. Never has blank verse been handled with fuller mastery ; never has it been sustained at a greater height of majesty, even by Milton, the greatest of all masters in blank verse. What largeness of utterance, and what a picture of God's creative joy, and of the earth's re-birth in spring, is there in lines like these :

> In the solitary waste strange groups
> Of young volcanos come up, cyclops-like,
> Staring together with their eyes on flame —
> God tastes a pleasure in their uncouth pride.
> Then all is still ; earth is a wintry clod :
> But spring-wind, like a dancing psaltress, passes
> Over its breast to waken it : rare verdure
> Buds tenderly upon rough banks.
>   The lark
> Soars up and up, shivering for very joy ;
> Afar the ocean sleeps ; white fishing-gulls
> Flit where the strand is purple with its tribe
> Of nested limpets ; savage creatures seek
> Their loves in wood and plain, and God renews
> His ancient rapture.

And then follows that vision of the true evolution, which it is a shame to quote piecemeal, but of which some sentences at least must be quoted here :

>   Thus God dwells in all,
> From life's minute beginnings, up at last
> To man, the consummation of this scheme
> Of being, the completion of this sphere

Of life, whose attributes had here and there
Been scattered o'er the visible world before,
Asking to be combined, dim fragments meant
To be united in some wondrous whole,
Imperfect qualities throughout creation
Suggesting some one creature yet to make,
Some point where all these scattered rays shall meet
Convergent in the faculties of man.
                                        Progress is
The law of life : man is not man as yet,
Nor shall I deem his general object served
While only here and there a towering mind
O'erlooks his prostrate fellows : when the host
Is out at once to the despair of night ;
When all mankind alike is perfected,
Equal in full-blown powers—then, not till then,
I say begins man's general infancy.

And it is more than evolution in the limited scientific
sense which meets us here.   The youth whose earliest
confession is that God has always been his lode-star can
conceive of no evolution which does not both begin and
end in God :

In completed man begins anew
A tendency to God.   Prognostics told
Man's near approach ; so in man's self arise
August anticipations, symbols, types
Of a dim splendour ever on before
In that eternal circle life pursues.

Paracelsus is a great poem, one of the greatest in English
literature ; and when we read it we cannot wonder that
one of the first organs of literary opinion in England
does not hesitate to set Browning close beside Shakespeare.   Browning has written as grandly in other poems,
but nowhere has he so fully expressed the scientific spirit
of the time, or written with completer power of thought
and utterance.

In sustained splendour of thought and imagery, but
upon a lesser scale, *Saul* is also one of the poems which
men will not readily let die ; and one might class with
Saul such wonderful studies as *A Death in the Desert* and
the *Epistle of Karshish*.   In *Saul* Browning has attained
the rare achievement of perfect form and harmony.   There
is a magnificent music in the billowy cadences of *Saul ;* it
seems to rise and fall not so much to the harp of David as
to the melodious thunder and trumpet-calls of some great
organ which floods the universe with invisible delight.
But such poems as these owe their true greatness to the
thought which informs them.   There is no writer of our
day, whether of prose or poetry, who will so well repay
the attention of the theological student as Browning.   He
has so vivid a vision of invisible things, so intense a grasp
on spiritual facts, that he pierces into the heart of religious mystery as no other man of our time has done, and
it is impossible to rise from a course of Browning without a sense of added or invigourated faith.   The literature
of Christian evidence has received, in our time, no more
important contributions than *Easter Day* and *Christmas*,
the *Death in the Desert* and the *Epistle of Karshish.*
The method is Browning's own, but it is used with consummate skill and effect ; it is a sword which no other
man can wield save the craftsman who forged it, but in
his hand it pierces to the dividing asunder of the bone
and marrow of current scepticism.   As poet and thinker
Browning secures a double advantage, and annexes realms
to his dominion which are not often brought under the
sway of a common sceptre.   The fashion of the world
may change, and the old doubts may wear themselves
out and sink like shadows out of sight in the morning of
a stronger faith ; but even so the world will still turn to the

finer poems of Browning for intellectual stimulus, for the purification of pity and of pathos, for the exaltation of hope, and will revere him who in the night of the world's doubt, still sang :

> This world's no blot for us,
> Nor blank,—it means intensely and means good,
> To find its meaning is my meat and drink.

Or, if the darkness still thickens, all the more will men turn to this strong man of the race, who has wrestled and prevailed ; who has illumined with imaginative insight the deepest problems of the ages ; who has made his poetry not merely the vehicle of pathos, passion, tenderness, fancy, and imagination, but also of the most robust and masculine thought.   He has written lyrics which must charm all who love, epics which must move all who act, songs which must cheer all who suffer, poems which must fascinate all who think ; and when " Time hath sundered shell from pearl," however stern may be the scrutiny, it may be safely said that there will remain enough of Robert Browning to give him rank among the greatest of poets, and secure for him the sure reward of fame.

So I close what I have to say of Browning.   It would be unseemly to detail what has been sufficiently evident to the reader—the deep indebtedness which I personally feel to Browning for the illumination and delight he has afforded me.   But the object of these studies would not be achieved if I did not express the hope that some, to whom Browning is a name and a shadow only, may be led to turn from these imperfect criticisms to the study of the man himself.   To Browning's work I may apply, without conscious impertinence, the noble words spoken of the Apollo Belvidere :   " Go and study it ; and if you see nothing to captivate you, go again; go until you find it, for be assured it is there."

Less fortunate than Tennyson in his life, so far as the recognition of his genius and the awards of fame are concerned, Browning was equally fortunate in his death. He retained to the last his genial faith, his resolute optimism, his intellectual vigour and subtlety. The last poem of his last volume is a sort of summing up of himself and his life-work: nor could a more discerning summary be found than in the words,

> One who never turned his back, but marched breast forward,
>   Never doubted clouds would break,
> Never dreamed, though right were worsted, wrong would
>   triumph,
>   Held we fall to rise, are baffled to fight better.
>   Sleep to wake.

Upon the announcement of his death the press was flooded with reminiscences from many who had known him slightly and more who had known him well, but all alike testifying to his simplicity, veracity, and kindliness of nature, and not less to the vigour of his mind and the breadth of his human and religious sympathies. "Never say of me that I am dead" was one of his last recorded observations to a friend, and it was eminently characteristic of the man and his philosophy. He died with the knowledge that his last book was a triumphant success; and his nation by common acclamation rewarded his life-work with the highest honour it can accord to its illustrious dead,—a grave in that great Abbey which is the Campo Santo of English genius. The greatest men of his generation by their presence and by their pens eagerly paid their tribute of honour to his genius, and it is still more touching to record that as his coffin was carried through the streets of London many of his more obscure disciples lined the streets, and cast upon it flowers and leaves of laurel. He was buried on the last day of the year 1889, and, to apply the words which Ruskin has written on the death of Turner, we may say that perhaps in the far future the year 1889 will " be remembered less for what it has displayed than for what it has withdrawn " in Robert Browning.

XXXI

MATTHEW ARNOLD

Born in Laleham, December 24, 1822. The Strayed Reveller, his first poem, published in 1848. Elected Professor of Poetry at Oxford, 1857. A collected edition of his poems, in three volumes, published in 1885. Died in Liverpool, April 15, 1888.

FEW men of letters in our time have filled a larger place in public attention than Matthew Arnold. During the greater portion of his life he was in the thick of perpetual controversy. He seemed to live and move in the arena of contention, and delighted in its keen and eager atmosphere. No controversialist had a happier knack of phrase, a sharper wit, a surer thrust than he. It was he who first used the word " Philistine " as a term of reproach, a symbol of all that was insular in politics, vulgar in manners, and ignorant in art. To Dean Swift's phrase " sweetness and light " he gave a new meaning and a new lease of life. He had a felicitous art of picking out some expressive word and charging it with wider meanings, thus making it the rallying-cry of his controversial disquisitions. It was in this way that the words " lucidity " and " distinction " became symbols of a literary doctrine, which he elaborated with unwearied self-satisfaction. No one less feared to repeat himself than Arnold. When he had hit upon a really good phrase he used it again and again, and it was the reiteration of the phrase as much as its aptness which did much to fix it in the public memory. With Matthew Arnold

333

as the essayist most thinking people have an adequate acquaintance; but, after all, it was neither in literary nor controversial essays that his true excellence lay.   What a few regarded as certain before his death has been generally admitted since, viz., that all the best qualities of Arnold's genius are manifested in his comparatively unknown poetry; and that it is by his poetry, rather than his prose, that he will claim attention from the next generation.

We may even go further than this, and express a regret that Matthew Arnold was ever drawn into the conflicts of controversy at all.   That he was a delightful controversialist we all admit.   The very sufficiency of his egoism is amusing.   He took a sort of perverse delight in intellectual isolation, and lectured his antagonists with the serene positiveness of one who was perfectly convinced that he knew everything better than anybody else knew anything.   He is never so happily ironical, so wittily satiric, so complacently sarcastic, as when he is engaged in proving the general obtuseness of the public, and the bright particular luminousness of his own ideas.

There is indeed a touch of literary dandyism in all Arnold's prose.   He always figures, as some one has well said, as "a superior person" talking down to the intellectual incapacities of his inferiors.   He is a master of ironical reasoning, and loves nothing so well as to put his antagonist in the witness-box, and convict him out of his own mouth.   He never uses the literary bludgeon: he delights rather in the sharp rapier-thrust, the swift retort, the quiet ironical smile which is so much harder to bear than the loud, derisive laughter of a Johnson or Carlyle.   And so far as distinction of style can preserve what is, after all, fugitive literary work, Arnold's controversial writings are safe.   He has originality, grace, sweetness : a style of the utmost lucidity and of frequent force. The paragraphs seems to move with such graceful ease that we begin to fancy it takes small art to produce them, until suddenly we perceive the master in some felicitous or stinging phrase, in the stroke of wit, or the quiet ripple of ironical humour. The very audacity with which Arnold quotes himself is a part of his style. He has a definite system of opinions, a scale of assured axioms, and he returns to them again and again as to the fundamentals of his faith. When he has polished to the last degree of artistic finish a definition or a phrase, it is no part of his purpose to leave it in modest retirement till the discernment of his reader dis- covers it. He has so little faith in the discernment of the public that he emphatically points out what a perfect phrase he has invented, and, lest it should be forgotten, makes it the pivot on which paragraph after paragraph revolves. These and many other characteristics of his prose make it delightful reading, and redeem the most barren themes of theological controversy with a casual grace. But not the less Arnold was out of his true sphere in theological debate. The urbanity, the cool- ness, the patience of the accomplished critic of literature forsake him when he enters the arena of theological controversy. He becomes as discourteous and unrea- sonable as the worst type of the narrowest bigot usually succeeds in being when he argues for some immeasura- bly insignificant detail of dogma. That the influence of Arnold on theology has been considerable must be granted, and his theological essays have secured him an attention which otherwise he would not have gained. But it is not, after all, as a theologian that he will be re- membered, nor is it as an apostle of ideas, nor is it as a critic of literature. More or less these are each fugitive forms of literature. But he who sums up something of the spirit of an age in poetry has chosen the most im-perishable mould for his thoughts which literature affords : and it is in his poetry that Arnold best ex-presses his own genius, and has rendered his highest service to the ages.

I have spoken of Arnold as an apostle of ideas, by which I mean that he sowed the minds of men with thoughts which have had a wide influence on the times. In the same way, we may say of his poetry that it is the poetry of ideas. He is a poet of the intellect, and his force as a poet is purely intellectual. He has no passion, no kindling flame of fervour, no heart-force ; he speaks from the mind to the mind, and the grace and beauty of his poetry are mainly the result of intellectual art. The graces of his style do not consist in those sudden in-tensities of sentiment or emotion which clothe themselves in flashing and unforgettable phrases ; they are the fine result of laborious art. He never surprises us ; but he powerfully attracts us, notwithstanding, with the gracious symmetry and completeness of his work. His gift of lucidity controls his poetry as it does his prose, and the same observation may be made of his gift of restraint. He never loses himself in the turbulence of his own passion ; he is grave, sad, deeply moved and deeply moving, but always restrained. He is never obscure ; he says what he has to say with admirable definiteness and precision of phrase. Indeed, the definiteness is too great : it affects one at times like a fault. It leaves no room for the play of imagination ; it requires no sym-pathy of understanding from the reader.

There is a poetry which affects us like the spectacle of

a great Gothic cathedral.   We never really see a perfect
specimen of the Gothic; we never fully exhaust it; we
never grasp its whole meaning and significance.   It gives
us room for infinite thought; it calls forth the interpreting powers of our own imagination, and makes them
vigilant.   We gaze untired into the dimness of the lofty
roof, where a hundred delicate branching lines of grace
seem to interlace and meet; we mark " the height, the
space, the gloom, the glory " ; a burst of sunlight kindles
" the giant windows' blazon'd fires " ; a passing cloud
darkens the vaulted aisles with awe-inspiring shadows ;
and in the delicate traceries of its stonework, the fantastic
carvings, the touches of inspired art which everywhere
reveal themselves to the studious eye, not less than in
the grandeur of it as a whole, we find food for continual
delight, and revelations of inexhaustible significance.
But there is no such mingling of mystery and beauty in
the poetry of Arnold.   It is rather like looking at some
piece of perfect statuary—cool, proud, pure; the lines
are gracious and symmetrical indeed, but very definite,
and requiring no help from the casual spectator to
interpret what is beautiful in them.   It may be that the
Gothic delights in a barbaric splendour: but it *is* splendour, it is the fruit of a fertile and fervent imagination, and
irresistibly appeals to the imagination.   It may be that a
Greek temple, with its long lines of polished columns
and exquisitely modelled friezes, is also beautiful : but it
does not refresh the eye or stimulate the mind, as does
the Gothic.   The Gothic is the work of men who
dreamed, the Grecian of men who thought.   Matthew
Arnold never dreamed.   He lived a strenuous intellectual
life, and his poetry is the outcome of his thinking.   In
its own way it is perfect, but it is not with the perfection

which most delights men.   For in poetry as in art it is
the dreamers who fascinate men, who hold them spell-
bound with the vision of beauty, and whose spell never
fails, whose charm never wearies, whose power of
stimulating the fancy and refreshing the heart is broken
by no change of time or transience of human taste.

From a literary point of view one of the most remarkable things about Arnold's poetry is its classicism.   The
rise of romanticism which so powerfully affected Tennyson, and which found its fullest expression in Rossetti,
Swinburne, and Morris, did not so much as touch Arnold.
He trifles once with the Arthurian Legends in *Tristram
and Iseult*, but unsuccessfully.   He had not the emotional abandonment nor the warmth of imagination of
the romanticist.   He approached in many ways nearer to
the spirit of Wordsworth than any other recent poet.
He has something of the same gravity and philosophic
calm, though he is far enough removed from Wordsworth's religious serenity.   In the last lines of the *Buried
Life* he recalls the very phrases of Wordsworth :

> And there arrives a lull in the hot race
> Wherein he does forever chase
> The flying and elusive shadow, rest.
> An air of coolness plays upon his face,
> And an unwonted calm pervades his breast.
> And then he thinks he knows
> The hills whence his life rose,
> And the sea where it goes.

But in his general disapproval of modern life and opinion, he was forced in literary ideals much further back
than Wordsworth.   He drew his real inspiration from
the great masters of antiquity.

In the preface to his poems published in 1854 he tells

us : " In the sincere endeavour to learn and practice, amid the bewildering confusion of our times, what is sound and true in poetical art, I seemed to myself to find the only sure guidance, the only solid footing, among the ancients. They, at any rate, knew what they wanted in art, and we do not." We can perfectly understand how a man of Arnold's temperament and culture should find his only sure footing among the ancients. The very lucidity and gravity of his mind inclined him, if early education and culture had not, to intense sympathy with the great classical authors. And the result, so far as the history of modern poetry is concerned, is remarkable. In the full stream of romanticism Arnold stands immovable, turning his face away from modern methods of expression and vagaries of style, to those alone who, according to him, knew what they wanted in art and found it. He too knew what he wanted in art and found it. He wanted verse as the best vehicle for his best thoughts. He had no profound deeps of emotion to be broken up, or, if he had, his natural reticence was too great to permit the outflow to find its way into poetry. He had no violent passions to which the winged words of poetry were an ecstatic relief. He had not the lyrical faculty :— that gift of melody which enchants us by its mere musical sweetness and beauty. But he had a message to utter, and he knew how to utter it with a certain sustained and stately music of phrase which was impressive. The spirit of the antique penetrates and elevates all his best poetry. In his *Thyrsis* he has produced one of the noblest of elegies since the *Lycidas* of Milton. In his *Empedocles on Etna* he has written a fine poem, full of classic gravity and beauty. In his purely didactic work, such as the memorable poems on *Obermann*, he

has succeeded in expressing the most modern of thoughts
and philosophic emotions, with the same classic lucidity
and charm.   It is only when he touches the questions of
the heart that he fails.   There he is weak, because he
has not the emotional abandonment requisite for the
finest lyrical work, and because in fact his natural gift of
melody was slight, and what melodiousness of expression
he possessed was rather the laborious result of culture
than of nature.

The perfect culture of Arnold reveals itself everywhere
in the delicate and finished workmanship of his verse.
Whatever lack of spontaneity and emotion we may ac-
cuse him of, we can find no fault with the form of his
work.   A born critic of others, he has exercised a severe
vigilance over himself, and the result is an admirable
terseness of phrase and distinctness of expression.
There are no metrical lapses, no slurred and slovenly passages, in his poems; he consistently does his best, and is
content with nothing less than the best.   He emphatically knows what he wants in art, and finds it.   He is
conscious of his own limitations, and is careful not to
exceed them.   He has the clearest possible conception of
his own powers, and he cultivates them with an unsparing
studiousness.   His verse reminds us of some lofty upland
farm, shut in by the purity of snowy heights, where the
soil yields a rich reward, but only at the price of infinite
industry.   It is the art and daring of man which have
made the soil rich ; its natural tendency is towards ster-
ility.   It is cultivated to the last degree, because without
watchfulness no crop were possible.   All is green and
beautiful ; but it is not the rank fullness of Nature, it is
the precious gain of art.   In the same way Arnold's
verse impresses not with artificiality—that would be a

wrong impression—but with a sense of admiration for his art. He cannot be lavish, because he is not wealthy. Nature has imposed upon him the need of frugality, and he shows us how culture can enlarge the comparative narrowness of endowment into noble fruitfulness. And the atmosphere of his verse, like the air that passes over a mountain farm, is clear and cold, and almost chilly. It is unlikely and indeed impossible that the mass of men should care to live in it. At the mountain's foot the thick vines cluster, and the warm sunlight ripples on the lake, and it is there most men prefer to dwell. They love poetry full of fragrant heat, in which the nightingale can sing. Arnold is too cold, too severe, for those whose emotions are quick and sensitive, for the young, the tender-hearted, the unwearied, whose days are filled with careless happiness. But not the less it does men good to climb sometimes, and sojourn in a keener air. The mountain wind also has its fragrance, and it can both cool and invigourate. So far as the art of poetry goes, Arnold's is a cooling and invigourating presence. He recalls us to simplicity, to the love of perfection for perfection's sake, to the love of wisdom instead of the love of beauty : and his poetry has a classic gravity of touch at all times, united to a classic art of workmanship.

Yet it must not be supposed that Arnold has no melody of his own, no natural freshness and distinction. On the contrary, there is a frequent breadth of tone in his poetry, such as few of our later poets have reached. It would be possible to mention many fine narrative poems before we came to one half so fine as Arnold's *Sohrab and Rustum*. It is one of the few poems which have the stamp of perfection on them. It may not be popular, it may never be popular ; but those who read it once will care to have it by them, and will find its solemn heroic tones deepening on the ear at each fresh reading. As a specimen of modern blank verse it is in itself remarkable. It has not, indeed, the melodiousness of Tennyson's, but it possesses a stately music of its own, and has a breadth of touch which Tennyson has scarcely excelled. It might be too much to say that it is the finest blank verse of modern times; but it is certainly among the finest, and recalls to us the severe grace of Landor in its air of impressive stateliness and the purity of its diction. In the concluding passage Arnold is more moved than is his wont, and exhibits a power of expression which many greater poets might covet.

> But the majestic river floated on,
> Out of the mist and hum of that low land,
> Into the frosty starlight, and there moved,
> Rejoicing, through the hushed Chorasmean waste
> Under the solitary moon: he flowed
> Right for the Polar star, past Orgunjé,
> Brimming and bright and large. Then sands begin
> To hem his watery march, and dam his streams,
> And split his currents; that for many a league
> The shorn and parcelled Oxus strains along
> Through beds of sand and matted rushy isles,—
> Oxus, forgetting the bright speed he had
> In his high mountain cradle in Pamere,
> A foiled circuitous wanderer: till at last
> The longed-for dash of waves is heard, and wide
> His luminous home of waters opens, bright
> And tranquil, from whose floor the new-bathed stars
> Emerge, and shine upon the Aral sea.

There is, indeed, no magical and haunting resonance in these lines; but they are an admirable illustration of the two qualities in which Arnold most excelled, the qualities of simplicity and severity.

In another direction, also, Arnold has achieved the highest kind of success. As one re-reads his poetry, with a more cultivated appreciation of its charm, the feeling grows that no one since Wordsworth has sur- passed Arnold in a peculiar power of both depicting and interpreting Nature. Two verses from *Thyrsis* may serve to illustrate this power, and will do so better than many pages of analysis and disquisition.

So, some tempestuous morn in early June,
 When the year's primal burst of bloom is o'er,
  Before the roses and the longest day —
When garden-walks, and all the grassy floor,
 With blossoms red and white of fallen may,
  And chestnut flowers are strewn —
So have I heard the cuckoo's parting cry,
 From the wet field, through the vext garden-trees,
 Come with the volleying rain and tossing breeze :
The bloom is gone, and with the bloom go I !

Too quick, despairer, wherefore wilt thou go ?
 Soon will the high midsummer pomps come on,
  Soon will the musk carnations break and swell,
Soon shall we have gold-dusted snap-dragon,
 Sweet-William, with his homely cottage-smell,
  And stocks in fragrant glow ;
Roses that down the alley shine afar,
 And open, jasmine-muffled lattices,
 And groups under the dreamy garden-trees,
And the full moon, and the white evening-star.

It would be difficult to surpass verses like these either for truth, simplicity, or voluptuous magic. Interesting and impressive as Arnold's ethical poems are, yet they by no means represent him fairly. Perhaps these will in time follow the fate of his doubtful experiments in theol- ogy, and melt out of memory ; but it is hardly possible that a poem like *Thyrsis* can ever be forgotten.   There can be no hesitation in naming him with Tennyson as among the greatest poets of English pastoral life.

Yet, after all, the best known work of Arnold, and in most respects the most memorable, is that section of his poetry which expresses the weariness and religious dis-quiet of the times.   It is here the deepest breathings of his heart are heard.   He is a spirit loosed upon the sun-less seas of doubt, and ever wearily scanning the gray horizon for a desired but undiscovered haven.   He is full of an incommunicable grief, and in the effort to express what he suffers, he reaches an intensity of utterance which we find nowhere else in his poetry.   The most characteristic poems Arnold ever wrote are the *Stanzas from the Grande Chartreuse*, and the *Obermann* poems. In each of these there occur striking lines which have passed into current quotations, as felicitous expressions of human thought and sentiment.   He accurately describes his own religious position when he pictures the Greek

> Wandering between two worlds, one dead,
> The other powerless to be born,

and his own unsatisfied desire, mingled with a charac-teristic touch of critical pessimism, when he says:

> Here leave us to die out with these
> Last of the people who believe!
> Silent, while years engrave the brow,
> Silent—the best are silent now.

Equally felicitous are such phrases as these:

> But we, brought forth and reared in hours
> Of change, alarm, surprise —
> What shelter to grow ripe is ours?
> What leisure to grow wise?

Too fast we live, too much are tried,
Too harassed, to attain
Wordsworth's sweet calm, or Goethe's wide
And luminous view to gain.

It would be easy to quote widely from this section of
Arnold's poetry, because in interest and expression it is
the most characteristic of all his work. It is indeed a
painful interest. He cannot conceal from us that there is
no peace in culture. A pervading sadness and despair
are its most memorable features. There breathe throughout the sadness of failure, the distress of faithlessness.
Occasionally it is a deeper note than regret which is
struck: it is the iron chord of a militant, yet despairing
pessimism, which vibrates in such satiric verses as these:

Creep into thy narrow bed,
Creep, and let no more be said!
Vain thy onset! all stands fast,
Thou thyself must break at last.

Let the long contention cease!
Geese are swans, and swans are geese.
Let them have it how they will!
Thou art tired : best be still.

But this belongs rather to the domain of religious truth
than of literary criticism. It is enough for us to note
lastly, concerning Matthew Arnold, that in power to interpret the spirit of his age, in intellectual candour, and
in the prevailing sadness of all his poetry which deals
with modern life and thought, he is the most representa-
tive man of the culture of the latter half of the nineteenth
century. A profound melancholy borne with pathetic
stoicism is the spirit of all his latter-day poetry. It is
the poetry of a man who has lost faith, but who passion-

ately wishes that he could believe. It is a long wail after the golden age when the Cross was in its first triumph :

> Oh ! had I lived in that great day,
>   How had its glory new
> Filled earth and heaven, and caught **away**
>   My ravished spirit too.

More than any other poet of our time, save Browning, Matthew Arnold is imbued with the religious spirit: but less than any other who has felt the force of religious truth, has he gained the secret of serenity, the mind that knows the calm of certitude, the heart that rests in the tranquillity of faith.

XXXII

DANTE GABRIEL ROSSETTI

Born in London, May 12, 1828. First volume of Poems appeared 1870, and second volume, 1880. Died at Birchington, April 9, 1882.

WITH Tennyson and Browning in the long line of great modern poets there are other names which cannot escape mention, and foremost is Dante Gabriel Rossetti. In point of quantity Rossetti has added comparatively little to the store of modern poetry; his chief praise is that what he has given us is distinguished by high and sustained artistic quality. It may also be said that his influence on literature has been out of all proportion greater than his achievement. Years before he had himself published a single volume, William Morris had dedicated a book to him, and both Morris and Swinburne were accustomed to regard him as their master. With Rossetti also the artist was inalienably associated with the poet. More than any other modern he has brought the art of painting and poetry—both arts of expression—into harmony. His poems were often suggested by his pictures; his pictures were an expression of the same ideas which dominated his poetry. Both as artist and poet his position is unique, and it is a matter of somewhat complex criticism to discern rightly the true bearings of his work, and the exact degree of his influence.

The environment of Rossetti's life explains to some

extent this position. He was born in an artistic atmosphere. The whole Rossetti family were singularly gifted,
and probably no house in England possessed such an atmosphere of artistic culture as that in which Rossetti was
reared. For every power of imagination or fancy which
Rossetti possessed there was the genial sunshine of a fos-
tering sympathy. Not unnaturally the dream of the
young Rossetti was to be an artist, and it was as an artist
he began his life. But he was very soon to develop
original ideas and methods in art. He observed that two
things seemed to have utterly departed from English art,
viz., the temper of religious wonder, and the power of
perfect fidelity and reverence in following nature. In the
earlier painters both these great qualities were supreme.
Rossetti determined to reproduce them. His ideas found
good soil in the enthusiasm of Millais and Holman Hunt,
each of whom at this time was on the threshold of his
artistic career. The first outcome of this enthusiasm was
the formation of what was known as the Pre-Raphaelite
Brotherhood, and the picture of each artist bore the
magic letters P.R.B. The object of this brotherhood
cannot be better stated than in the words which Rossetti
used in starting the *Germ*, which was a small magazine
devoted to the exposition of the new creed: " The endeavour held in view throughout the writings on art," he
said, " will be to encourage and enforce an entire adherence to the simplicity of Nature."

Himself an Italian, with the southern sensuousness of
temperament, intensity of passion, and love of art, when
Rossetti began to write poetry these qualities of nature at
once manifested themselves. To the colder English taste
there is a warmth in the poetry of Rossetti which is not
always pleasant, and which to the fastidious might even

be offensive. English poetry presents no more curious study than Rossetti's treatment of woman. He approaches her with consistent chivalry, with an almost religious reverence, and yet with a frank and sensuous admiration of her mere physical charms which would have been impossible to a correcter taste and more masculine mind. It is difficult to express the exact feeling that this peculiar tendency of Rossetti's poetry excites in us. The older poets, Shakespeare preëminently, did not scruple to touch the same difficult theme with breadth and daring. But what we always mark in Shakespeare is that peculiar justness of vision which perceives all things in their natural apportionments and adjustments ; that divine innocence which can gaze without shame on things which, to a prurient mind, would suggest nothing but impulses of impurity. Had Rossetti's been a more masculine mind, he would have been saved from certain errors of taste which unquestionably disfigure his poetry. Just as the healthy appetite rejects luscious and over-ripe fruit, and prefers a sharper flavour, so the healthy mind is soon surfeited with the over-ripe descriptions of female charms in which Rossetti's sonnets abound. We turn away when Rossetti lifts the nuptial curtain ; we grow tired of " emulous ardours," " abandoned hair," and " flagging pulses." We feel that it is bad art, if nothing else ; for true art is accurate art, which does not exaggerate details at the expense of general truth, and this perpetual recurrence of the mind to one theme, and that a morally enervating theme, is an evidence of a lack of intellectual poise, of an effeminating defect of character ; and it is in this moral effeminacy that Rossetti's great defect lies. One cannot speak of one who treats woman with chivalrous and almost pious reverence as immoral ; but it must be admitted that Rossetti permits himself a license of expression which a more robust nature would have rejected. His world is dominated by the " eternal feminine." He sings of woman, not of man ; the praise of beauty, not the praise of courage. His sweetness is a cloying sweetness. When we enter the world of his poetry, it is like entering that sleeping-room of Rossetti's which Mr. Hall Caine so strikingly describes : a funereal apartment, full of black oak furniture carved in quaint designs, of velvets and faded tapestries, of antique lamps that shed a drowsy light upon the heavy air, a room of charms and mysteries, remote and hidden from the busy life of men. At first we are irresistibly fascinated. We breathe a perfumed air, and hear the sweetest music ; but presently we begin to long for the open heavens, the fresh wind, the " multitudinous laughter of the sea," the reassuring tramp of human feet. Beautiful as Rossetti's poetry is, we feel that it is something of an exotic, and that in its super-sensuousness there is something enervating to the vigour of the taste and the fibre of the moral nature.

This defect of Rossetti's poetry is probably due to the fact that his life was to a large degree a morbid one. The great romance and tragedy of his history lay in his love and marriage. He was first attracted to his future wife by her remarkable beauty ; it was a beauty of a very unusual type, full of stately purity and dignity, and yet characterized also by a sort of gracious sensuousness. After a long engagement they were married, and twelve months later she died. From that hour the glory and vivacity of life were gone for Rossetti ; he became practically a recluse, a brooding and uncomforted man, whose days were passed in the shadow of the dead. How fully his wife's beauty filled his mind is seen in the long array

of his pictures. It was her face which dominated the
thirty years of his artistic toil. The features of his dead
wife look out of every female face he painted; she is
the Francesca and the dead Beatrice, the lady of love and
the lady of sorrow. Into her coffin he thrust his poems
in token of his passionate abandonment of earthly ambitions, and there for a considerable period they remained.
Later on there came the terrible shadow of insomnia, and
with it the confirmed habit of chloral-taking. It seemed
as though Rossetti had become the living embodiment
of the unhappy hero of Poe's poem of the *Raven*. The
rooms he inhabited were rich with the curious collections
of an artistic taste; the lamplight streamed upon the
" tufted floor," but " just above the bust of Pallas, just
above the chamber-door," was seated the bird of evil
omen, recalling vainly in his mournful cry the perished
splendours of the past. Sensuous in all things, Rossetti
was sensuous in his grief, and cultivated sorrow as other
men cultivate happiness. The shadow that had fallen on
his soul was " lifted never more." Can we be surprised
that there is a lack of healthy vitality in his poems?
Melody and imagination there always is; a charm that is
at once weird and powerful; a heart-piercing sadness, a
gloomy force, a memorable pregnancy of phrase; but
there is not the robust spontaneity of a healthy mind.
We are always conscious of a feverish intensity and
strain. The gloom of sorrow is overpowering, and even
when the theme is not in itself sorrowful, there is something in the tone of the poet's voice that lets us know
that he suffers. In other words, Rossetti's poetry has a
morbid taint in it which is deep-rooted and pervasive,
and, for this reason more than any other, it has failed to
lay hold of the popular taste in any marked degree.

Turning from the easily discernible defects of Rossetti, we are first struck with his great power as a melodist. He brings the laborious patience of the true artist to his work, and is satisfied with nothing less than the best which his genius can achieve. He is frugal of words; he passes them through the fieriest assay of criticism that he may gain the pure gold of a perfect phrase, and extract the utmost expression of which language is capable. There is no slovenly work in Rossetti. Indeed, his very laboriousness almost impresses us like a fault at times. In his aim at pregnancy he becomes obscure; in his love of melody he becomes mannered. His mannerism lies largely in his use of mediæval forms of speech, and in his peculiar scheme of rhythm. He adopts " novel inversions and accentual endings," and the effect upon the reader is often a somewhat painful sense of artificiality. But when we have made full allowance for the mannerism of Rossetti, the most hostile critic is bound to admit the artistic excellence of his work. It is this point that Mr. Stedman fixes on, when he says that " throughout his poetry we discern a finesse, a regard for detail, and a knowledge of colour and sound. His end is gained by simplicity and sure precision of touch. He knows exactly what effect he desires, and produces it by a firm stroke of colour, a beam of light, a single musical tone. Herein he surpasses his comrades, and exhibits great tact in preferring only the best of a dozen graces which either of them would introduce. In terseness he certainly is before them all." It will be observed that Mr. Stedman, in his criticism, cannot help remembering that Rossetti was an artist as well as a poet. Upon the whole it is a true instinct which declines to discuss Rossetti's poetry altogether apart from his paintings. The " beam of light," and the "single musical tone"; the laborious ingenuity which characterizes both his pictures and his poems, sprang from the common source of an intensely artistic nature.   In art, his carefulness of detail made him a Pre-Raphaelite, in poetry an original and mannered melodist.

But the great merit of Rossetti is in the fact, that he struck afresh in English poetry the note of the romantic and supernatural.   He reproduced the temper of religious wonder which filled the mediæval poets.   His *Blessed Damozel*, is one of those few poems which surprise and delight us at first reading, and never afterwards lose their charm.   It is a poem absolutely original in style, senti-ment, and rhythm, something that stands alone in litera-ture.   The imagery is new, peculiar, impressive; the whole poem a unique combination of daring and rever-ence, of sensuous warmth and spiritual remoteness.

Two verses stand out with a peculiar vividness and beauty of imagery : the description of God's house —

> It lies in Heaven, across the flood
> Of ether, like a bridge.
> Beneath the tides of day and night
> With flame and darkness ridge
> The void, as low as where this earth
> Spins like a fretful midge :

and the description of the ended day —

> The sun was gone now ; the curled moon
> Was like a little feather,
> Fluttering far down the gulf ; and now
> She spoke through the still weather —
> Her voice was like the voice the stars
> Had when they sang together.

All the qualities of Rossetti's poetry are in this one won-derful poem, which he wrote at eighteen.   He speaks alternately like a seer and an artist; one who is now bewitched with the vision of beauty, and now is caught up into Paradise, where he hears unutterable things. To him the spiritual world is an intense reality. He hears the voices, he sees the presences of the supernatural. As he mourns beside the river of his sorrow, like Ezekiel, he has his visions of winged and wheeling glories, and leaning over the ramparts of the world his gaze is fixed on the uncovered mysteries of a world to come. There is no poet to whom the supernatural has been so much alive. Religious doubt he seems never to have felt. But the temper of religious wonder, the old, childlike, monkish attitude of awe and faith in the presence of the unseen, is never absent in him. The artistic force of his temperament drives him to the worship of beauty; the poetic and religious forces to the adoration of mystery.

In his reproductions of the mediæval ballad, Rossetti's success varies. In common with Swinburne he was powerfully attracted by the *bizarre* genius of Villon, and the best translations we have of Villon's curious ballads are his. No one has reproduced so accurately the temper and spirit of the old ballad as Rossetti: where he most frequently fails is in the introduction of complexities of thought and fancy when the very key to excellence should be absolute simplicity. Perhaps he aimed less at the reproduction of form than of temper. His *Rose Mary*, for instance, is a marvellous reproduction of the mediæval spirit; but in its elaborateness of structure, its subtlety of suggestion, and its ingenuity of fancy, is as far as possible removed from the directness of the old balladists. On the other hand, in the brief and pathetic poem of *John of Tours*, we have the form as well as the temper of the old ballad perfectly rendered. With what flashing simplicity the ballad opens :

John of Tours is back with peace,
But he comes home ill at ease.

"Good morrow, mother." "Good morrow, son ;
Your wife has borne you a little one."

" Go now, mother, go before,
Make me a bed upon the floor :

" Very low your foot must fall,
That my wife hear not at all."

As it neared the midnight toll,
John of Tours gave up his soul.

And with what tragic directness and pathos does the poem
end :

"Tell me though, my mother dear,
What's the knocking that I hear?"

" Daughter, it's the carpenter,
Mending planks upon the stair."

" Nay, but say, my mother, my dear,
Why do you fall weeping here?"

"Oh, the truth must be said —
It's that John of Tours is dead."

" Mother, let the sexton know
That the grave must be for two ;

" Aye, and still have room to spare,
For you must shut the baby there."

In work like this we have something absolutely new in
modern poetry. The strange world of mediævalism, with
all its chivalrous ardours, its awe-struck faith, its simple
movements of human passion, its frank revelations of feeling, its glory and romance, lives again for us. It is as
though the figures on some piece of faded tapestry began

to move, and the gateways of their quaint turreted towns opened, and gave egress to the knights and ladies, the troubadours and artificers, of the days of chivalry. Tennyson was touched with the same spirit when he wrote the *Lady of Shalott*; but Tennyson's mediævalism has a modern veneer of moral adaptation—Rossetti's is the thing itself. Tennyson's is the mediævalism of museums—with Rossetti we actually move again in the times of Agincourt and Poictiers.

Perhaps the word which best describes Rossetti's poetry is the word " glamour." In common with Coleridge and Keats he possesses a curious power of exciting the imagination into intensity of vision. There is a sense of wizardry in the charm which Rossetti wields over us. He never fails, even in his simplest verses, to cast over us the spell of the supernatural. He affects us powerfully by his own intensity of vision and feeling, and lifts us completely out of the atmosphere of common life into that world of subtle sensation and imagination in which he habitually dwelt. Take, for instance, so simple a poem as *My Sister's Sleep*. Its theme is purely modern : it pictures the dying of his sister, amid the common surroundings of ordinary life. It is Christmas Eve: his mother has her little work-table with work to finish set beside her.

> Her needles, as she laid them down,
> Met lightly, and her silken gown
> Settled : no other noise than that.

But in an instant Rossetti has invested the whole scene with glamour when he writes :

> Without, there was a cold moon up,
> Of winter radiance, sheer and thin ;
> The hollow halo it was in
> Was like an icy crystal cup.

Through the small room, with subtle sound
   Of flame, by vents the fireshine drove
   And reddened.   In its dim alcove
The mirror shed a clearness round.

I had been sitting up some nights,
   And my tired mind felt weak and blank :
   Like a sharp strengthening wine it drank
The stillness and the broken lights.

Twelve struck, that sound, by dwindling years
   Heard in each hour, crept off ; and then
   The ruffled silence spread again,
Like water that a pebble stirs.

All this is exquisitely simple, and exquisitely realistic.
Yet there is a subtlety, a magic, a charm of imagination
investing it all, which rivets the attention and fascinates
the fancy.   It affects us like some pungent and pervasive
perfume.   We may analyze the verses as we will ; the essence is too volatile to be captured by any such means as
these.   And there is the same indefinable charm in all
Rossetti's poetry ; a quality original and bewitching, which
is all his own, and is like nothing else in modern poetry.
" Glamour " best describes it : something beautiful and unearthly, that lays its restraint upon us, and cannot be
shaken off.   It is a rare gift, one of the very rarest in
English poetry, but it is unquestionably the special note
of Rossetti's poetry, and the real secret of his influence.

There can be no doubt that Rossetti has exercised a
wide influence over modern poetry, and an influence that
does not seem likely to decline.   He set a new fashion,
but he did more than this : he struck a new note.   He has
had many imitators ; many have followed the fashion, but
scarcely any has struck the note.   William Morris comes
nearest in his early ballads ; then perhaps Bell Scott ;

lastly Swinburne. But neither has the same intensity of vision and terseness of diction. If Rossetti had only set a fashion of poetry, if he had invented only an æsthetic craze for mediævalism, we might doubt the permanence of his influence. All mere fashions pass away, and are forgotten. But he has done much more than this. He is an original poetic artist, who has produced original work. He has a message, an idea, a mission to communicate. He opens the closed doors of the past, and leads us into fresh fields of romance. He has furnished poets with a new set of artistic impulses and motives. And he has exercised a wide influence on the forms of poetry, in giving back to us forgotten rhythmic movements, and setting an example of the most careful literary workmanship. When we have made all possible deductions for defects of taste and diction, we have still left in Rossetti that rare combination of genius and originality which alone can constitute the true poet, and claim prolonged fame.

XXXIII

ALGERNON CHARLES SWINBURNE

Born in London, April 5, 1837. His first production, the Queen Mother and Rosamund, published in 1861; Atalanta in Calydon, 1864; Poems and Ballads (First Series), 1866; Bothwell, 1874; Poems and Ballads (Second Series), 1878; Poems and Ballads (Third Series), 1887.

THERE can be no doubt that Swinburne is a fine poet; there can be as little that he is an extremely unequal poet, who has not wholly fulfilled the promise of his youth. His earliest poems aroused intense interest and enthusiasm, and from the first his unique powers received the most ample recognition. This chorus of praise, however, did not last. It was succeeded by a fierce critical warfare, which split the literary world into two camps, and liberated the most violent passions. It was natural that the world should recognize the greatness and nobility of such a poem as *Atalanta in Calydon*. No reproduction from the antique since the *Prometheus Unbound* of Shelley, had been cast in so large a mould, had struck so full and lofty a note, had given such ample evidence of power and skill. As an embodiment of the antique spirit, in some ways it was superior even to the masterpiece of Shelley. It had more of classic gravity and restraint, and it was almost equal in its superb power of musical utterance. Nothing grander than the choruses in *Atalanta* has been given us by the genius of any living poet. They have fire and stateliness, dignity and passion, tragic depth and intensity, and a certain overwhelming music of their own, which the greatest masters of poetical expression might covet. It was this completeness of musical utterance which took the world by storm, and roused something like amazement in readers who had listened to the sweet flute-notes of Tennyson, and had given up hope of any further development in the art of verbal music. Swinburne's music was like the full sweep of a great wind, or the organ-clamour of the sea. It overwhelmed and it exhilarated; it came like a resistless force, before which criticism was bowed and futile, and it conveyed also a sense of immense power and resource in the poet. He seemed to produce the most magnificent effects of diction without effort, and to be able to go on producing them without weariness or exhaustion. The poem was, indeed, the first full utterance of a poet in the first freshness and glory of his genius. On the day which followed the completion of *Chastelard*, *Atalanta* was commenced. His genius was in full flow, and it seemed to his readers of a quarter of a century ago that there was no point of achievement or crown of fame that might not well be his.

Two years after the publication of *Atalanta in Calydon* Swinburne published his *Poems and Ballads*. For the moment there was a shock of pained surprise, and then the storm of anger and disappointment broke. The *Poems and Ballads* was not really a new work; it was a collection of poems, most of which had been written at an earlier date. They represented the " storm and stress " period of the poet's development, the passionate fermenting and clearing of his genius. The themes were perilous, the spirit sensuous. The entire atmosphere of the book was morbid, if not immoral. The poet in the madness of his turbid thoughts seemed to have no respect

for the decencies of life ; he even took a violent and savage pleasure in defying them.   Sensuous passion was
treated with a frankness unknown in modern poetry, and
the reticence of natural modesty was flung to the winds.
The outcry that arose reproduced the passionate vituperation of the attacks made on Byron.   Just as Southey attacked the *Satanic School of Poetry*, so another poet, of
about equal calibre, attacked Rossetti, and by implication
Swinburne, in an anonymous article on the *Fleshly School
of Poetry*.[1]   It can serve no useful purpose to fight these
battles over again.   Foolish and regrettable things were
said on both sides.   There, however, the book stands and
its influence has been wide-spread.   The damage it in-
flicted on Swinburne's reputation has been irreparable.
Its effects are seen in the productions of a swarm of mi-
nor poets, who have seemed to imagine that the purveying
of moral poison was the highest duty of the poet, and
that the nearer a poet came to sheer indecency the truer
was his gift.   Critics also arose who made it the first
article of a sound poetic faith that for the poet Nature
had no reticencies, and that in art moral considerations
had no weight, and were of no account.   It is possible
that the wisdom of maturer life has often led Swinburne
himself to wish that he had burned some of these erotic
verses of his youth.   The very charm and music of them
constitutes a perennial peril.   They have a secret and
subtle sweetness as of forbidden fruit which begets in us
unspoken covetings.   To read them is like sitting at
some enchanted feast, where lamps glitter, and voluptuous
music trembles on the ear, where the air is heavy with
odour, and the senses gradually are overcome by potent

---

[1] *The Fleshly School of Poetry*, by "Thomas Maitland" (Robert
Buchanan), in the *Contemporary Review* for October, 1871.

charms, as the moral sense is slackened, and the resolute‐
ness of manhood is dissolved in evil languor; and it
is only when the clear dawn shines in, and the fresh
breath of Nature wakes us from our heavy sleep, that
we see it is a poisoned banquet we have shared, and we
pay the penalty of abiding disgust for the short-lived
enchantment of the hour. No mature man of pure life
can read these poems without revulsion. We may even
say more: that all moral considerations apart, these
poems are bad art. It is not true art which fixes on the
sensuous side of life alone, and forgets the thousandfold
nobler and wholesomer aspects which exist. There is
nothing so monotonous as sin. There is nothing that
sooner wearies the discerning mind than the perpetual
strumming on the one vulgar chord of fleshly affinities.
Sunk as man may be, he covets something better than
this ; and if he feed on the swine-husks he does not want
lyrics of the swine-trough. When we compare the grav‐
ity and beauty of the *Atalanta* with the morbid, turbid,
unwholesome imagination of the *Poems and Ballads*, we
can scarcely be surprised at the vehemence of the public
resentment.

It would be a mistake, however, to suppose that in the
two volumes of his *Poems and Ballads* Swinburne
touches only such themes as I have alluded to. There
are powerful evidences of other influences than those
which find utterance in the erotic lyrics of his unripe
youth. Like Rossetti, he had carefully studied the
mediæval manner, and reproduces it with great effect in
St. Dorothy and the *Masque of Queen Bersabe*. There is
also an Hebraic influence, a close observance of the vivid
utterance of the Hebrew prophets, which is reproduced
with terrible force in the poem *Aholibah*. In the second

volume of *Poems and Ballads* much that was most distasteful in the first volume disappears. True it contains many translations of Villon, whose poetry never fails to leave a bad taste in the mouth, but the general tone of the book is altogether stronger and more normal. The heavy intoxicating fragrance of evil is still there, but is subdued and is in part dissipated by fresh draughts of air that blow to us from the world of Nature. In pomp and splendour of diction, and in richness of musical harmony, both books excel. The chief characteristic of the harmony is its surprising originality. New lyrical effects, new and perfect rhymes, bewitching assonances and undertones, meet us at every turn, and once heard take possession of the memory. Music itself could scarcely produce a more exquisite sensation on the ear than lines like these :

> If love were what the rose is,
>   And I were like the leaf,
> Our lives would grow together
> In sad or singing weather ;
> Blown fields or flowerful closes,
>   Green pleasure or gray grief;
> If love were what the rose is,
>   And I were like the leaf.

It is the subtle solemn music of the verse also which arrests the ear in these lines :

> Could'st thou not watch with me one hour ?   Behold,
> Day skims the sea with flying feet of gold,
> With sudden feet that graze the gradual sea.
> Could'st thou not watch with me ?

> Lo, far in heaven the web of night undone,
> And on the sudden sea the gradual sun :
> Wave to wave answers, tree responds to tree.
> Could'st thou not watch with me ?

Or, again, in this cry to the sea :

> Save me and hide me with all thy waves,
> Find me one grave of thy thousand graves,
> Those pure cold populous graves of thine,
> Wrought without hand in a world without stain.

Or in the passage of the *Ave atque Vale*,

> For always thee, the fervid, languid glories,
> Allured of heavier suns in mightier skies ;
> Thine ears knew all the wandering watery sighs
> Where the sea sobs round Lesbian promontories,
> The barren kiss of piteous wave to wave,
> That knows not where is that Leucadian grave
> That hides too deep the supreme head of song.

There are also here and there fine images, such as,

> Behold,
> Cast forth from heaven with feet of awful gold
> And plumeless wings that make the bright air blind,
> Lightning, with thunder for a hound behind,
> Hunting through fields unfurrowed and unsown ;

but in Swinburne it is not the imagery, and still less the thought, that moves us : it is the metrical charm and sweetness. Many of the highest qualities of poetry are not his, but in metrical affluence he takes rank with the highest; and if he have any claim to prolonged remembrance as one of the makers of modern poetry, it is that in the grasp of his genius the English language becomes so supple and sensitive that no language could well excel it as a vehicle of lyrical expression.

On the other hand, it is impossible to overlook the fact that Swinburne's great gift of expression is altogether out of proportion to other gifts which are necessary to permanence in poetry. Nothing can be truer than Coventry Patmore's saying, that in reading Swinburne's poetry it is " impossible not to feel that there has been some disproportion between his power of saying things and the things he has to say." And so also in Patmore's description of Swinburne's relation to Nature. " It must be confessed that flowers, stars, waves, flames, and three or four other entities of the natural order come in so often as to suggest some narrowness of observation and vocabulary. For example, in a passage of thirteen lines we have ' flowing forefront of the year,' ' foam-flowered strand,' ' blossom-fringe,' ' flower-soft face,' and ' spray-flowers.' " The same fault occurs in all Swinburne's poetry. His effects are kaleidoscopic : the subject is changed, but the sets of words and images are always the same. To have an overwhelming flow of words is one thing ; to have a large vocabulary is another ; and very often Swinburne's torrent of speech reminds us not so much of a natural fountain whose springs are deep and abundant, as of an artificial fountain, which is always ready to shoot aloft its glittering spray, and always reabsorbs itself for some further service ; so that while the fashion of the jet may differ, the water is pretty much the same. He is too good an artist to let us hear the creaking of the force-pump, but all the same we know that it is there, and for that reason he readily lends himself to imitation. His trick of alliteration is soon caught, and his peculiarity of cadence proves itself an artifice. Men cannot go behind Shakespeare and steal the patent of his mechanism, because his poetry is not a thing of mechanism, but of Nature, and has its springs deep down in the living heart of things. The more mannered a poet is, the sooner is his method mastered, and the sooner does he weary us ; but the greatest art is always the simplest, and the noblest works of art are those which are most allied to the simplicity of Nature.

Again, it is a true criticism which discovers in Swinburne little genuine observation of Nature. He loves Nature in a fashion, but it is not the fashion of the true lover. He has not studied her with minute attention, and, consequently, he tells us little new about her. He has not lived in the solitary joy of her presence, as Wordsworth did; he has not been subdued and penetrated with her charm, as Shelley was. For while Shelley's grasp of Nature was vague, yet his adoration of her was passionately sincere, and his sincerity atoned for his lack of detailed observation. But Swinburne touches only the surface of her revelation, and loves her rather for her worth to him as artistic ware than for herself. If he had been more deep-hearted and sincere in his love he would not have dwelt with monotonous insistence on one or two aspects of her glory, nor would thirteen lines of his poetry have contained five adaptations of the same image. It is the limitation of his power, or his impatience of the drudgery of observation, which makes it possible for us to say that he is kaleidoscopic rather than various in his artistic effects.

And, finally, he is often not so much a master of words as their slave. His adjectival opulence may surprise us, but it also wearies us. There is a total lack of concentration in his speech. He rarely attains to the art of concentrating in some one flashing phrase the whole spirit or thought of a poem. It is this which makes his dramas so essentially undramatic: he obscures in a flood of gorgeous rhetoric a situation which ought to declare itself in a sentence. His surpassing gift of melody enchants us; but when it ends we are like men who have heard a Wagnerian opera, and find it difficult to recall a single air. No one is so difficult to quote, because his poetry contains so few lines which are distinguished by their concentration of phrase. He never seems to have used the pruning-knife; he flings down his opulent verses in all their original unrestrained luxuriance, and not infrequently mistakes abundance for opulence. He surfeits us, but does not satisfy us. A prolonged course of Swinburne leaves us bewildered with a sense of riches, but in reality none the richer. His poetry is like fairy-gold: we dream that we are wealthy, but our wealth perpetually eludes us. For that which makes poetry a real posession is not only the art of expression, but the gift of thought, and Swinburne never was a thinker. We always feel that he has no message, that his very vehemence is a sign of weakness, and that his seeming power of words conceals an actual feebleness of thought. There are, of course, poets who live by their exquisite power of expression alone, and who have contributed little to the intellectual impulses of the world. Keats was such a poet, but Keats had in a supreme degree that gift of concentrated phrase which Swinburne lacks. So that when we carefully consider Swinburne's claims to permanent remembrance, they are all narrowed down into the fact that he is a great metrical artist, and he must stand or fall upon that one indisputable quality. Perhaps it seems little to say; yet when we consider how difficult it is to introduce into a literature of poetry so enormous as the English any new form of expression, any metrical originality, it is not so little as it appears. That, at all events, is Swinburne's solitary claim; and it is in virtue of his metrical genius that we must rank him among those who have helped to mould and develop modern English poetry.

XXXIV

WILLIAM MORRIS

*Born at Walthamstow, Essex, 1834. The Defence of Guin-
evere, published 1858; Life and Death of Jason, 1867; The
Earthly Paradise, 1868-70. Joined the Socialistic League, 1884.
Died October 3, 1896.*

WILLIAM MORRIS is the third great name
connected with the revival of Romanticism in
modern poetry. His *Defence of Guinevere*,
published in 1858, and dedicated to Rossetti, is marked
by that same return to the mediæval spirit which so
strikingly distinguished Rossetti, and which bore partial
fruit in the early poems of Swinburne. The chief thing
to be noticed about all three poets is that their poetry disdains modern thought and purpose, and deliberately seeks
its inspiration in other times, and more ancient sources of
emotion. Rossetti alone remained absolutely true to the
mediæval spirit: his last poems had as distinctly as his
first the impress and mould of mediæval Romanticism.
Swinburne, as we have seen, did his best work under the
shadows of Greek Classicism, and has besides grown more
modern in spirit as he has grown older, handling purely
modern themes, as in his *Songs before Sunrise*, with all
his early vehemence and metrical skill. With William
Morris the fascination of present-day life is a thing of very
recent growth, and it can scarcely be said that it has done
anything to help his poetry. As a poet he has three distinct periods. First comes the period when, in common
with Rossetti, the fascination of ballad-romance was strong

upon him, and its fruit is the thirty poems contained in his earliest volume. When he next appealed to the public he had cast off the glamour of mediævalism, and had become an epic poet. This is the period of *Jason* and the *Earthly Paradise*. The last period, if such it may be called, is marked by an awakening to the actual conditions of modern life, and is signalized by a series of *Chants for Socialists*, which are remarkable rather for political passion than poetic power. It may be well for us briefly to glance at these three periods.

William Morris's first volume, the *Defence of Guinevere*, is a remarkable book. It is not only significant for its revival of mediæval feeling, but also for its artistic feeling, its sense of colour, its touches of frank yet inoffensive sensuousness, its simplicity and directness of poetic effect. As a matter of fact, the question whether Morris should devote his life to art or literature for a long time hung in the balance, and it is only natural that his poetry should be remarkable for richness of colour and objective effect. The *Defence of Guinevere* is a fragment, but its very abruptness and incompleteness are effective. Its involution of thought, its curious touches of indirect introspection, its vivid glow of colour, its half-grotesque yet powerful imagery, are essentially mediæval. Such lines as the following at once recall the very method of Rossetti, and bear in themselves the marks of their relationship to the *Blessed Damozel*:

> Listen: suppose your time were come to die,
> And you were quite alone and very weak:
> Yea, laid a-dying, while very mightily
>
> The wind was ruffling up the narrow streak
> Of river through your broad lands running well:
> Suppose a hush should come, then some one speak:

" One of those cloths is heaven, and one is hell,
Now choose one cloth forever, which they be
I will not tell you, you must somehow tell

" Of your own strength and mightiness : here, see ! "
Yea, yea, my lord, and you to ope your eyes,
At foot of your familiar bed to see

A great God's angel standing, with such dyes
Not known on earth, on his great wings, and hands,
Held out two ways, light from the inner skies

Showing him well, and making his commands
Seem to be God's commands ; moreover, too,
Holding within his hands the cloths on wands :

And one of these strange choosing-cloths was blue
Wavy and long, and one cut short and red ;
No man could tell the better of the two.

After a shivering half-hour you said
"God help! heaven's colour, the blue ; " and he said,
    " Hell."
Perhaps you then would roll upon your bed,

And cry to all good men who loved you well,
"Ah Christ! if only I had known, known, known."

It is characteristic of mediæval imagination to dwell in
the borderland of spiritual mystery, and to utter itself
with perfect unrestraint, much as a child speaks of such
things, with a fearlessness which is unconscious of wrong,
and a quaintness which gives a touch of sublimity to what
in other lips would sound simply grotesque. It is precisely this frank and fascinating quaintness which William
Morris has admirably reproduced in this remarkable
poem. His description of the angel is the description of
a mediæval artist, who notices first the celestial dyes upon
hands and wings, and the colour of the choosing-cloths,
and afterwards ponders the spiritual mystery of his pres-

ence. The chief quality in both Morris's and Rossetti's poetry is its sensitive appreciation of colour; each has carried to its furthest point the art of painting in words.

There are other poems in this slight volume which are equally remarkable with the *Defence of Guinevere*. The *Haystack in the Floods* is one of the most realistic poems in modern literature. All the troubled terror of the Middle Ages, the fierce passions and hasty vengeances, the barbaric strength and virility of love, the popular ignorance and cruelty, are brought home to us with an intense vividness in this brief poem. Every line of the poem is simple and direct, and it is by a score or so of natural touches of description that the whole scene is put before us. It is a piece of grim tragedy, painted, rather than told, with realistic fidelity and force. The landscape is as clear to us as the figures of the actors; we see the whole episode in its tragic misery and rudeness when we read the opening lines —

> Along the dripping, leafless woods
> The stirrup touching either shoe,
> She rode astride as troopers do,
> With kirtle kilted to her knee,
> To which the mud splashed wretchedly ;
> And the wet dripped from every tree
> Upon her head and heavy hair,
> And on her eyelids broad and fair ;
> The tears and rain ran down her face.

It is so Jehane rides on into the deepening shadows of fate. Her lover

> Seemed to watch the rain: yea, too,
> His lips were firm ; he tried once more
> To touch her lips ; she reached out, sore
> And vain desire so tortured them,
> The poor gray lips.

But the vision she sees through the dripping forest glades is

> The court at Paris : those six men,
> The gratings of the Chatelet ;
> The swift Seine on some rainy day
> Like this, and people standing by,
> And laughing, while my weak hands try
> To recollect how strong men swim.

One would have supposed that poetry so original and powerful as this would have been sure of recognition. The book, however, fell dead from the press. Little of it is even now known save the spirited ballad, *Riding Together*. It was not until twenty-five years later that the significance of this first volume of Morris's was realized. By that time he had reached his second period ; he had outgrown much of his early mediævalism, or rather he had " worked out for himself a distinct and individual phrase of the mediæval movement."

Eight years after his first volume William Morris published the *Life and Death of Jason*, and this was followed in 1868 by the first installment of the *Earthly Paradise*. Of the first poem it is enough to say that it is a noble epic, full of sustained narrative power, but too long, and occasionally too deficient in interest, to obtain the highest honours of the epic. It marks, however, his emancipation from the spell of mediæval minstrelsy. He had now entered a larger world, where pleasant sunlight had taken the place of tragic shadows of terror, and where his genius moved freely with a sense of conscious power. It was evident also that his mind had developed new and unsuspected qualities. The old simplicity and directness are here, the old keen sense of colour is still predominant ; but there is something new—a gift of larger utterance, a power of word-painting, inimitably fresh and truthful, a sort of childlike joy in dreams, and a corresponding power of setting them forth, which interests and fascinates us. And there is the same sort of childlike delight in Nature. He sees her with a fresh eye, and tells us what he sees in the simplest phrases. We rarely meet an epithet which surprises us by the keenness of its observation, or the intensity of its vision, but we never meet a description of Nature that is not truthful and sincere. We are never startled into delight, but we are always soothed and refreshed. "The art of William Morris," said Mary Howitt, "is Nature itself, rough at times, but quaint, fresh, and dewy beyond anything I ever saw or felt in language."

The scenery Morris loves to paint, and which he paints best, is familiar scenery; the dewy meads, the orchards with their snowy bloom, the white mill with its cozy quiet, the flower-gardens where the bee sucks, and where the soft wet winds murmur in the leaves of "immemorial elms." The charm of such pictures is in their unintentional art, the entire absence of any effort to be fine. The breaking day has been described a thousand times, and often the most laboured descriptions have been most admired; yet there is still delight to be found in so simple a sketch as this:

> So passed the night; the moon arose and grew,
> From off the sea a little west wind blew,
> Rustling the garden leaves like sudden rain,
> And ere the moon had 'gun to fall again
> The wind grew cold, a change was in the sky,
> And in deep silence did the dawn draw nigh.

How clearly is the colourist seen also in this companion picture:

The sun is setting in the west, the sky
Is clear and hard, and no clouds come anigh
The golden orb, but further off they lie,
Steel-gray and black, with edges red as blood,
And underneath them is the weltering flood
Of some huge sea, whose tumbling hills, as they
Turn restless sides about, are black, or gray,
Or green, or glittering with the golden flame :
The wind has fallen now, but still the same
The mighty army moves, as if to drown
This lone bare rock, whose sheer scarped sides of brown
Cast off the weight of waves in clouds of spray.

Sometimes there is a flash of imaginative intensity, as in the lines :

And underneath his feet the moonlit sea
Went shepherding his waves disorderly ;

but such touches are rare.   William Morris has the infrequent gift of using commonplace phrases in a way that is not commonplace.   Tennyson would scarcely deign to use so well-worn a phrase as "the golden orb"; he would probably have invented some felicitous double adjective which would strike us as much by its ingenuity as its truth.   Morris is never troubled by any such scruples.   He uses the handiest phrases, and somehow he makes us feel that they are after all the truest.   He is always pictorial, and his pictures are painted with so great a breadth that the absence of any delicate filigree work of ingenious phrase-making is not remarked.   Perhaps this also is part of his charm.   While almost every other poet of our day aims at the invention of new phrases which shall allure us by their originality, Morris is simply intent upon telling us his story; and the very absence of pretension in his style fills us with a new delight, and strikes us as a new species of genius.

The aim and scope of the *Earthly Paradise* Morris has himself set forth in his *Apology* and *L'Envoi.*

> Of heaven and hell I have no power to sing ;
>   I cannot ease the burden of your fears,
> Or make quick-coming death a little thing,
>   Or bring again the pleasure of past years ;
>   Nor for my words shall ye forget your tears,
> Or hope again for aught that I can say —
> The idle singer of an empty day.
>
> Dreamer of dreams, born out of my due time,
>   Why should I strive to set the crooked straight ?
> Let it suffice me that my murmuring rhyme
>   Beats with light wing against the ivory gate,
>   Telling a tale not too importunate
> To those who in the sleepy region stay,
> Lulled by the singer of an empty day.

In *L'Envoi* he boldly claims Geoffrey Chaucer as his master, and sounds the same note of gentle pessimism as regards the fortunes of his own day. From a moral point of view this pessimism is the most striking thing about the *Earthly Paradise.* He turns to dreamland, and bids us travel with him into the realms of faery, because he cannot unravel the mystery of human life, and believes that any attempt to do so can only end in bewilderment and despair. When he ventures upon any counsel it is simply the old pagan counsel of *carpe diem.* The thought of death is always with him, and the true wisdom of life is to gather the roses while we may. Death, the great spoliator, will soon be upon us, and the days will come all too soon when we have no pleasure in them.

> In the white-flowered hawthorn brake,
> Love, be merry for my sake :
> Twine the blossoms in my hair,

> Kiss me where I am most fair —
> Kiss me, love! for who knoweth
> What thing cometh after death?

This is the note which sounds throughout the *Earthly Paradise*. Ogier the Dane, at the bidding of the fairy, renounces life just when its consummation is at hand, and puts aside the crown of Charlemaine, saying:

> Lie there, O crown of Charlemaine,
> Worn by a mighty man and worn in vain.
> Because he died, and all the things he did
> Were changed before his face by earth was hid.

Ambition, the fierce race for wealth, the battle even for what seem to be great causes and sufficing ideals, are all in vain, and end in disillusionment and sorrow. It is better still to dream. In dreams everything is beautiful; in actual life the sordid and the vulgar intrude at every turn. It is better still to dream, because dreams never disappoint us. There, at least, we can forget the shadow of death and wander in the meads of a perpetual spring; and, so far as dreams bring the jaded mind refreshment and release, it is wise to dream. The imaginative faculty needs exercise as well as the practical, and no full or fair life can be lived where it is stunted or ignored. And we are only too ready to hail a singer who bids us

> Forget six counties overhung with smoke,
> Forget the snorting steam and piston-stroke,
> Forget the spreading of the hideous town ;
> Think rather of the pack-horse on the down,
> And dream of London—small, and white, and clean —
> The clear Thames bordered by its gardens green.

But, after all, he is not the highest poet who only bids us dream. The highest poet is he who, knowing life and death, bids us not ignore the one nor fear the other, but prepares us equally for both by the inspiration of his courage and the serenity of his faith. This William Morris does not do in his greatest poems, and has not sought to do. He knows the limitations of his nature, and confesses his inability to sing the songs which humanity has ever counted the noblest. He has left to others the battles of faith and philosophy. He has sought only to be the singer of an empty day, the dreamer of dreams, in whose bright spells weary men may rest awhile, and those who are vexed by life's disasters may find a brief refreshment and repose. Nor is this a slight aim nor a contemptible achievement. It is something to have amid the fierce strain of modern life one poet who does not excite, but soothe us; who does not make us think, but bids us enjoy; who lures us back again into the simplicities of childhood, and who, in all his writings, has not written a page that a child might not read, and has written many with so lucid an art that a child might enjoy and comprehend them.

Of the third period of William Morris it is only necessary to add a sentence or two. The dreamer of the *Earthly Paradise* at last wakes from his dream, and casts away his spells, and breaks his magic wand. He discovers that the nineteenth century is not an empty day, nor is it a time when any man who has helpful hands may dare to be idle or unserviceable. The social problem, which is the great and real problem of our time, powerfully affected Morris's mature life. With his socialistic harangues at street corners, his "wrestles with policemen, or wrangles with obtuse magistrates about freedom of speech," we have nothing to do here. Here we have only to deal with his work in literature, and with the exception of a few spirited verses such as these:

Then a man shall work and bethink him, and rejoice in the
    deeds of his hand,
Nor yet come home in the even, too faint and weary to stand,
For that which the worker winneth shall then be his indeed,
Nor shall half be reaped for nothing by him that sowed no
    seed.
Then all *mine* and *thine* shall be *ours*, and no more shall any
    man crave
For riches that serve for nothing but to fetter a friend for a
    slave,

the socialistic propaganda has gained nothing by his
poetic art. Perhaps it was too late in life for Morris to
catch the true lyric fire of the revolutionary poet. It is,
however, profoundly interesting to remark how the huge
shadow of this social problem has been gradually projected over the entire field of literature, politics, and
philosophy.

It is by his earlier work in mediæval romance, and his
Earthly Paradise that Morris will be remembered. Concerning the latter it is but uttering a commonplace to say
that no writer since Chaucer has displayed so masterly a
power of continuous narrative, or has rested his fame so
completely upon the arts of simplicity and lucidity. In
this he occupies a unique place among modern poets.
He has imitators, but he has no real competitor. He
has drunk deep of the well of English undefiled, and has
again taught the old lesson of the potency of plain and
idiomatic Saxon as an unrivalled vehicle of poetic utterance. If he has added nothing new to the wealth of metrical
expression he has enriched modern literature by the re-
coining of ancient forms of speech, and by the recurrence
to the free simplicity of our older poetry. If he falls far
behind Rossetti in the art of beautiful expression, and
behind Swinburne in vehemence and lyric fire, he is the

superior of both in the more enduring qualities of strength and breadth of style, and has a nobler inventiveness and a wholesomer view of life. To be the modern Chaucer is a far greater thing than to be an English Baudelaire or Villon, simply because Chaucer was an infinitely greater man than either, and carried in his sweet and sunny nature the secret seed of a more enduring immortality. This William Morris is—the nearest approach to Chaucer which the nineteenth century can produce, or that any intervening period has produced. This is much to say, but it is not too much to say of the author of the *Life and Death of Jason* and the *Earthly Paradise*. Separated as they are by a vast stretch of time, different as they are by so much as five centuries of civilization can constitute of difference, still they are alike in spirit; and Chaucer is indeed the master of William Morris's art, and he the most faithful and successful of his disciples.

XXXV

CONCLUDING SURVEY

WE have now made ourselves acquainted with those poets of modern literature who stand first both in force and achievement. In the growth of later English poetry one thing is very marked, viz., the steady development of excellence in technique. False rhymes and halting cadences are no longer pardonable offences. As readers have become more cultured, the standard of technical perfection has been greatly raised. It is hardly an exaggeration to say, that during the last thirty years many men and women have written poetry which, had it appeared thirty years earlier, would have attracted general attention, and have laid the foundations of a solid fame. It is not necessary to drag from their obscurity the Hayleys and the Pyes of earlier generations : one may quote such names as those of James Montgomery and Kirke White, both poets of a true gift, as instances of writers who achieved a reputation which the more exacting conditions of later literature would have made trebly difficult or altogether impossible. And the influence of this higher standard of excellence has been retrospective also. The names of many men famous in their generation have almost dropped out of sight. There has been a general displacement of reputation. Thus it happens that a history of poetry written fifty years ago would have given extended notice to many writers who can receive only casual notice to-day.

Thomas Moore is one of these writers. Moore, in his day, was one of the most popular of poets, and one of the best paid. Much of his reputation was due to his association in the popular judgment with greater men than himself; much, of course, to his own conspicuous ability. He was witty, genial, and graceful, and in his lighter moods is the most pleasant of satirists. As a lyrical poet of a certain order he has never been surpassed. Many of his songs, especially his national and patriotic songs, had the good fortune to be wedded to exquisite music, and entered at once into the general memory. They have remained popular through all changes of taste and thought, and are likely to do so for many generations yet to come. But Moore's was, upon the whole, a light and shallow nature, deficient in masculine force. His poetry reveals the same defect. Much of it—*Lalla Rookh*, for example—offends us by its glittering artificiality. It is little read to-day, and is virtually dead.

Thomas Moore 1779–1852.

To include Southey among the great poets, and omit Landor, appears very like a glaring failure of justice; but the justification is found in Landor's own confession: " Poetry was always my amusement, prose my study and my business." Landor, if not among the greatest poets, had moments of singular greatness; and it is something of a scandal that his poetry is not better known. In his two longest poems, *Gebir* and *Count Julian*, there are passages of extraordinary power, and even splendour. Dante himself has scarcely pictured the scenery of the infernal world with more intensity than Landor in the following passage :

Walter Savage Landor 1775–1864.

> A river rolling in its bed,
> Not rapid—that would rouse the wretched souls,
> Not calmly—that would lull them to repose ;
> But with dull, weary lapses it still heaved
> Billows of bale, heard low, but heard afar.

In *Count Julian* there is also a passage, comparing Julian with the mountain eagle, which De Quincey regarded as one of the finest in all poetry :

> No airy and light passion stirs abroad
> To ruffle or to soothe him ; all are quelled
> Beneath a mightier, sterner stress of mind.
> Wakeful he sits, and lonely, and unmoved,
> Beyond the arrows, shouts, and views of men ;
> As oftentimes an eagle, ere the sun
> Throws o'er the varying earth his early ray,
> Stands solitary, stands immovable
> Upon some highest cliff, and rolls his eye,
> Clear, constant, unobservant, unabased,
> In the cold light, above the dews of morn.

Many of Landor's lyrics, lightly as they are touched, possess an almost faultless excellence of workmanship, and a peculiar charm of simplicity and clearness. He who once takes kindly to Landor will find in him a comrade capable of the greatest things. In sweetness, tenderness, and classic gravity, in a power of producing in the mind an emotion more often caused by the beautiful austerity of great sculpture than by literature, in occasional Miltonic pomp of line and splendour of imagery, Landor excels ; but he could also be careless and eccentric, and his finest passages are frequently preceded or followed by poor or turgid lines. It may be said that there is more pure gold in twenty pages of Landor than in all the poetry of Southey ; but there are other matters also which have to be considered. Whatever we may think of Southey to-day, in his own day he occupied a place of great repute, and the history of modern poetry cannot wholly pass him over. On the other hand, Landor, as we have seen, never made his poetry the main purpose of his life; he elected to be judged, not by his poetry, but his prose. I have thought it best, therefore, to include him among the great prose-writers (*vide The Makers of English Prose*) instead of with the poets. This is his rightful place, which he would have wished to occupy, and to which he has claims manifold. Nevertheless, it is but justice to remember, that though Landor's best poetry could be included in a very small compass, yet it ranks among the best of modern literature.

In William Blake, an artist and poet whose life was nearly coequal with Crabbe's, we have a writer who has the genius to be loved. Blake's *Songs of Innocence* and *Songs of Experience* are among the imperishable treasures of English poetry. He writes like an inspired child, with a pen dipped in fantasy, with a wealth of uncoördinated thought, with an indefinable charm and grace, full of glamour and magic. His art is instinctive, never deliberate. To form, and even to rhyme, he is indifferent. Very few of his poems have the technical correctness of his famous lines upon *The Tiger*.

William Blake 1757–1827.

> Tiger, Tiger, burning bright
> In the forests of the night,
> What immortal hand or eye
> Could frame thy fearful symmetry?
>
> In what distant deeps or skies
> Burnt the fire of thine eyes?
> On what wings dare he aspire?
> What the hand dare seize the fire?

And what shoulder, and what art
Could twist the sinews of thy heart?
And, when thy heart began to beat,
What dread hand and what dread feet?

What the hammer? what the chain?
In what furnace was thy brain?
What the anvil? what dread grasp
Dare its deadly terrors clasp?

When the stars threw down their spears,
And watered heaven with their tears,
Did He smile His work to see?
Did He who made the lamb make thee?

But there is scarcely a poem of his, scarcely a couplet, that is not pregnant with imaginative force. The very simplicity of his verse deceives us, and retards the impression of its real philosophic depth and frequent prophetic force. Certainly Blake's contemporaries never so much as gave him casual recognition. If they thought of him at all it was as a madman, who produced extraordinary designs which might pass for art, accompanied by verses that were at once puerile and incoherent. No doubt Blake was, as Emerson once said of himself, " gently mad." He dreamed dreams and saw visions all his days. He walked in the brightness of his dreams, profoundly careless of fame, or even of success, so long as he could earn his daily bread. His death, like his life, was clothed in the same visionary glory. " He said he was going to see that country he had all his life wished to see, and expressed himself happy, hoping for salvation through Jesus Christ. Just before he died, his countenance became fair, his eyes brightened, and he burst out into singing of the things he saw in heaven. " Another account tells us that " he composed and uttered songs to his Maker, so sweetly to the ear of his Catherine that, when she stood to hear him, he, looking upon her most affectionately, said, ' My beloved, they are not mine! No, they are *not* mine!'" This is the very impression which all Blake's lyrical poetry makes upon us. It is a gust of pure inspiration coming from unknown regions, of which he is the mere vehicle. He is an eternal child, and to him are revealed the things hidden from the wise and prudent.

A poet of great power and achievement is Philip James Bailey. Bailey is one of the most undeservedly neglected poets of our generation. This **Philip James Bailey** is the more curious because when his **1816.** great poem *Festus* was published, in 1839, it was hailed with almost world-wide applause. Rossetti " read it again and yet again," and spoke of it in the highest terms. Many very competent critics did not hesitate to compare the author of *Festus* with Shakespeare, Milton, and Goethe. Possibly this comparison was suggested as much by the nature of the theme as the quality of the work, for *Festus* is another rendering of the great Faust legend, and, it must be confessed, a splendid rendering. It is the more extraordinary as the work of a very young man, for Bailey was not more than twenty-four when it was published. The opening lines —

> Eternity hath snowed its years upon them,
> And the white winter of their age is come,
> The World and all its worlds ; and all shall end—

touch sublimity. The lines —

> We live in deeds, not years ; in thoughts, not breaths ;
> In feelings, not in figures on a dial.
> We should count time by heart-beats. He most lives
> Who thinks most, feels the noblest, acts the best —

have probably been quoted more frequently in the pulpit during the last fifty years than any others that could be named.   But the whole poem is full of noble thoughts finely expressed, and has many of the qualities of truly great poetry.

The most curious thing about Mr. Bailey is that he has written nothing of note since *Festus*.   He presents an extraordinary case of arrested development.   A great and sudden success animates some men and petrifies others.   It would seem as if the author of *Festus* felt that he had done his utmost in his first poem, and never had the courage to attempt to surpass himself.   He has spent his entire life in working over his one great poem, revising and adding, till it has now grown into an enormous volume.   Thus, *The Angel and the World*, a poem published in 1850, is now incorporated in *Festus*.   This is scarcely to the advantage of the poem, which in its original form possessed many dramatic qualities which are quite obscured in later editions.   It has now become a somewhat disorderly treasure-house of poetic ideas and material, among which much rubbish may be found, but still more of excellent work, characterized by rarity and beauty.   Some of the choruses are especially fine— notably the one beginning —

> They come from the East and the West —

and ending —

> And unto, and not of, the Lamb
> Shall be the sacrifice.

The main religious idea unfolded in *Festus* is universalism, now far more popular than in 1839, when it was regarded as a dangerous novelty.   Mr. Bailey is far from being a Shakespeare or a Goethe, and his reputation has greatly suffered by the extravagance of adulation with which he was first greeted. But he is a true poet, of wide powers and noble achievement.

Of what was once called the *Spasmodic School of Poetry* very little trace remains. The epithet "spasmodic," first applied by Carlyle to Byron, was taken up by Professor Aytoun, who fixed it as a term of reproach upon Bailey, Sydney Dobell, and Alexander Smith, the latter of whom he satirized mercilessly in his *Firmilian*. The category was unfortunate, for Bailey has little in common with Dobell and Smith. Nor was the satire just, for both Dobell and Smith were fine poets, who deserved more generous treatment from a man of Aytoun's eminence. Dobell's poetry has died long ago, nor have any recent efforts to resuscitate it been attended with success. But if few or none read his *Roman*, he has created an imperishable monument for himself in one simple but magnificent ballad, *Keith of Ravelston*. This ballad is worthy to rank with Keats' *La Belle Sans Merci*. It even surpasses it in its power of producing an impression of weird and haunting mystery, in its simple yet impressive cadence, in its suggested tragedy.

Sydney Dobell
1824–1874.

Alexander Smith
1830–1867.

> The murmur of the mourning ghost,
>   That keeps the shadowy kine,
> " Oh, Keith of Ravelston,
>   The sorrows of thy line ! "
>
> Ravelston ! Ravelston !
>   The merry path that leads
> Down the golden morning hill,
>   And thro' the silver meads.

Ravelston ! Ravelston !
  The stile beneath the tree,
The maid that kept her mother's kine,
  The song that sang she !

    *   *   *   *   *

Year after year, where Andrew came
  Comes evening down the glade,
And still there sits a moonshine ghost
  Where sat the sunshine maid.

Her misty hair is faint and fair,
  She keeps the shadowy kine ;
"Oh, Keith of Ravelston,
  The sorrows of thy line ! "

I lay my hand upon the stile,
  The stile is lone and cold,
The burnie that goes babbling by
  Say nought that can be told.

    *   *   *   *   *

She makes her immemorial moan,
  She keeps her shadowy kine ;
"Oh, Keith of Ravelston,
  The sorrows of thy line ! "

In this brief poem we have a fuller indication of Dobell's genuine poetic gift than in all the rest of his poetry put together. It is a poem that the greatest poets might have been proud to claim.

Alexander Smith achieved a popularity which never came to Dobell. His *Life-Drama* had an extraordinary success. Incredible as it appears now, yet the time was when Smith was considered Tennyson's most serious rival, and was supposed by his two generous critics to have eclipsed him. It was no doubt the absurdity of this adulation that inspired Aytoun with the idea of turning his pretensions into ridicule. Yet in the *Life-Drama* the

beauties were at least as conspicuous as the faults.   Smith
excelled in what an older generation called the pretty
" conceits " of poetry.   He was apt in the invention of
fanciful images, many of them instinct with beauty, but
still more of them strained and crude.   An example of
what is meant is found in the lines :

> The bridegroom sea
> Is toying with the shore, his wedded bride,
> And, in the fullness of his marriage joy,
> He decorates her tawny brow with shells,
> Retires a space to see how fair she looks,
> Then, proud, runs up to kiss her.

It is manifest with what ease a passage like this could be
satirized and burlesqued.   But Smith sometimes hits upon
a really beautiful image, as in the lines :

> That night thro' one blue gulf profound,
> Begirt by many a cloudy crag,
> The moon came leaping like a stag,
> And one star like a hound.

In a contemporary of Alexander Smith's, David Gray,
the author of *The Luggie*, we have a poet of much more
genuine power, and of greater distinc-
David Gray
1838–1861.
tion.   Gray's is an oaten pipe with few
notes, but it has the mellowness and
sweetness of the thrush's call in it.   He is a true poet of
Nature, seeing clearly, feeling deeply, and clothing his
thought almost always in felicitous and musical phrase.
What is most noticeable is the native sweetness of his note,
its unstrained freshness and ease, and the fact that his last
poems, written when the shadow of death lay heavy on
him, are by much the finest both in thought, form, and
expression.   And it must be remembered also that he
died in his twenty fourth year, and accomplished what he

did amid an environment wholly unfavourable to literary development.   This is how he describes his life:

> Poor meagre life is mine, meagre and poor !
>   Rather a piece of childhood thrown away ;
> An adumbration faint ; the overture
>   To stifled music ; year that ends in May :
> The sweet beginning of a tale unknown ;
>   A dream unspoken ; promise unfulfilled ;
> A morning with no noon, a rose unblown —
>   All its deep rich vermilion crushed and killed
> I' th' bud by frost.

A piece of childhood Gray's life was in its unsophisticated sincerity of aim ; but it also has the child's freshness of emotion and joy of vision.   The Luggie, the wonder of the snow, the wakening of spring, his home, his mother,—these make the staple of his poetry.   As he lies dying he sighs:

> O God! for one clear day, a snowdrop, and sweet air!

It is in his nature-pictures that Gray's finest power is displayed.   Not even Keats has described spring with a more exquisite burst of music than this:

> Now, while the long-delaying ash assumes
>   The delicate April green, and, loud and clear,
> Through the cool, yellow, mellow twilight glooms,
>   The thrush's song enchants the captive ear ;
> Now, while a shower is pleasant in the falling,
>   Stirring the still perfume that wakes around ;
> Now, that doves mourn, and from the distance calling,
>   The cuckoo answers, with a sov'reign sound,—
> Come, with thy native heart, O true and tried !
>   But leave all books ; for what with converse high,
> Flavoured with Attic wit, the time shall glide
>   On smoothly, as a river floweth by,
> Or as on stately pinion through the gray
> Evening the culver cuts his liquid way.

Perhaps this sonnet is the best known of Gray's writings, but there is one other poem, quoted by Robert Buchanan, which in a quite extraordinary degree combines all Gray's qualities at their best—his depth of affection, his passion for nature, his exquisite sensitiveness of feeling and mastery of phrase. The lines were written at Torquay, one of the places to which he was sent by the generosity of his friends in the year in which he died, and are dated January, 1861.

Come to me, O my mother! come to me,
Thine own son slowly dying far away!
Thro' the moist ways of the wide ocean, blown
By great invisible winds, come stately ships
To this calm bay for quiet anchorage ;
They come, they rest awhile, they go away,
But, O my mother, never comest thou!
The snow is round thy dwelling, the white snow,
That cold, soft revelation, pure as light,
And the pine-spire is mystically fringed,
Laced with encrusted silver. Here—ah me!—
The winter is decrepit, under-born,
A leper with no power but his disease.
Why am I from thee, mother, far from thee ?
Far from the frost enchantment, and the woods
Jewelled from bough to bough? Oh, home, my home!
O river in the valley of my home,
With mazy-winding motion intricate,
Twisting thy deathless music underneath
Thy polished ice-work—must I never more
Behold thee with familiar eyes, and watch
Thy beauty changing with the changing day,
Thy beauty constant to the constant change?

Surely there is not a more human and heart-moving cry in modern poetry than this. Nor would it be easy to find, even among the great poets, any lines written before their twenty-fourth year more remarkable for grace, finish, melody, and emotional expression than these.

On the name of Arthur Hugh Clough a longer pause is necessary. It is he who is commemorated in Arnold's *Thyrsis*—a poet's monument to a singularly noble-minded poet. Clough was a man of great sweetness of nature, of fine wit, of ample scholarship, of true poetic instinct, but his life was clouded by persistent melancholy. This was mainly due to the unsettlement of his religious beliefs. One of his finest poems, which most poignantly expresses this condition of mind, is his *Easter Day*, with its often-quoted lines :

**Arthur Hugh Clough
1819–1861.**

> Eat, drink, and die, for we are souls bereaved :
> Of all the creatures under heaven's wide cope
> We are most hopeless, who had once more hope,
> And most beliefless, that had most believed.

In his *Dipsychus*, a longer and semi-dramatic poem, the same doubts are expressed in a spirit of mingled acumen and irony. The poem has also its brighter moments and its lighter themes, and is marked by a passionate love of nature which at times overcomes the melancholy of the poet's mind. The happiest of poets could not have written more delightfully of the gondola than Clough in the lines commencing —

> Afloat ; we move. Delicious ! **Ah,**
> What else is like the gondola ?
> This level floor of liquid glass
> Begins beneath us swift to pass.
> It goes as though it went alone,
> By some impulsion of its own.
> (How light it moves, how softly ! **Ah,**
> Were all things like the gondola !)

But a page or two later we have the half-bantering confession of the self-tormented thinker:

> The world is very odd we see,
>   We do not comprehend it ;
> But in one fact we all agree,
>   God won't, and we can't mend it.
>
> Being common-sense, it can't be sin
>   To take it as I find it ;
> The pleasure, to take pleasure in ;
>   The pain, try not to mind it.

The utmost hope of which Clough is capable carries him no further than this :

> 'Twill all be well; no need of care ;
> Though how it will, and when, and where,
> We cannot see and can't declare.
> In spite of dreams, in spite of thought,
> 'Tis not in vain, and not for nought,
> The wind it blows, the ship it goes,
> Though where and whither no one knows.

Clough's longest poem, and the best specimen of English hexameters in existence, is *The Bothie of Tober-na-Vuolich*, in which he succeeds in maintaining a lightness of spirits unusual with him ; and there are also many fine passages to be found in his *Mari Magno*. He is perhaps the most interesting of the lesser modern poets ; yet one is conscious constantly of something inefficient in him, in the man, in his life, and in his writing. It is difficult to define exactly what is meant, but the general impression is of a man in bonds. His genius is indisputable, but he nowhere attains the calm efficiency of a great artist. Poetry was for him, one imagines, not so much *the* medium of expression, as *a* medium ; something not native but acquired ; used with skill, and often with conspicuous brilliance of effect, but rarely with absolute mastery, never with the inevitable art and instinct of the great poet. He can invigourate, he can fortify, he can charm the mind, but he lacks the authentic spell by which the poet takes possession of the heart. But he did not aim at touching the heart; his poetry is mainly addressed to the intellect, and he is peculiarly the poet of culture and of reason. Not his least significance in English poetry is that he interpreted with singular sensitiveness and truth a period of great intellectual and spiritual crisis. Russell Lowell has said of him, " We have a foreboding that Clough, imperfect as he was in many respects, and dying before he had subdued his sensitive temperament to the sterner requirements of his art, will be thought a hundred years hence to have been the truest expression in verse of the moral and intellectual tendencies, the doubt and struggle towards settled convictions, of the period in which he lived." This is, of course, to judge poetry rather from the moral than the artistic standpoint; what is perhaps more likely to keep his poetry fresh is its rare quality of humour, which is all the more attractive by reason of the background of sadness against which it shines.

Clough was a Fellow of Oriel, and during his Oxford days came under the influence of Newman. Newman was by temperament a far greater poet **John Henry Newman** than Clough, and although he chose to **1801–1890.** express his genius in prose rather than poetry, yet he produced one poem of quite superlative excellence, *The Dream of Gerontius*. Praise is impertinent and criticism vain of such a poem as this. Newman by this single poem places himself beside Dante, as **the**

great exponent of Catholic theology. When was the
physical terror of death so described as he describes
it ? —

> 'Tis this strange innermost abandonment,
>   (Lover of souls !   Great God !   I look to Thee,)
> This emptying out of each constituent
>   And natural force, by which I come to be.
>
>   *   *   *   *   *
>
> 'Tis death,—O loving friends, your prayers !—'tis he !
>   As though my very being had given way,
> As though I was no more a substance now,
>   And could fall back on nought to be my stay,
> (Help, loving Lord !   Thou my sole Refuge, Thou,)
>   And turn no whither, but must needs decay
>   And drop from out this universal frame
> Into that shapeless, scopeless, blank abyss,
>   That utter nothingness of which I came :
> This is it that has come to pass in me ;
> O horror ! this it is, my dearest, this ;
> So pray for me, my friends, who have not strength to
>   pray.

And so the moment after death : —

> I went to sleep ; and now I am refreshed.
> A strange refreshment : for I feel in me
> An inexpressive lightness, and a sense
> Of freedom, as I were at length myself,
> And ne'er had been before.   How still it is
> I hear no more the busy beat of time,
> No, nor my fluttering breath, nor struggling pulse ;
> Nor does one moment differ from the next.
>
>   *   *   *   *   *
>
>   What is this severance ?
> This silence pours a solitariness
> Into the very essence of my soul ;
> And the deep rest, so soothing and so sweet,
> Hath something, too, of sternness and of pain.

So the poem proceeds, touching every note of mystical

rapture, and yet always under the control of a powerful analytic intellect—one of the most remarkable, and as a religious poem the greatest, in the English language.

In Mr. F. W. H. Myers we have another poet of religion. Mr. Myers, like Matthew Arnold, is one of Her Majesty's inspectors of schools, and is the author of several volumes of verse. One only of these, however, is memorable, a poem called *St. Paul.* The poem is an attempt to re-express the spirit of St. Paul, to re-create out of the Epistles the soul of the great Apostle, with all its passion for Christ and for men, its pressure of thoughts too deep for tears, its heroic renunciations, its shame and shrinking, its vehemence of purpose and rapture of spiritual vision. It may be at once granted that it does not accomplish this design perfectly ; perhaps that is more than we could expect of any modern artist. There are false touches in the poem, ways of putting things which we are quite sure St. Paul would never have used. It would be perfectly natural for Mr. Myers to write of himself :

**F. W. H. Myers
1843.**

> Often for me between the shade and splendour,
>   Ceos and Tenedos at dawn were gray ;
> Welling of waves, disconsolate and tender,
>   Sighed on the shore and waited for the day.

But is it possible to conceive St. Paul as taking any interest in the voice of the waters on the shore, and " the purple mystery of dawn " ? When St. Paul stands upon the shore at daybreak it is amid the company of the elders ; and his whole soul is too much with the little church at Ephesus and with the disconsolate group that bid him farewell, knowing that they will see his face no more, for the splendour of the dawn to strike a joy along his senses.

But if these splendid pictures of Ceos and Tenedos, of pearly dawn, and spring that "pours in the rain and rushes from the sod," of Araby and Orion, —

> The night-noise and thunder of the lion,
> Silence and sounds of the prodigious plain, —

are essentially the creations of the Wordsworthian age, there is no doubt about the spiritual truth of the great bulk of the poem, and the marvellous skill with which it interprets the soul of the Apostle. Is not this picture of St. Paul, remembering the days when he was a persecutor, both true and perfect? —

> Your remembered faces,
> Dear men and women, whom I sought and slew!
> Ah, when we mingle in the heavenly places,
> How will I weep to Stephen and to you!

Or this picture of the man who was in a strait betwixt two, being ready to depart, which was far better:

> Once for a night and day upon the splendid
> Anger and solitude of seething sea,
> Almost I deemed my agony was ended,
> Nearly beheld Thy Paradise and Thee, —
>
> Saw the deep heaving into ridges narrow,
> Heard the blast bellow on its ocean way,
> Felt the soul freed, and like a flaming arrow
> Sped on Euroclydon thro' death to day.
>
> Ah, but not yet He took me from my prison, —
> Left me a little while, nor left for long, —
> Bade as one buried, bade as one arisen,
> Suffer for men, and like a man be strong.

Is it not like St. Paul, too, to pray that he may see the wounds that he has made, in order that he may be humbled by the memory of the past?

> Yes, Thou forgivest, but with all forgiving
>   Canst not renew mine innocence again ;
> Make Thou, O Christ, a dying of my living,
>   Purge from the sin, *but never from the pain !*

And finer still, both in its intensity of expression and its historic truth, is this :

> Oft when the Word is on me to deliver,
>   Opens the heaven, and the Lord is there ;
> Desert or throng, the city or the river,
>   Melt in a lucid Paradise of air, —
>
> *Only like souls* I see the folk thereunder,
>   Bound who should conquer, slaves who should
>   be kings, —
> Hearing their one hope with an empty wonder,
>   Sadly contented in a show of things ; —
>
> Then, with a rush, the intolerable craving
>   Shivers throughout me like a trumpet call, —
> Oh, to save these !—to perish in their saving,
>   Die for their life, be offered for them all !

Writing from the standpoint of absolute religious negation, James Thomson, in his *City of Dreadful Night*, produced one of the most memorable poems of modern poetry. It is a poem of immitigable bitterness, of profound thought, of stately grief. Thomson was a republican, an atheist, and a pessimist. His message, such as it is, is contained in these two verses of his greatest poem :

James Thomson ("B. V.") 1834–1882.

> I find no hint throughout the Universe
> Of good or ill, of blessings or of curse,
>   I find alone Necessity supreme ;
> With infinite Mystery, abysmal, dark,
> Unlighted even by the faintest spark
>   For us, the fleeting shadows of a dream.

> O Brothers of sad lives ! they are so brief;
> A few short years must bring us all relief :
>   Can we not bear these years of labouring breath ?
> But if you would not this poor life fulfill,
> Lo, you are free to end it when you will,
>   Without the fear of waking after death !

Thomson did not always write, however, as the laureate of despair. Some of his lighter verse has great charm and even humour. Nor was he incapable of appreciating the pieties which he had renounced: he always gazed after them with wistful sadness. Thus no one has shown a truer appreciation of William Blake, and his short poem on Blake is a gem.

> He came to the desert of London town,
>   Gray miles long ;
> He wandered up and he wandered down,
>   Singing a quiet song.
>
> He came to the desert of London town,
>   Mirk miles broad ;
> He wandered up and he wandered down
>   Ever alone with God.
>
> There were thousands and thousands of human kind,
>   In this desert of brick and stone,
> But some were deaf and some were blind,
>   And he was there alone.
>
> At length the good hour came ; he died
>   As he had lived, alone :
> He was not missed from the desert wide —
>   Perhaps he was found at the Throne.

But for Thomson no return to faith was possible, and his despair is as sincere as it is tragic. His power of imagination is intense and unflagging. Two of his shorter poems, *In the Room* and *Insomnia*, are almost terrifying in their gloomy power. His own life was made much

more unhappy than it might have been by his intemperate habits. These indirectly caused his death. He died
in University College Hospital on June 3, 1882. Upon
his funeral-card was printed a verse of his most despairing poetry, which, in a sense, summarized his unhappy
life :

> Weary of erring in this desert life,
>   Weary of hoping hopes forever vain,
> Weary of struggling in all-sterile strife,
>   Weary of thought which maketh nothing plain,
> I close my eyes, and calm my panting breath,
> And pray to thee, O ever-quiet Death !
> To come and soothe away my bitter pain.

There remains for consideration the work of a group
of American poets who have added much both to the
bulk and the lustre of the poetry of the
last century. The earliest of these is
W. C. Bryant, whose work, now almost forgotten, once
exercised a powerful charm over the minds of his contemporaries. Bryant had little original gift, but he excels in a certain stately gravity which
lends to worn and trite themes an air of
dignified grace. His verse always has a
certain large simplicity, which soothes and uplifts the
mind; but he does not arrest the thought, and he has
little power to kindle the imagination or the emotions.

American Poets.

**W. C. Bryant
1794–1878.**

Totally different is Edgar Allen Poe, whose contributions to prose literature are considered in the third volume
of this series. Poe possessed in the high-
est degree the gift of charm. He is essentially morbid in thought and artificial
in method; he is often a mere trickster in his excessive
mannerism : but he nevertheless possesses a gift of melody

**Edgar Allen Poe
1809–1849.**

quite unrivalled by any other poet of his nation. It is of little consequence that his musical cadences are themselves a piece of superb trickery : the fact remains that they haunt the memory, they have a magical sweetness, they exercise a wizard's spell on the imagination. His poem on *The Raven* is known wherever English literature is known. It is the most sincere of all his poems ; and, in spite of its obvious artificiality in form, is still a memorable expression of stately grief and incurable regret. As a lord of melody he is Swinburne's precursor, and remains his master. His greatest excellencies are often found in his lesser poems,—as for instance in *Annabel Lee*, and the exquisite lyric commencing,

> In the fairest of our valleys
> By good angels tenanted :

his greatest vices in a poem like *The Bells*, which is a piece of unmixed lyric artifice. With the temperament of the *poseur* and the tricks of the juggler ; with no particular truth to express or conviction to convey ; Poe is nevertheless so supreme an artist that his poetry moves us as only genuine poetry can, and it survives in spite of defects more notorious than can be enumerated in the writings of any other poet of established eminence.

Longfellow is the most popular poet of modern times, but he is very far from being a great poet. Much of his poetry is derivative, drawn from well-known sources ; only in his *Evangeline* and *Hiawatha* is he a distinctively American poet. He excels in simple pathos, in a faculty of quaint conceit and graceful fancy, and in the interpretation of the domestic affections.

Henry Wadsworth Longfellow 1807–1882.

Lines like the following win their way to the heart by
their very simplicity and unaffected tenderness :

> O little feet, that such long years
> Must wander on through hopes and fears,
>   Must ache and bleed beneath your load,
> I, nearer to the wayside inn,
> Where toil shall end and rest begin,
>   Am weary, thinking of your road.

Poems such as *Excelsior* and *The Psalm of Life*, in
spite of triteness in theme, have nevertheless earned their
right to be numbered among the secular hymns of
humanity.   Occasionally Longfellow gives signs of a
larger power of vision and interpretation.   This is found
chiefly in his ballads, such as *Carmilhan* and *The Phantom
Ship*.   But the real deficiency of Longfellow is always
apparent ; he lacks distinction, and his mind though
highly cultivated, is nevertheless of commonplace
quality.

Whittier, whose poems have also shared a wide popularity, ranks much lower than Longfellow.   He is a
hymnist rather than a poet, and his best
productions are hymnal in form.   His
best gifts are moral passion, nobly displayed in all his poems written against
slavery, and spiritual fervour which is never lacking in his
religious and devotional poetry.   He soothes, pleases,
and instructs ; but he seldom opens new gates of vision to
the mind, and there is little that is distinctive in his style
and method.   It is perhaps a sufficient tribute to his gift
that he has written some of the best hymns of his generation, which often contain lines that are really exquisite in
thought and expression.

**John Greenleaf
Whittier
1807–1892.**

Lowell is a more masculine poet than either Longfellow or Whittier, but is too didactic, and is usually stiff
and unmelodic in his versification. He
James Russell Lowell 1819–1891. is rather an accomplished man of letters
who has written excellent verse than a
poet by separate gift and vocation. As
a humourist, however, he stands above all rivals; many
of his brilliant epigrams have passed into common speech,
and his *Biglow Papers* are a rich storehouse of shrewd
drollery and sententious wisdom.

Whitman is a potential rather than an actual poet.
He has all the qualities of a true poet, but these qualities
are not coördinated. Occasionally he
Walt Whitman 1819–1892. surprises us by a fine phrase or a noble
expression of emotion, but he disdains
versification, often is crude to the point of vulgarity, and
rarely works himself free from a wholly mistaken conception of the nature and structure of poetry. Many of his
so-called poems are mere catalogues of names, places, and
things, arranged with a certain barbaric opulence of
effect; only occasionally from a wilderness of tedious
verbiage does there flash forth the unforgettable epithet
or perfect phrase. Nevertheless he is much more of a
poet than either Longfellow, Whittier or Lowell—not in
achievement, however, but in temperament and gift. His
lines on the death of Lincoln, in spite of the looseness of
their structure, possess a noble sincerity which places
them among the great elegies of universal poetry.

Among the lesser poets of America there are many
writers of excellent verse, such as Bret Harte and Joaquin
Miller, the former of whom is a delightful humourist, and
Oliver Wendell Holmes, whose verse is always touched
with delicate grace and wit. The most considerable poet
of recent years is Sidney Lanier, the most wonderful in

native power, Emily Dickenson. Lanier has something of Poe's gift of melody, but unlike Poe, he is always sincere. He is at his best in his shorter poems; in his longer poems his craftsmanship is often in excess of his material. Emily Dickenson, on the other hand, in spite of an almost total ignorance of craftsmanship, displays a range of imaginative power, with an occasional intensity of vision and felicity of phrase, altogether unique in modern poetry, and entirely wonderful when we remember the limitations of her mind and life. She ranks with William Blake in the essential spirituality of her gift and the method of its expression.

Among living poets of America and England there are many memorable names, such as Rudyard Kipling, William Watson, John Davidson, and Whitcomb Riley. The first and last of these are the most original, each being an interpreter, the one of the strenuous life of common men, and the other of all that is most characteristic in the rural life of America. In the work of William Watson and John Davidson, the tradition of the great poetry of the nineteenth century is still maintained; nevertheless it is clear that the great minstrelsy of modern poetry closed with Tennyson. The sun which sank on the 6th of October, 1892, took with it not a life only, but an era. The new age has yet to produce its new poets. That it will do so, we cannot doubt. Of that large gift of song which filled the nineteenth century we may say as Ferdinand in *The Tempest* says :

> This music crept by me upon the waters,
> Allaying both my fury and their passion
> With its sweet air ; thence have I followed it,
> Or it hath drawn me rather ;—but 'tis gone.

Let us also hopefully complete the speech of Ferdinand,

No, it begins again.